# John Junor Remembered

# Contents

| | |
|---|---|
| *Publishing Director:* | Don Short |
| *Design:* | Associated Group Design |
| *Cover design:* | Simon Gunn |
| *Picture research:* | Danny Howell |
| *Illustrations:* | © Associated Newspapers Ltd. |
| *Printing:* | Integrated Colour Editors Europe Limited Aylesbury, Buckinghamshire |

*First published October 30, 1997*

*British Library Cataloguing in Publication Data.*

*© The Mail on Sunday, 1997*

*Published in Great Britian for The Mail on Sunday by Solo Books Ltd., 49–53 Kensington High Street London W8 5ED*

*ISBN No. 1 873939.06X*

# Foreword

*by* Peter McKay

John Junor had spent 32 years as editor of a national newspaper before he launched into his second career as a columnist. It showed. His experience was wide. He knew what lay behind opaque newspaper stories. He'd met most of the household-name politicians, business executives and entertainment industry big names. He'd lunched privately with both the Queen and Diana, Princess of Wales. Over thirty years as an editor - preceded by active, wartime service in the Fleet Air Arm - he'd become a shrewd judge of human character.

JJ knew what made articles 'sing,' what dragged them down, what was permissably vulgar, and what was not. All of his life and career, he believed you had to put your heart and soul into journalism. You really had to work at it. Nothing came easy. If it did, then it was no good. He laboured on paragraphs as a jeweller polishes a precious stone. It would take readers seconds to pass over them but he wanted them to absorb the meaning immediately, and for it to strike home. He harried others to do the same. As an editor, he sent articles back for re-writes to big-name writers. He'd have seen some weakness in the text, some sentence in which the meaning was not utterly clear, or contradictory. Many editors think twice about annoying famous contributors - and it does annoy writers, famous and otherwise,to have shortcomings pointed out - but he knew, and they knew, that all journalism is improved in this way. He was usually generous in his praise and silent in the event of failure. He told one political journalist who had struggled long and hard : 'This is a brilliant piece. If I was going to use it I would not change a word'

His last secretary, 24-year-old Harriet Arkell, remembers the JJ modus operandi: "JJ would dictate his column onto a tape-recorder in the evenings at home (I would hear the television in the background) and in the car on the way to work. I would ring him on the car phone at ten to eleven, ostensibly to find out if he wanted any research done. Normally he did not, as he knew exactly what he was going to write, and so he would just tell me which restaurant to book for lunch. He got in at about 10.45, and went to his office where he might dictate a final sentence or two before I came in ten minutes later. He would give me the tape and I would sit at his desk and type in the first story, while he read his post and looked at the papers. (He read all of them in the car on the way in, except the Mirror and the Independent which came to the office.) When I had typed the first story, I would swivel the computer screen round and he would read it. He was always thrilled to see his stories on screen, and I would have to sit in absolute silence while he read them - if I so much as coughed he would become enraged and ask me how on earth he was meant to concentrate! Then he might tell me to change a sentence, or delete a word, before I started typing in the next story, and he returned to the papers. When all the stories were in the system, I would leave him to work on them - he might change a word himself or do some other minor adjustment. I would take the tape onto which he had dictated replies to his letters and go to my room to type these. Just before lunch he would ask me to go and get proofs from the printer, and I would cut these out and glue them onto A4 paper. These he would take home in the evening to scribble changes onto. He would come back from lunch at about three o'clock, never later if he could help it. I might have had to look something up for him in the meantime (e.g.: 'I remember a story in the Express in 1994 about X, can you find it?'). He would have a sleep until about a quarter to four, when I would go in with the letters to be signed, making as much noise as I could so he would hopefully wake up before I 'caught' him asleep at his desk, which he found embarrassing. He would sign the letters and then go home, with the hard copy proofs. The next morning (and subsequent mornings) he would give me, instead of the tape, the corrected proofs, and I would make the changes on the system. By Thursday night it was generally all sorted, and on Friday morning the sub editor would have put a proof on his desk for him to inspect and edit'.

Some columns appear to be written exclusively for other columnists: journalists self-indulgently writing to amuse and impress each other. John Junor wasn't like that. He never wrote to please other writers. He sought to engage the mass of ordinary readers. They responded by writing back to him and he always answered their letters promptly. Sometimes he followed up the tales they told, especially those which disclosed ill-treatment by officialdom. He spoke to fellow passengers on buses and trains, following up their stories, too. Like the regular in his morning bus queue who excitedly told JJ about a secondhand caravan he'd bought for £300. He was taking his wife and frail, 13-year-old daughter on holiday for the first time. Next time they met, JJ asked 'How's the caravan?' The man said it didn't matter to him any more. His daughter had died before they were due to leave for their holiday. John wrote that he was 'humbled beyond measure by the courage with which other people faced up to personal and total disaster' The courage of ordinary people hit by tragedy was a constant theme in his column. Another was the integrity of families. When Robert Maxwell died, JJ did not join in the chorus of vilification for the Mirror boss. He admitted Maxwell had 'great failings' but said he had 'great qualities, too.' He wrote: 'His courage and energy and zest for life bordered on the unbelievable. . . No matter what else he may have done in his life, can a man be wholly bad who can retain the love and affection of his own wife and children over such a long period of time?'

But his columns were never all doom and gloom. They had to contain 'light and shade,' he said. Balance a sad item with a happy one; follow a bitterly critical one by throwing a bouquet to some deserving figure - often a gorgeous young woman - in the public eye. Never make readers think you're sour about all human existence. He was also fanatical about being fresh. If any paper came close to printing some view he planned to express, the idea would be dumped without ceremony. He was a master of the surprise attack. Few readers might expect an item beginning harmlessly enough with 'Although it is, alas, outside the realm of my experience' to continue, 'I expect I might have been momentarily taken aback if Miss Janet Lawler had walked into my office holding her skirt above her head and saying, "You haven't seen my knickers today, have you?"' JJ strove to present himself as an innocent in the world. He would recount in lip-smacking detail every particular of a saucy newspaper story while making out he didn't know what to make of it. He also had the hair-raising (for newspaper lawyers) habit of reciting a catalogue of crimes, asking himself if the person he named was guilty of them, and airily concluding 'I do not know,' as if this exempted him from all responsibility. His instincts were Conservative, although on the three occasions he stood for Parliament as a young man it was as a Liberal Party candidate. He was keen on law and order, but this didn't mean he always approved of police actions. He was convinced they often fabricated evidence, harassed citizens who challenged their authority, and were sometimes led by chief constables who would have made their mark 'in Hitler's Waffen SS'. He ends one item, reprinted in this collection, 'I so much want to write kind things about the police. Without them we would be lost. But do you sometimes feel that some of them seem deliberately to go out of their way to get themselves disliked?' JJ was fond of question marks. He believed the power of a statement was doubled when couched as a question. Inviting the reader to come to a conclusion, he argued, is far more telling than simply stating to them what you think. Sometimes most of the paragraphs in his column ended with question marks. Friends occasionally teased him about this but he never changed his style. The questions were not simple. Often they were thundering denunciations. Sometimes it was mock indignation. After telling in 1980 how he'd met a young presenter called Selina Scott in an Aberdeen TV studio, and of how 'she made Angela Rippon and Anna Ford look like a couple of sock-knitting crones,' he concluded his item in mock despair: 'Why should the whole country be denied a sight which the people of the Grampian Region enjoy almost every evening?'

Why indeed. Miss Scott was duly tempted South, and JJ followed her subsequent career with interest. He thought to the end of his days that her great talents were ill-used. Born in Glasgow in 1919, he retained a sentimental affection for Scots and Scotland. He was a member of The Royal and Ancient Golf Club of St Andrews. It was on his way to and from there that he passed through the Fifeshire hamlet of Auchtermuchty. This became his personal Brigadoon, a magical, earthy place in which kilted, sex-mad laddies and lubricious lassies performed various burlesques on the eternal human relationship. In 1979, he read about a new system in Natal whereby Zulu maidens had to submit to virginity tests. If they failed, the man responsible had to give two heads of cattle to the girl's parents. Critics said the practice was unethical and cost humble people too much money. JJ wrote: 'I can understand how they feel. If they had similar tests in Scotland, there are some farmers I know not too far from Auchtermuchty who would never again have to get up early. For in their byres, poor laddies, there wouldn't be a single cow left to milk' He hated zoos and loved little birds who came to his garden. Blue tits would hover by his window, he thought, to remind him to refill the peanut container. The migratory feats of birds filled him with child-like wonder, often coupled to some darker thought about the hopeless fecklessness of humankind.In 1995, he was distraught after losing 'an old friend' - a spotted woodpecker he found lying dead on his path. 'Do you suppose that birds, just like humans, can suddenly drop dead from heart attacks?' Again, a question. But on a subject likely to interest millions; the kind of item which encourages readers to write to papers telling of their experiences.

JJ owned a cottage in Normandy, in the small fishing port of Barfleur. He always wrote about going there, and of the 70 franc menu at his favourite local restuarant. 'Night after night' he gloated in 1990, 'I found myself faced with a choice of starters, including half a dozen oysters, a whole crab, a bowl of mussels and soup. Main courses included Dover sole, entrecote steak, canard a l'orange, coq au vin, gigot d'agneau - with the widest possible choice of deserts to follow. Unbelievable, isn't it, when for that sort of money you would hardly get a hamburger and chips in London?' Friends and colleagues travelling in Normandy never located JJ's 70 franc Heaven.

He was a Scottish Presbyterian but he loved France. In particular, he admired the French for believing in their country, and for what others saw as their brusque disdain of outsiders. Although he could ascend to Himalayan heights of columnar fury over the actions of nationalists in Ireland, particularly the IRA, he always praised those who possessed simple Roman Catholic faith.

After after meeting his mentor, Lord Beaverbrook, in the early 1950s he was never a poor man. He was always paid highly and was shrewd with the shares which deservedly came his way after he had made tens of millions of pounds for his then proprietors at the old Express group. But he never joined the middle, or upper-middle-class, viewpoint on any subject. He loathed the old boy network, golf club snobbery, anti-Semitism and any behaviour which struck him as high-handed and unfair.

Nothing he put in his column suggested he led a life of comparative privilege, or that he was so famous Princess Diana stopped him in Kensington High Street for a chat and the Prime Minister asked him to Number Ten for a gossip. Some columnists fill their space with references to their ministerial friends, and what insights they have received from them. JJ got a vast amount of information from the same sources but considered it vulgar and amateur to mention such meetings. On the rare occasions he flew to some far off country, he wrote with innocent delight about the experience. He could wring an amusing column item out of an overnight ferry crossing to Cherbourg. The point was simplicity. His opinions and ideas were straightforward. They were expressed in simple English. Readers might say, putting the paper down: that's exactly what I think. He's said what I have been thinking. That's what he aimed for. There were heroes and villains, saints and crooks, but he rarely wrote himself into a corner: there was usually a get-out, even if it was only his omnipresent question marks.

He blew hot and cold on famous personalities, depending on their behaviour. He never forgot - and never let his readers forget - that the famous are motivated by the same ancient forces as everyone else. He was a journalistic legend, but never one of the boys. He never sought membership of the gentlemen's clubs which now admit newspapermen, or was part of any media association. At the age of 78, he was awarded the highly-coveted Gerald Barry Award for long, distinguished service in journalism. Ever-competitive, he was disappointed they hadn't given him Columnist of the Year at the same ceremony. He liked lunch a deux and always produced a menu of gossip after encouraging his guest to choose his or her food from the plat du jour.

JJ rarely indulged in back-biting with rival newspapers or columnists. If he did weaken, it was with great style and humour. His old paper, the Sunday Express, printed some ill-natured remarks when he joined The Mail on Sunday. JJ responded: 'The editor of a once-great but now, alas, ailing newspaper says patronisingly of my move to the Mail on Sunday: "Good wine clearly does not travel" Doesn't it? I had always thought that good wine travelled enormously well - which is why the great vintages and premier crus are enjoyed by millions of connoisseurs all over the world. I also thought the stuff made of sour grapes was hardly worth putting in bottles at all.'

John Junor was a premier cru, no doubt about that.                    *August, 1997*

# Injustice

*J.J's pen was always ready to fight injustice.*

*He campaigned rigorously on behalf of those whom he considered to be victims of the system.*

*Victims like the BA pilot who narrowly avoided crashing his jumbo jet into a hotel, and the train driver in the Purley rail crash. The pilot waited a year for his trial, the train driver was jailed. J.J. argued that both were treated like criminals for 'one aberration'.*

*In another injustice, he called on John Major to intervene in the case of a have-a-go hero's widow denied money from the State.*

*He also highlighted the injustice of naming men in rape trials regardless of the circumstances while the women accusers remained anonymous. On the same theme, he cited the case of a family doctor named, but cleared in court, of having sex with women patients while their identities remained secret.*

*And he prophesied a future injustice if and when the killer of Josie Russell's mother and sister is caught: the killer, he feared, was likely to spend only a few years in jail while Josie would remain in a mental hell all her life.*

Why should their faces be hidden?
Rules that only add to a misery
Will they never leave her alone?
The hidden face of justice

# Why should their faces be hidden?

IF there is such a thing as instant fame, 32-year-old Dr Jeremy Stupple has certainly achieved it.

This time last week he was virtually completely unknown outside his West Sussex practice.

Now, after the evidence given to the General Medical Council and plastered over the pages of every tabloid in the land, he has become a national figure.

Nor, even though he has been found innocent of the charges made against him, is his fame suddenly going to disappear. Some of the mud thrown is going to stick. For months, maybe years, to come he is going to be pointed out as the man whose desire for sex was said to be so insatiable that within minutes of making love with one attractive, blonde, married patient in his surgery, he was having sex with another, with only a brief breather for a cup of coffee in between.

People will nudge each other and whisper behind his back about his red underpants and of how, on another occasion, he was said to have had sex with one of the women in his surgery while her three-year-old son was separated from them only by a curtain. It is desperately unfair that Dr Stupple should receive such notoriety.

But what seems to me to be even more damnably unfair is the fact that while he received the full glare of the publicity the two women who claim to have had sex with him and almost destroyed his career were allowed to shelter under the titles of Mrs A and Mrs B.

Why weren't their pictures emblazoned on the front pages?

Why shouldn't we have been allowed to know their names?

At the very least, haven't other doctors a right to be forewarned of the perils from now on of offering either of them even as much as an aspirin?

# Will they never leave her alone?

MRS Sonia Sutcliffe, wife of the Yorkshire Ripper, is not a lady to whom I instinctively warm.

I did not care for the number of libel actions she kept on bringing against newspapers.

Nor did I care for the vast amounts of money, some £334,000, she received as a result.

Especially since there have been suggestions that she lied to social security officials, claiming housing benefit at a time when she had an undisclosed £23,500 in a building society account. So I rejoiced when her libel action against the News Of The World was thrown out by a High Court jury and she was left facing huge legal costs, which virtually wiped out every penny she had previously won.

It seemed to me that justice of a kind had been done. My hope was that, apart from any action the law might take against her, Mrs Sutcliffe would disappear from the headlines.

That, it would appear, is not to be

Last week, when she went shopping at the sales with her mother at a Texas Homecare superstore in Yeadon, near Bradford, there was a Daily Express photographer taking pictures of everything she did. How did he just happen to be there? The inference has to be that he was there because the Express had staked out her home and was watching every move she made.

The harassment was so great that, on leaving the crowded shop, she lay face down on the back seat of a Ford Fiesta driven by her mother.

Doesn't that stink a little? Haven't even the wives of mass murderers the right to some privacy?

Isn't it time to let Mrs Sonia Sutcliffe sink back into the anonymity from which she came?

Or is it the intention of some newspapers to keep on harrying her until finally she sticks her head in a gas oven?

May 12, 1991

■ ■ ■ ■ ■ ■

**THERE are some who may think that 53-year-old Captain William Stewart, the British Airways pilot who almost landed his jumbo jet on top of the Penta Hotel at Heathrow Airport, got off lightly with a fine of only £2,000.**

I think it damnable that he should have ever been brought to trial at all.

It is one thing to discipline, maybe even sack, a man who after 25 years of exemplary flying makes one mistake, in the most ghastly weather conditions and with his co-pilot sick, which imperils lives, including his own.

It is quite another to treat him as a criminal, and then subject him to more than a year of mental torture while awaiting a trial with the very real prospect of a jail sentence at the end.

What is the point of it all? What earthly good did it do, sending to jail last year the train driver in the Purley rail disaster who, in one moment of mental aberration, went through a red signal? Did it bring back to life any of the dead? Is it likely to make other British Rail drivers less prone to human error?

**ERROR: William Stewart**

Is the treatment of Captain William Stewart likely to raise the morale among British Airways pilots or make them any less liable to human error? If you believe that then you really will believe anything.

Why, then, do we continue having criminal trials of men who make nothing more than an honest mistake? Could it be simply because Authority must always find a scapegoat for what very often are its own failings?

June 17, 1993

# Rules that only add to a misery

I AM all for the Department of Social Security applying tight rules when it comes to handing out benefits.

Nor do I disagree with the principle that anyone who has capital in excess of £8,000 should be ineligible for Social Security.

But should that apply to 43-year-old Mrs Linda Reed, who's husband Les was killed last June when he tried to stop vandals breaking the bollards and traffic signs near his home on the Ely council estate in Cardiff?

Four youths have since been charged with Mr Reed's murder and the attempted murder of Mr Reed's friend, Mr Philip Tull, who went to his aid and was left unconscious after the attack.

Since her husband's death Mrs Reed, who has three children, has received rent and income support of £48.74 per week.

Now she has been told that she may no longer be entitled to that money when she receives the £9,700 raised by friends and neighbours to help provide for her and her children. Isn't that more than a little bit harsh?

If Margaret Thatcher had been Prime Minister and was aware of what was being done in the Government's name, I suspect she would have been on the telephone immediately to the Minister for Social Security. Shouldn't Mr John Major be on the telephone, too?

February 19, 1995

# The hidden face of justice

THE picture of 25-year-old PC Michael Seear, now on trial at the Old Bailey on a charge of rape, has been on the front page of almost every newspaper in the land.

Guilty or innocent, the publicity means that fingers are going to be pointed at him for years to come. But what about the WPC who accused him but who took three months after the alleged rape to do so and who during those three months lived in the same police section house as PC Seear and her regular bedtime boyfriend, continued to socialise with PC Seear and is said to have visited his room alone, once when he was dressed only in underpants, horsed around with him in the shower, sent him a postcard from holiday and gone shopping with him? What does she look like? We are not allowed to know.

Even if the case against PC Seear is thrown out on its ear we will still not be able to know the name or appearance of his accuser.

Isn't it damned ridiculous?

February 26, 1995

THERE is now a debate going on over a subject I raised last week — the unfairness of men involved in rape trials being named regardless of the circumstances while the women who make allegations which subsequently turn out to be entirely false escape publicity altogether.

But isn't there another — and perhaps even more important — subject which should be discussed? And that is why some of these cases ever come to court at all. PC Michael Seear was only the most recent example.

How, on the evidence presented, could he ever have been found guilty? Before him there was the equally ridiculous case of student Austin Donnellan. There was also the case of poor Angus Diggle, who got three years in jail for attempted rape when, in my view, he should never have been in the dock.

Is it purely coincidence that the apparent willingness to accept the alleged victim's word and to push ahead with the rape cases when the evidence is so flimsy has all happened since that controversial figure Mrs Barbara Mills became Director of Public Prosecutions? Isn't it time we got shot of that lady?

THE picture published on the front pages of almost every newspaper in the land of a mugshot of actor Hugh Grant taken by Los Angeles police, with a police number spread across his chest and looking for all the world like a wanted murderer made me very angry indeed.

Not at Hugh Grant but at the LA Police Department, which issued the pictures within hours of their being taken.

What sort of society is it that does such a thing? Is the crime Hugh Grant committed, picking up a coloured prostitute in his car on Hollywood's Sunset Boulevard, sufficiently serious as to warrant perhaps destroying his career?

Was that the purpose of the LA Police Department when it issued the pictures? The whole thing stinks and it would be monstrous if he were victimised or the public's perception of him destroyed by it. We should realise that great actors are temperamental creatures. We should not expect them always to act like Sunday school teachers. And, after all, isn't being caught with a prostitute on Hollywood's Sunset Boulevard at least a damned sight better than being found with a guardsman in Hyde Park?

# The life sentence Josie now faces

IT IS heartwarming news that nine-year-old Josie Russell, left for dead by the killer who murdered her mother and sister, has recovered so well.

Her progress has been such that detectives have been able gently to question her about that awful afternoon three months ago when horror struck in that quiet Kentish country lane.

But her awakening memory brings its problems.

Her father tells us that when he takes her shopping down the High Street in Canterbury and some-one she does not know stops to talk to him, Josie dashes to the other side of the street and cowers in a doorway. That is a terrible price for a child to pay.

Isn't it even more terrible that if and when they catch the man who murdered her mother and sister – and until they do Josie's own life may be at risk from him — the probability is that he will spend no more than a few years in prison while Josie herself may spend the rest of her life in a mental hell?

ANGER, even outrage, is being expressed because former Guinness chairman Ernest Saunders has been successful in his claim to the European Court of Human Rights that his trial for fraud in England represented a breach of his human rights.

I cannot understand why. There is not the slightest doubt in my mind that at the time Ernest Saunders was treated in the most appalling fashion by English justice. And by the financial Establishment. And I said so at the time.

Right from the moment of his arrest in a highly publicised and quite unnecessary dawn raid and a humiliating night in a cell he was treated in a manner clearly designed to show the British public that he was guilty even before he had been tried. The treatment to which he was subjected was utterly contemptible. Deliberately designed to break and destroy him.

Just as disgraceful was the fact that, stripped of his job, his pay, his chauffeur, his car, and utterly deserted by the Guinness propri-etors, the Iveagh family, whom he had enriched beyond their wildest dreams, he had to endure that public humiliation for nearly three years before his trial eventually took place.

The whole episode, tinged as it was by more than a whiff of anti-Semitism, was a blot on British justice. So I applaud his victory in Strasbourg.

I am only sorry that the judgment falls short of allowing him to take the British judicial authorities financially to the cleaners.

# World leaders

*Bill Clinton, President of the United States and leader of the Western world. The most powerful figure on earth — yet to J.J. he was an object of contempt and derision. Clinton was a weak, draft-dodging, no good, sex-mad womaniser you wouldn't buy a second hand yo-yo from. A shoddy saxophonist with a third-rate mind, married to Hillary, a congenital liar. J.J. never pulled his punches!*

*The savaging of Clinton was in marked contrast to his admiration of Mikhail Gorbachev. The Russian President who ended the Cold War was succeeded by Boris Yeltsin.*

*Gorbachev may not always have been right, but at least there were no doubts about his sanity, J.J argued. Yeltsin, by contrast, was a hard-drinking, unstable maverick who put the fear of God into our columnist.*

*In his assessment of other world leaders, George Bush was old, incapable of original thought and unable to communicate.*

*South African leader Nelson Mandela was a civilised moderate leader handicapped by the presence of Winnie, his wife at the time, and the 'odious' Archbishop Tutu.*

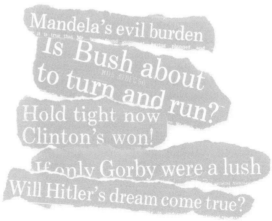

# The decency and dignity of Mr M

THE more I see Mr Nelson Mandela, the more I like him. There is an innate decency and dignity about him.

My instinct tells me that he is a civilised moderate whom I could trust with my life.

I wish I could say the same about those closest to him. Including his wife, Winnie, and that odious little self-publicist, Archbishop Tutu.

If Mr Mandela were left on his own to do what he in his wisdom thinks best, I have not the slightest doubt that he and Mr de Klerk could negotiate a settlement which, although it could not produce an immediate one-man, one-vote situation, would at least end apartheid and ensure peace and prosperity for all South Africans, black and white alike.

But will he be left on his own?

My fear is that, even if he resists the malign influence of his wife, he will be swept aside by younger hot-headed militants who are not interested in compromise.

Only in total, absolute, black Marxist victory.

And that ahead could lie violence and bloodshed such as not even South Africa has seen before.

If that were to happen, would not a terrible responsibility for it rest on the shoulders of foreign politicians like Neil Kinnock and Gerald Kaufman, who now give the impression of egging the militants on?

**■ ■ ■ ■ ■**

EVEN after the £30,000-a-year increase awarded him last week by the Soviet parliament, Mr Mikhail Gorbachev's £48,000-a-year salary is still, by Western standards, derisory.

Even so, in a country seething with discontent — a veritable gunpowder keg just waiting for a match — I think he is mad to take an increase of any kind at a time when the mass of his people can hardly afford to buy enough food to live.

I desperately hope for all our sakes that Mr Gorbachev is going to survive.

He would have a

**PAY RISE: Gorbachev**

better chance of so doing if he and his elegant, sable-clad wife learned the elementary lesson that the only leaders who do survive are those who lead from the front and who do not impose on their people hardships they are not prepared to accept themselves.

Or who, if they do cheat, at least have the wit not to publicise the fact to the world.

# Will Hitler's dream come true?

Mr BORIS YELTSIN is not the sort of man to whom I instinctively warm.

He gives me the impression of being the sort of slob one would expect to see staggering out of pubs late at night and usually tripping over a few bar stools on the way.

Intellectually, he is not even in the same league as Mr Mikhail Gorbachev. But it would be unwise to underestimate either his popularity in Russia or his rabble-rousing qualities.

And since he is able, quite unfairly, to put all the blame on Mr Gorbachev for all the hardships which now afflict the Russian people, he may well succeed in toppling him.

But if he does, and the result is — as it would be — the disintegration of the USSR, then who would benefit? Certainly not us. Nor France. Nor even the US. I see only one beneficiary. A Germany united, and so rich and powerful that it would be economic master of all Europe.

Fantastic, isn't it, how 45 years after his death in a Berlin bunker many of Hitler's dreams may yet be realised?

# Is Bush about to turn and run?

JUST one year ago, in my first column for The Mail on Sunday, I posed the question:

*'If the world were an enormous hot-air balloon and its continuing survival depended on jettisoning one crew member from the control basket, who would you choose to chuck overboard — President Gorbachev or President Bush?'*

My own vote went unhesitatingly for the dumping of George Bush.

Now, one year later, it is Mrs Thatcher who has been chucked out, Mr Gorbachev is just hanging on by his fingernails — God alone knows for how much longer — and President Bush is alone at the controls.

Is that a situation which makes you feel like singing and dancing in the streets? I tell you this. It puts the fear of God into me.

Not because I think George Bush is a bad or evil man. It is just that I have a terrible feeling that he is a born waffler who may turn out to be as great a disaster for the world as his predecessor Woodrow Wilson.

He may look all right jogging in his running shorts for the benefit of the TV cameras — although the very fact that a man in his sixties feels the need to impress in that way is in itself suspicious. But as the leader of the free world he makes me very nervous indeed.

Contrast his dithering over Saddam Hussein with the sharp, swift, decisive action his predecessor Ronald Reagan took against Colonel Gadaffi from whom there has been barely a squeak ever since.

When Mr Bush was simply Vice-President hoping to secure the Republican Presidential nomination, his critics taunted him with the accusation that he was a wimp who could never make his mind up about anything. As decision day of January 15 approaches in the Kuwait crisis, aren't his critics being proved to be absolutely spot-on?

How is that crisis going to end? If by January 15 there is not a complete and unequivocal Iraqi withdrawal from Kuwait, has George Bush the bottle to declare war?

Or will there be a cowardly, miserable fudge which will leave Saddam Hussein with part of his spoils and free to strike again whenever he chooses in just the same way as Hitler once was?

Do you wonder if in her new flat in Eaton Square an impotent Mrs Thatcher occasionally feels like banging her handbag against the wall?

# The devil we don't know

ON January 7, 1990, in my first ever column for The Mail on Sunday I posed this question:

'If the world were an enormous hot-air balloon and its continued survival depended on jettisoning one crew member from the control basket, who would you choose to chuck overboard? President George Bush or President Mikhail Gorbachev?'

I plumped for President Bush. I argued that whereas George Bush was an adequate US president, there were many other men equally adequate who could replace him. But that Gorbachev was irreplaceable. Now the irreplaceable has been replaced. And it is virtually certain that in the control basket President George Bush will now ride with Mr Boris Yeltsin.

Does that make you feel like singing and dancing in the streets? It puts the fear of God into me.

Mr Gorbachev may have had his faults. He may have been too slow in switching to a market economy. He may have been too keen on compromise in order to keep the whole Soviet Union together. But at least there was never any doubt about his sanity. Can the same be said with equal certainty about Mr Yeltsin?

My suspicion is that he is a hard-drinking, unstable maverick who, when not falling into the Volga or lurching through the Chancelleries of Europe, has gained vast public popularity by making to the Russian people promises he cannot possibly ever

keep and who, if things go on the way they are, is going to preside over the creation of anarchy as the whole Soviet system falls apart.

Furthermore, in the ensuing mess, it is probably he and he alone who will have his finger on the Russian nuclear button. Is that likely to be a recipe for international tranquillity?

I could be wrong and I very much hope that I am. But my fear is that the day could yet come when the world will wish that Mr Yeltsin's counter coup had failed and that if Mr Gorbachev had to go it would have been safer for us all if it had been the so-called hardliners and not Mr Yeltsin who had replaced him.

# Mandela's evil burden

IF IT is true that Mr Nelson Mandela plans to divorce his wife Winnie, I would say it is probably the best thing he has ever done.

Mr Mandela himself gives the impression of being tolerant and liberal.

He is someone many white South Africans believe they can trust.

But Winnie? She is a virago who has already been found guilty of, and is now awaiting sentence for, the kidnapping and beating up of young blacks.

She also gave the impression that she condoned, if

she did not actually incite, the horrific necklaces of fire placed round the necks of blacks suspected of having collaborated with whites.

Now she is accused of having planned and conspired to assassinate members of the African National Congress.

She gives the impression of being an evil woman who loves violence for the sake of violence. Mr Mandela will be well shot of her. But is there any jail in South Africa big enough to keep her from fomenting trouble in the future?

# Does a Hitler lie in waiting?

ALTHOUGH his lead in the opinion polls may be narrowing, it still seems probable that by next Wednesday Governor Bill Clinton will be the new President of the United States.

What will that mean for the future of the world? God alone knows.

It used to be said of President Richard Nixon that he was the sort of man from whom you wouldn't want to buy a second-hand car.

Bill Clinton, with his record of draft-dodging and floozie-chasing, and who during the election campaign has been all things to all men, seems to me to be the sort of President from whom you wouldn't even want to buy a second-hand yo-yo.

Yet it is easy to understand why, even if they don't trust Governor Clinton, US voters are turning away from George Bush. His critics point to the mountainous US unemployment figures and to the devastating effects of the recession and blame him.

Yet, weak and wet although he may sometimes appear, and may indeed be, is he to blame? Any more than perhaps Mr John Major and the hapless Mr Norman Lamont are to blame for the recession and the collapse of the pound in Britain?

Or President Mitterrand for the unemployment and penal interest rates in France? Or the Swedish government for having to raise Swedish interest rates to at one moment the unbelievable height of 75 per cent? Or even Helmut Kohl for the catastrophe which many people believe may soon engulf Germany?

Isn't the truth of the matter the fact that the whole world is in economic turmoil? And what has caused it? Ironically, isn't it the dividend of peace? As long as the Soviet Union remained an awesome, frightening military power and the Western nations spent astronomic sums arming to defend themselves against possible attack, there was prosperity everywhere.

Now the Soviet Union has collapsed and the threat has gone. So there is no need to build bigger and better tanks, faster and more technologically advanced bombers. The workers who made them have been laid off. So now there is a worldwide slump.

It was exactly the same after the First World War. Only the arrival of Hitler, who was himself a product of the unemployment and hyper-inflation in Germany, set alarm bells ringing, the world re-arming and industry buzzing again. I just hope to God that we will not need another Hitler this time. Wouldn't it be terrible if history were to find that the only thing the world's politicians just cannot cope with is lasting peace?

# Hold tight now Clinton's won!

NOT too many tears will be shed in Britain over the defeat of President George Bush.

He was a decent man and, I think, an honest one. But he seemed totally incapable of original thought. Above all, he had absolutely no capacity to communicate in simple language with the American people. On the public platform he sounded just about as articulate as a dead duck.

Finally he was old, a fact that not all the jogging in the world could hide, and any personal magic he may ever have had as a war-time naval pilot had long since gone. The new President, in sharp contrast, is young and good-looking and with bags of sex appeal.

He has clearly modelled himself on his predecessor of 30 years ago, President John F. Kennedy, and, in many ways, they are indeed similar.

Kennedy, too, had a long history of womanising.

And just like President Kennedy, Bill Clinton has a magic way with words. Some of his public utterances during the campaign have been almost pure poetry. But will we discover, as we have done with Kennedy, that his words had been written by someone else?

What will his election mean for Britain? That will depend on whether he meant all the things he said during the campaign or whether he was simply saying them to win the votes.

If he continues to be supportive of Irish Republicanism and attempts to carry out his promise to send a US peace envoy to Northern Ireland, that could be disastrous for British-US relations.

If he tries to protect US jobs by raising trade barriers, that could be disastrous for the whole world. He may turn out, of course, to be very much better than we expect. It may be that behind that pretty-boy image there is a man who really cares about humanity and genuinely wants to serve it.

We will just have to wait and see. My own fancy is that for the next four years we could be in for a pretty rough ride.

So fasten your seatbelts. And tell Alice to keep the sick bag handy.

*John F. Kennedy*

*George Bush*

*Bill Clinton*

# May it never rain under Clinton

THE least surprising thing about the monumental cock-up which ended with 87 people, including 17 children, being incinerated in the Waco disaster was the rapidity with which President Clinton initially distanced himself from responsibility.

His first reaction was to lie low and say: 'Talk to the Attorney General or the FBI. I knew it was going to be done, but the decision was entirely theirs.'

It was only after 24 hours, and much adverse Press comment, that he emerged from the White House publicly to admit responsibility but even then he did so in such a half-hearted fashion as to make it meaningless. So, it is his Attorney General, Janet Reno, who, along with the FBI, is left to carry the can. This despite the fact that Clinton himself was in the affair right up to the neck and had been informed that the FBI intended to break the siege on that particular day and in that particular ham-handed way with a battering ram and tear gas. And with no fire engines in attendance.

In terms of international politics, I don't suppose the whole shoddy shambles matters a damn. Save for one thing. The insight it gives us into the mind of this weak, constantly vacillating man who is now President of the US and, God help us, leader of the Western world until 1997.

I only hope it doesn't rain between now and then.

*It now looks probable that Boris Yeltsin may win today's referendum in Russia. If he does, I, for one, will not be singing and dancing in the street. My own view of Mr Yeltsin has never wavered.*
*He is an unstable lush who cannot long survive in the Russian top job. But, while he does, isn't it going to be an exciting world with Boris Yeltsin gargling in vodka in Moscow while Mr Clinton plays the saxophone in Washington?*

# Is Blair next to be rumbled?

THE sick, sad look on the face of President Clinton told it all far better than any political commentator could.

After just 21 months in the White House he has been rumbled by the American people.

They voted for him in 1992 because they were tired of boring, honest, dull, old George Bush. They were seduced by the boyish face, easy-going manner and apparently fresh ideas of Bill Clinton.

Now, after just 21 months, they have discovered that behind the boyish manner there lies nothing but a third-rate, indecisive mind.

Does the catastrophe which has now engulfed President Clinton give that equally attractive, boyish figure, Mr Tony Blair, cause for thought? And perhaps the British electors, too?

# How Major can sidestep Clinton

THE Prime Minister was absolutely right to snub President Clinton by refusing to speak to him on the telephone last week.

His anger with the shoddy saxophonist is amply justified.

But is the matter going to end there? When Mr Major goes to Washington the week after next, is it all going to be, on the surface, lovey-dovey again? Will the President and the Prime Minister be pictured shaking hands, arms round each other and delivering the usual platitudes about the warmth of the friendship which exists between Britain and the United States? I hope not.

There is no way in which Mr Major can duck out of his visit to Washington. Nor is there any reason why he should.

No matter how angry we are about the deification of Mr Gerry Adams by President Clinton, business between the two countries has to go on as usual. What there is no need for at all is for Mr Major to provide President Clinton with a propaganda platform from which he can persuade the American people that his treatment of Mr Adams, a crude attempt to win Irish-American votes, has not in any way endangered US relations with Britain.

So, after their talks, why doesn't Mr Major politely decline the usual obligatory TV appearances posing with the President on the White House lawn?

And if he needs an excuse for so doing, couldn't he always say he has a pain in a wisdom tooth?

**TELLING LOOKS: Bill and Hillary Clinton**

HILLARY CLINTON may be everything her critics in the US say she is.

She may be a congenital liar. She may be up to her neck in Whitewater skulduggery. She may terrify White House staff with her early-morning rages and her caustic tongue. She may know a great deal more than she admits about the cover-up surrounding the mysterious death of her close friend and Presidential aide Vincent Foster. She may be talking about adopting a child simply to obtain public sympathy. She may be a nutcase who spends her evenings in imaginary conversations with Eleanor Roosevelt and Mahatma Gandhi.

She may be all these things. But do you observe the look in Bill Clinton's face every time he is pictured with her?

Clinton himself may be a no-good, sex-mad womaniser. But can anyone doubt the real affection in his eyes when he looks at Hillary?

But do you notice something else? That in all their pictures she never seems to be looking at him? Could that also be telling us something?

# If only Gorby were a lush

WHEN, three weeks ago, by the narrowest of margins, Mr Boris Yeltsin won the first round of the Russian General Election, I had this to say in my column about his victory.

It may well be that, with the help of General Aleksander Lebed, the anti-Mafia, anti-corruption, law-and-order man who came third and to whom he has given a top cabinet job, he will win the second round too. But will he still be in power or even alive in another six months' time? I wouldn't bet on it.

During his time in office he has suffered heart attack after heart attack. Yet, during the election campaign, and almost certainly hyped up by drugs, he was cavorting about like a two-year-old . . . all in a desperate attempt to prove to the Russian TV audiences that he was still fit and active. He may have succeeded in so doing. But at what cost to his health?

We now know the answer to that last question. Yeltsin took no part at all in the second round of the campaign except for one stumbling TV appearance in which he looked much more dead than alive. Last week he startled the world by failing to turn up for a meeting with US Vice-President Al Gore. And when eventually he did see Mr Gore, the meeting place was a sanatorium and Yeltsin could barely walk. Clearly he is a goner. Even so, he remains Russian President in name. But who, in fact, is in control? Is it the completely unknown and politically inexperienced paratroop general Aleksander Lebed who has the title of Vice-President?

Or will there be a coup, to oust him, too? It is a situation bristling with danger for all of us.

Yet there is one man in Russia whom the West could trust. Mikhail Gorbachev. Alas, he languishes in the background.

Why? There are two reasons. One is the fact that in his time in office he waged war on the drinking habits of the Russian people and tried to make them cut down on vodka. They didn't like that.

But most of all they, especially the Russian women, didn't like his wife Raisa and the high-profile glamorous life she led buying fashion gowns with an American Express card in the sophisticated capitals of the Western world.

Wry old thought, isn't it, that the world today might be a damned sight safer place if only Mikhail Gorbachev had been himself a vodka drinker and his wife had been as dull and drab and ugly as the rest of the Kremlin bosses' wives?

# The Queen

*The Nineties was the most difficult and traumatic decade of the Queen's reign. There must have been times, J.J. commiserated, when she thought her world was collapsing around her.*

*As disenchantment with the monarchy grew, she faced a ferocious and potentially damaging onslaught against the Royal Family.*

*As a mother, she had witnessed the marriage break-ups of three of her four children. She had to cope with the humiliation of Prince Charles's hopeless obsession with Mrs Camilla Parker Bowles, a woman J.J. insisted would never be tolerated by the British people.*

*The Queen also had to deal with her daughter-in-law, Diana, who seemed at one time, according to J.J, to be doing her best to destroy the monarchy. She was further dismayed by Prince Andrew's divorce from 'the spend-thrift, pleasure-loving, outrageous' Duchess of York.*

*One scandal after another rocked the foundations of the House of Windsor destroying its mechanism.*

*At the height of this stressful period, the Queen was publicly criticised for her failure to pay income tax on her personal income, which is something she later rectified. At the time of the Windsor Castle fire, she was subjected to further criticism when it was suggested she should even pay for the repairs herself. J.J. dismissed such an idea as yob talk.*

*Despite all the difficulties the Queen faced during this turbulent period, she could still look back and find consolation, said J.J. Throughout all the upheavals she should be in no doubt that her personal standing had not diminished. Nor had the affection in which she was held by the majority of her subjects.*

*Throughout her reign, her devotion and duty had been outstanding — her personal conduct without flaw.*

*While ably supported by the Queen Mother, Her Majesty had many crosses to bear in her life, not the least heavy of them her husband, Prince Philip.*

# Is the Queen saving up for a rainy day?

I WONDER what the innermost thoughts of the Queen were as she looked out of her bedroom window at Sandringham last Thursday morning, the 40th anniversary of her accession to the Throne.

Did she think back with sadness on how the news of her father's death had been broken to her that day in Kenya so long ago?

Did she think back wistfully to those heady days at the time of the Coronation when she was young and beautiful and the nation was talking excitedly about the arrival of a new and glorious Elizabethan age?

But is she happy in her own mind about everything she has since achieved? She should be.

The youth and beauty may have gone but other and greater and more enduring qualities have taken their place. For 40 years her devotion to duty has been outstanding; her personal conduct without flaw. And in the Prince of Wales she has produced a worthy successor to herself. But even so, can she be entirely happy about the state of the monarchy?

She is far too wise not to be aware that there is a growing public disenchantment with the Royal Family. It was most probably her awareness of that disenchantment which caused her to ask for the cancellation on the grounds of economy of the project to commemorate her 40th anniversary by the building of a fountain in Parliament Square.

But if there is public disenchantment what is the cause of it? Certainly the outrageous activities of a few of the minor Royals, some of them commoners who have quickly shown just how common they are, has not helped. Over-exposure on TV and in the tabloid Press has also done much to destroy the mysticism which used to surround the Royal Family. The break-up of Royal marriages has not helped either.

But, bizarrely, in one tiny, relatively unimportant aspect Her Majesty herself has not been without fault. Like many other people who are very far from being republicans I find it quite baffling that she should seem to be so firmly personally opposed to paying income tax on her purely personal income. Not income tax on the money voted to her by Parliament for the upkeep of the monarchy. Not tax on her personal possessions, her palaces, her paintings, her jewels. But tax only on the investment income she receives from her stocks and shares.

What possible objection can she have to that? Every time the issue is raised there is a flurry of Palace-inspired stories indicating that the Queen is not really as rich as everyone thinks. And maybe she isn't. But does the amount of her wealth — whether it is £1,000 million or just £100 million — really matter? Isn't it the principle involved that is the important thing?

There is a perhaps greater mystery — what can she possibly want the money for? After all, she can't take it with her and her descendants seem to have quite enough already.

So what is the explanation? Can Her Majesty really still be saving up for a rainy day? The day, perhaps, the Revolution comes?

# Brooke fires the mob

THERE is something ugly, brutish and ignorant about the cries coming from some socialists and also, and quite extraordinarily, from some sections of the Tory Press, demanding that the Queen make a sizeable financial contribution to the restoration of Windsor Castle.

There are some, indeed, who would like to see her pay for it all.

That is yob talk. One does not need to be much of a royalist to regard it as such. Or to feel intensely sorry for the Queen having to make a public

speech at the Guildhall lunch celebrating her 40 years on the throne on the very day much of the bilious comment was being printed.

I am not suggesting that the Queen be immune from criticism. I have long thought she was singularly ill-advised to resist paying income tax on her private income. And I rejoice that she has at last yielded on this issue although, unhappily, her change of stance is now likely to be regarded not so much as a gracious gesture as a hasty retreat in the face of an advancing mob. But to contribute to the restoration of Windsor Castle? That just has to be a nonsense.

Windsor Castle does not belong to the Queen. Any more than Hampton Court or Buckingham Palace do. They belong to the nation in exactly the same way as Number 10 Downing Street does.

If Number 10 were destroyed by fire or by an IRA bomb, would we expect Mr John Major, or whoever happens to be Prime Minister at the time, to pay for the reparation? If not, why then should we expect Her Majesty to pay for Windsor Castle?

So what, then, explains the present uproar? Part of the problem comes from the ham-handed way in which the matter was handled by the National Heritage Secretary, Mr Peter Brooke. When Mr Brooke took over the Heritage job after the abrupt and unlamented departure of Mr David Mellor, he was described as 'a safe pair of hands'.

Safe pair of hands? You could have fooled me. I think he is a bumbling idiot.

What on earth induced him, while the flames were still burning, to announce in that plummy, upper-class voice of his that, no matter the cost, the taxpayer would pick up every penny of it.

Why, at that stage, was it necessary to make any statement at all? Why didn't he just keep his mouth shut?

I don't know. But I tell you this. The more I see of Mr Peter Brooke the more I think the Prime Minister should release him from his present job and set him free to do the thing he does best. Singing Darling Clementine on Irish TV.

# Tell it like it is, Your Majesty

ON Friday afternoon at 3 o'clock the Queen will deliver her most painful, and perhaps, from the Monarchy's point of view, her most crucial Christmas message ever.

For just this once the whole nation is going to be on tenterhooks to hear her.

What is she going to say?

I mean no disrespect. Quite the reverse. But is it going to be the usual time-worn collection of platitudes cobbled together by Palace courtiers and read without discernible emotion from a tele-prompter? I so much hope not.

The Queen, as anyone who has ever had private conversation with her will testify, has a first-class mind and a capacity to express herself movingly.

Why doesn't she do so on Friday? Why not tear up any speech that may have been prepared for her and instead tell us what is really in her mind?

It has indeed been a terrible year for her and her family. But why not speak openly and frankly about it and of her especial sadness at the break-up of the marriage of Prince Charles and the Princess of Wales?

And of her concern for the future of the children.

To do so may be stressful for Her Majesty. But, even so, wouldn't such temporary stress be infinitely preferable and, in the long run, infinitely less damaging for the Monarchy than if she were to sidestep the whole issue altogether?

# Has there ever been a braver royal lady?

IT MUST have been galling for the Queen Mother when she found a newspaper photographer had snapped a picture showing something she would have preferred to keep quiet.

The fact that, at the age of 94, she just occasionally uses a wheelchair.

She was spotted by a photographer as, her leg heavily bandaged, she was wheeled the last few yards from Walmer Castle last weekend to the car waiting to take her to morning service in nearby Saint Mary's Church. But there was no wheelchair when she walked with the aid of a stick into the church, smiling at fellow worshippers and insisting on standing during hymns.

Yet she must have been in pain. Perhaps the same sort of pain she would have been in during the VE Day celebrations when she stood on the Buckingham Palace balcony alongside the Queen and Princess Margaret, and the whole nation saw her mouth the words as Vera Lynn sang There'll Be Bluebirds Over The White Cliffs Of Dover.

There can never have been a braver or more remarkable royal lady. There can never have been a royal lady more devoted to duty or who served the nation better. Even last Wednesday's cataract operation has not caused her to cancel a single public engagement.

There is currently a discussion as to which famous public figure most deserves to have his or her achievements commemorated with a statue on the vacant space in Trafalgar Square.

Could there be a better candidate than the Queen Mother?

**December 3, 1995**

# Spare us the pomp

IF IT is true that Prince Edward and Miss Sophie Rhys-Jones are shortly to announce their engagement and plan a spring wedding then I wish them both much happiness.

I just hope that no one in Buckingham Palace is naive enough to imagine that a fairytale wedding in the spring will do anything to restore the Royal Family's present tarnished image. It could do exactly the opposite.

My own opinion is that the public is fed up to the teeth with royal weddings. And would infinitely prefer it if, after a family Sandringham wedding, Prince Edward and his bride were to retire, as so many other minor Royals have done, into private life.

**February 25, 1996**

# A royal cross to bear

AS the Duke of Edinburgh was entering the stable yard of Windsor Castle at the reins of his horse-drawn carriage, Kitra Cahana's father, Ronnie, waved to him and said: 'Good morning, Sir. My little girl is six today.'

The Duke's reply was terse. 'So what?' he snapped, and with a flick of the reins proceeded on his way.

No wonder the little girl, whose father had paid £32 to take his family round the Castle, burst into tears.

But doesn't her father himself share some responsibility for these tears? Shouldn't he have had more sense than ever to have approached such a cantankerous old man with such a meaningless remark?

What did he expect Prince Philip to do? Jump down and give Kitra a kiss?

But that having been said, can you imagine the Queen or the Queen Mother, or indeed any other member of the Royal Family, acting so ungraciously?

The Queen has had many crosses to bear in her life. Not the least heavy of them, I suspect, is her husband.

# The Queen's one great consolation

THIS has to be just about the unhappiest birthday the Queen has ever had.

On what should be a day of joyous celebration, her personal world is collapsing around her.

The marriage of one daughter-in-law, the spend-thrift, pleasure-loving, outrageous Duchess of York, has ended in divorce.

Her heir, the Prince of Wales, is still apparently hopelessly obsessed with a woman the British people will never accept and, instead of supporting the monarchy, her second daughter-in-law, the Princess of Wales, seems to be doing her damndest to destroy it.

Yet it is not all gloom. Hasn't the Queen also grounds for optimism? First of all she must know that her own personal standing has not been diminished. Nor has the affection in which she is held.

There is a public awareness that throughout all the traumas affecting the Royal Family her own conduct and devotion to duty have been exemplary.

And hasn't she enormous consolation today at the presence at her birthday part of her grandchildren and in particular the second in line to the throne, Prince William — a boy whose warmth of heart is demonstrated every time he is seen solicitously fussing around and taking care of his great-grandmother, the Queen Mother.

Although hopefully it will be many years ahead, isn't he one day going to make a perfect King?

# The humiliating of Diana

THERE is one aspect of the Royal divorce settlement which reflects no credit on either the Queen or her advisers — the decision to strip the Princess of Wales of the title Her Royal Highness.

That is an act of petty pointless vindictiveness.

It means that from now on the Princess of Wales will be expected to curtsey to members of the Royal Family who were her former in-laws, including Princess Michael of Kent.

She will even be expected to curtsey to her own sons. Even to Camilla Parker Bowles if Prince Charles is stupid enough to marry her. Which he may well be. It is all so humiliating and so unnecessary. It may also be self-defeating.

The Queen and Prince Charles may feel they are scoring points by depriving the Princess of Wales of her title. I think that in time they may find that, by so doing, they themselves have lost a great deal more.

HAVE you noticed the change in the Queen's appearance in the past month or two?

Quite suddenly she has aged. I was shaken when I saw pictures on Sky News of her visit with the Duke of Edinburgh to the Royal Tournament. She looked so tired and almost dumpy.

Clearly the events surrounding not only the Royal divorce, but before that all the hassle over the Duchess of York's debts and flibbertigibbet conduct, have taken a heavy toll.

The Prince of Wales's continuing association with Camilla Parker Bowles cannot bring her much pleasure or hope for the future either. I feel so sorry for her.

It is appalling that, after a lifetime of devoted service and dedication to duty, she should now be reaping such a sad harvest.

The hope must be that in the years to come her grandson Prince William will once again make the sun shine for the Queen and for the House of Windsor.

He is their very last hope.

# Merry old Kohl's a dangerous soul

WAS the Duke of Windsor a traitor who would have been happy to have been installed by Hitler as a puppet-king?

Was the Duchess of Windsor really such a bitch as to have desired at any price to become Queen?

I do not believe it. I do not believe that the Duke of Windsor was anything other than a simpleton who was as thick as two planks. But then what's new about that among Royals? Nor do I believe that the Duchess ever had aspirations to become Queen of a Nazi-controlled Britain.

She was too fond of high-life American society for that. The summit of her ambition was to be given the title HRH to flaunt to her friends in the US.

But don't events of 60 years ago, now revealed to the public in documents released by the Public Record Office, make fascinating reading?

And even 60 years later doesn't it maky you shiver slightly to realise just how close this country was to becoming a province of Germany? But are we all that far away from the same thing happening again? Fat, jolly, beaming Helmut Kohl may not look like Hitler. In character he is quite the opposite. He is a passionate believer in democracy and is against all racism. I am prepared to believe that he is a good, decent man who says his prayers every night and goes to church twice on Sundays.

But isn't his aim, just as it was Hitler's, the German domination of Europe? And, if he succeeds in persuading Britain to adopt a common currency and obey every diktat that comes from the bureaucrats in Brussels, will he not at last be succeeding where Hitler failed.

December 22, 1996

# Wasn't the Duke right on target?

THE Duke of Edinburgh is notorious for making remarks which upset people.

And sometimes is rightly criticised.

But it is quite ridiculous that he should be so violently assailed for having said that, desperately as he sympathised with parents who had lost their children, he felt that reaction to the Dunblane shooting was being overdone. And that a total ban on hand-guns, even for sporting purposes, would be just about as sensible as a total ban on cricket bats.

Has it really become a crime to tell the truth? And just where do we go from here?

Will the next step by the increasingly hysterical anti-gun lobby be a ban on shotguns, too, and on all forms of field sport? Is a youngster like Prince Harry going to be pilloried and made to feel a leper because he enjoys accompanying his father on a day's shooting at Sandringham?

Or has the time come to tell Snowdrop campaign leader Ann Pearston, who is making a career out of Dunblane, and her fellow sob-sisters of both sexes, including that buffoon Labour's Shadow Scottish Secretary George Robertson, to go to hell?

I would very much like to think so.

# Hypocrisy

*J.J. could not abide hypocrisy. No individual was too exalted to escape judgment, whether they belonged to the Royal Family, the Establishment, the Church or the world of sport.*

*Among those he criticised for their double standards were Princess Anne, Sir Robin Leigh-Pemberton, a governor of the Bank of England, designer Sir Hardy Amies, Sebastian Coe and Dr Eamonn Casey, the Roman Catholic Bishop of Galway.*

*And there was no escape from J.J.'s wrath for the hypocrisy shown by the burghers of a Lancashire town embroiled in a battle over a World War One hero's Victoria Cross.*

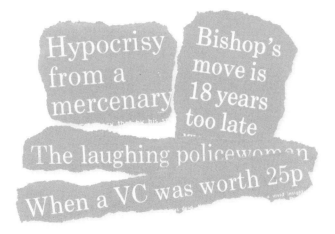

Hypocrisy from a mercenary

Bishop's move is 18 years too late

The laughing policewoman

When a VC was worth 25p

# When a VC was worth 25p

PRIVATE Tommy Whitham of the Coldstream Guards was just 29 when he won the VC at Ypres in 1917.

Single-handed, he had stormed a German machine-gun nest.

They gave him a brass band hero's welcome when he returned to his native Burnley.

The mayor and all the top dignitaries were there. Echoing down through the years, can't you almost still hear the oom-pah-pah of the band and the blah-blah-blah of the councillors? But when later, and shortly before his demob, he wrote to the then mayor asking for a job as a stonemason in the council's building department, he was told to get lost.

Seven years later he was dead. Now, 73 years later, Burnley council and the late Tommy Whitham's family have been in a tussle over who should have the VC.

The council bought the medal from a pawnbroker for £50 in 1931 and has retained possession of it ever since. and has just voted to continue so doing.

Mr Whitham's family, headed by his eldest son — now himself an old man of 78 — say they wanted to buy it back so they could present it to the museum of the Coldstream Guards.

I don't suppose it matters a damn who has the medal. But there is one aspect of the story that tugs at the heart-strings and gives a vivid insight into just how grim things were in Britain after the First World War.

When, in order to buy food for his family, Tommy Whitham pawned that VC in 1921, he received for it just five shillings.

Just 25p. It brings a tear to the eye to think of that brave man looking at two old half-crowns in the palm of his hand. The end product of all his valour.

Sad, isn't it, that the people of Burnley did not think as warmly towards him then, when he so desperately needed help, as apparently they do now?

**FRUGAL: The Queen**

■ ■ ■ ■ ■

THERE is just a hint of sourness in the way Sir Hardy Amies tells the world that the Queen is on the mean side when it comes to spending money on clothes.

He even suggests that she is not too keen on paying the full marked price and that hints have been dropped that a discount would not come amiss on the dresses she does buy.

I suppose that does tell us a bit about the Queen, and for my own part I am delighted to learn that she is so frugal.

## Patronage

But doesn't it tell us quite a bit about Sir Hardy Amies, too?

His success as a designer and everything else he has in life, including that title, have been largely due to royal patronage.

Might he not, in these circumstances, have been just a little bit kinder? Might he not have remembered the adage I learned on my mother's knee — that one old queen should always speak warmly and with affection about another?

■ ■ ■ ■ ■

FOR my own part, I don't give a damn whether or not Princess Anne is having an affair with naval Commander Tim Laurence (remember the hoo-ha last year when The Sun newspaper revealed that the Commander — then an equerry to the Queen — had been writing 'affectionate' letters to the Princess)?

Nor do I give a damn whether she plans to marry him the moment she gets her quickie divorce from Captain Mark Phillips.

If I had any feeling at all it would be of sympathy for the Commander. I myself would as soon seek the *embrace of a female tarantula.* But then, at the age of 36, he ought to be quite old enough to look after himself.

What does annoy me is the behind-lace-curtains secrecy with which the whole business is being conducted.

The couple meet discreetly and, according to reports, the Commander on shore leave

**SECRECY: Anne**

from his ship at Devonport, spends occasional weekends at Gatcombe Park. On other occasions they go shooting together at Sandringham.

Presumably, with the full knowledge of the Queen.

Why then so hush-hush about it all? Is it so that the Princess can escape from the Divorce Courts without stigma? If so, I can understand the motivation.

Yet would the nation really collapse in a swoon if it thought the Queen's daughter was committing adultery?

On balance, isn't adultery at least preferable to hypocrisy?

**PIOUS: Leigh-Pemberton**

■ ■ ■ ■ ■

**WHEN Mrs Thatcher originally appointed Mr Robin Leigh-Pemberton as Governor of the Bank of England, I thought she was making a mistake.**

My view then was that, behind the pretty face and smooth manners, there was not the greatest of intellects. Nothing in the intervening years has made me change my mind.

Now, only days after he has been up in his pulpit piously preaching wage restraint and how we must avoid listening to siren voices urging the cutting of interest rates since inflation is not yet under control, it is revealed that all the time he was moralising, he himself was accepting an inflation-busting rise of 17 per cent. How's that for practising what you preach?

It may be difficult for the Prime Minister to sack Mr Leigh-Pemberton before the end of his term.

But as a leading member of the officer-and-gentleman class in our society, might he not have the decency to resign before he does the Government even more harm than he already has?

May 10, 1992

# Bishop's move is 18 years too late

MY initial reaction was one of sympathy when I heard the news that the R.C. Bishop of Galway, Dr Eamonn Casey, had had to resign following the revelation that for 17 years he had been paying money totalling over £100,000 to a woman in America with whom he apparently had had an affair and who was allegedly the mother of his son.

Even the most saintly can on occasion succumb to temptation and spend the rest of their lives regretting one moment of weakness.

But the extrovert Dr Casey, who while piously preaching chastity from the pulpit was having it off with Annie Murphy in the vestry, does not quite seem to fit into that mould.

A taste for the good things, like a BMW and frequent attendance at the best and most fashionable hotels and restaurants in Ireland, plus a drink-driving offence, hardly suggests a life of penance.

And there are other things, including his declaration that all priests should be poor while he himself seemed to have had no difficulty in raising £100,000, which stop me falling overboard with compassion for him.

His guilt goes back more than 18 years. Shouldn't he have quit the priesthood then instead of accepting promotion?

And shouldn't he be kicked out of it now instead of being allowed to retain for the rest of his life the title of Bishop?

July 26, 1992

# The laughing policewoman

ISN'T Miss Alison Halford the lucky lady?

At the age of just 52, and after 19 months' suspension on full pay, she gets a lump sum of £142,600    and, because she is taking early retirement on 'health grounds', an enhanced index-linked pension of £36,800 a year.

Health grounds? What's wrong then with this big strapping lass who looks as if she could take on if not a tank then at least a beer lorry single-handed? She is said to have an arthritic knee. But then what woman of 52 hasn't?

Isn't it a mercy that at least it won't stop her indulging in what seems to have been the favourite pastime of all the Merseyside Police top brass — swallowing booze as if it were going out of fashion.

It is all, of course, a carve-up. In return for her £142,600 and pension Miss Halford lets Merseyside Police Authority off the hook by agreeing to drop her suit for sexual discrimination — a suit that has cost the taxpayer more than £1 million.

Isn't it all a bloody scandal? No wonder the TV pictures show Miss Halford laughing happily. No doubt on the way to the bank. But shouldn't the rest of us be silently sobbing into our porridge?

# Loving proof of a royal he-man

THERE is criticism of the Queen because she permits Prince Edward and his girlfriend Sophie Rhys-Jones to cohabit in Buckingham Palace and that, by so doing, she is encouraging immorality.

Isn't that a load of hypocritical cant?

The Prince and Miss Rhys-Jones are not children. He is 31, she is 30.

If they are living together how can the Queen possibly stop them and would it make any moral difference if they were living somewhere other than in the Palace?

But are they, in fact, living together? I don't know. What I do know is that, if they are, then, from a public relations point of view, it has to be the best thing that has ever happened to Prince Edward.

Might it not go a long way to convince the British public that Prince Edward, despite his previous somewhat effeminate image, is as much a ladies' man as his brother Prince Andrew?

And can that be bad?

October 15, 1995

# What's in this for Branson?

THERE is a fascination about the way in which Mr Richard Branson, who in the past so assiduously sucked up to Margaret Thatcher and the Princess of Wales, is now cosying up to the Labour Party.

First there was the warmth of the welcome he gave Mr Tony Blair when Mr Blair accepted an invitation to visit Virgin Airways at Gatwick.

They sat together in the cockpit of one of Virgin's 747 jumbo jets, exchanged ideas and agreed to meet again.

It ended with a hint from Mr Branson that he might explicitly declare for Mr Blair: 'I keep that private but we may decide to go public on this nearer the election.' Later came the revelation that the renegade MP Mr Alan Howarth is and has been for some time on Mr Branson's payroll.

Is that simply a coincidence? Had Mr Howarth discussed his planned treachery with Mr Branson and had been assured in advance by Mr Branson that a change of party would not affect his no-doubt handsomely paid consultancy?

My suspicions may be unworthy. But it all makes me wonder just what Mr Branson's end game is.

Perhaps, for starters, to have the running of the National Lottery taken from Camelot and handed over to him if and when Mr Blair becomes Prime Minister?

And for afters? A life peerage perhaps?

# Nature

*J.J. was one of life's keenest observers. The tiniest detail never eluded him, whether he was studying man, society or indeed the natural world. He was fascinated and enchanted by the mysteries of nature – the behaviour of birds and animals – which he felt were symbolic of a greater force.*

*He described much of what he saw – often out of the window of his home – as moments of pure magic.*

THERE can have been few people who were not moved by the story of that 14-year-old cross-collie, Ruswarp, found starving in a remote hill area of mid-Wales by a rambler who then discovered in a nearby stream the body of the dog's master, 41-year-old hill-walker Grahame Buttall, missing since January.

If the rambler had not turned up, the dog would still have been there until its own death, guarding the body of its master.

Isn't such loyalty touching?

Wouldn't it be a quite different, but maybe much duller world, if only women were just half as faithful?

# Scared to death

THE story of Hilda the hippo made headlines last week when the lorry carrying her to be mated at Windsor Safari Park jackknifed on the A303 at Andover.

There were sweet pictures of her grazing on the grass verge. That, of course, was before a tranquillising dart was shot into her and before she died from the sheer terror of it all. By next week she will be forgotten and the headlines will be dealing with some more important issue. But is there one?

Shouldn't her death and the manner of it cause us to stop and think of the suffering we cause to wild animals which, for our own selfish pleasure, we imprison in zoos?

I LOOKED out of my kitchen window the other night and there, less than 30 ft away in the orchard, was this beautiful young stag, scratching his head against the slim trunk of a plum sapling and causing it to bend back almost to the point of snapping. Then something else further off attracted his attention and he moved leisurely away, still oblivious of my presence. And apparently quite unconcerned, too, by the occasional car passing on a nearby road. It was, for me, not only a moment of magic, but also of relief. It was the first tangible evidence I'd had that, despite the hurricanes which had caused such devastation and brought down so many trees, the small herd of wild deer that inhabit my wood had somehow managed to survive. It is almost unbelievable that they have, just 30 miles from London, and apart from the rose bushes of myself and my neighbours, utterly dependent, even in the depths of winter, on natural vegetation for their food. Could it be because, for these timid, gentle creatures, someone, somewhere, cares?

# The birds with brains

THE blue tit hovering outside my kitchen window with its tiny beak almost touching the glass seemed to be trying to attract my attention.

I looked beyond the bird to the peanut container hanging from a branch of the weeping ash.

It was empty. As it had been throughout the summer and mild autumn. But now it was cold. Freezing cold.

Had the bird remembered from previous years that by now nuts should be available? I filled the container and within minutes there were more than a dozen assorted tits feeding from it. Even though I have not seen a tit in the garden for months. Where they came from, or how they so quickly received the news that food was available, I do not know.

What I do know is that the more I observe birds, the more I realise that there are still things in this world which are quite beyond the ken of man.

February 17, 1991

# That's what best friends are for

NIGHT was just beginning to close in and there, staggering around in the snow outside my back door, was this little dog.

My first unworthy thought was to shoo it away. Then I noticed it was dragging its rear legs behind it and going aimlessly in circles. Its tail did not wag even faintly when I approached and its eyes did not seem to see me at all.

It was shivering, frozen stiff and looked to me on the point of death. I managed to get it into my back porch and telephoned my friend Les, a countryman who lives in a village two miles away and has worked with animals all his life. The moment he heard a dog's life was in danger, he was into his car.

Within half-an-hour of my finding it, and little thanks to me who just stood passively by, that dog was on a drip feed in a heated kennel in the surgery of one of the best vets in the country.

It was suffering from extreme shock and hypothermia and had deep cuts in its back.

The probability was that it had been knocked over by a car on the road outside my house and had staggered into my garden.

It wore a collar but there was no owner's name or address on the tab.

The next morning I learned from the vet that the old dog was a little better and was taking food. But its condition was still critical. I thanked him and asked him in due course to let me have his bill. He looked astonished. There would be no bill. 'I couldn't,' he said, 'let that old dog suffer.'

As I thought of the time and trouble both he and Les had gone to, without thought of reward, I reflected that although a dog may well be man's best friend, man can on occasion be not all that bad a friend for an old dog either.

June 18, 1991

# A bird's-eye view of the fur war

IN THE Hebridean islands of Lewis-with-Harris and North and South Uist some 6,000 wild mink are on the rampage and multiplying all the time.

They are not only destroying crofters' free-range poultry, raiding fish farms and killing salmon.

There is also serious concern about the threat their insatiable appetites are having on rare bird species such as guillemots, razor-bills, kittiwakes, dunlin, golden plover, lapwing, greenshank and redshank.

What can be done about them?

Once upon a time when the islands had a thriving cottage mink industry there would have been no problem. They would have ended up around the shoulders of elegant ladies with rich husbands or even richer lovers. But, thanks to the loud-mouthed hectoring and occasional violence of zealots in the animal rights movement, many women are now scared stiff of wearing mink in public.

But need they be any longer?

After all, could anyone seriously complain about a lady wearing mink if she were able to explain that she was only doing so as a means of saving the golden plover?

# Mystery end

I LOST an old friend last Friday morning. A spotted woodpecker.

For the past two years it has been a regular early morning visitor to the bird table outside my kitchen window. A most cautious visitor.

It would hid behind the tree on the far side of the bird table. Not until it was quite sure there was no danger would it emerge to gorge on the peanuts. Even then it would be constantly turning its head from side to side, and upwards too, to make sure that no danger lurked. Several times I tried to photograph it. Unsuccessfully. It always saw me close to the window and was off.

Last Friday morning it was lying dead on the path. What had killed it? I have no cat. Besides, no cat would ever have been quick enough to get near it.

So what happened? Do you suppose that birds, just like humans, can suddenly drop dead from heart attacks?

I AM not sure what wakened me at 3 am, but when I looked out of my bedroom window there in the moonlight was a magical scene. Four deer nuzzling each other as they grazed on my front lawn. There may not be too many consolations about being back from holiday. But at least there are some.

WITH temperatures way below freezing there has been each morning this past week an increasing flurry of birds hungrily attacking the two containers of peanuts I put out for them. Blue tits, coal tits, nuthatches, woodpeckers, chaffinches, with sparrows, wagtails and a robin equally hungrily searching for crumbs from the table.

What would happen to them, I have wondered, if people like myself did not feed them? Would any of them survive? The answer, I am told by experts, is that incredibly, even in the toughest conditions, some of them do. Isn't that the wonderful thing about nature?

A Happy New Year to you all. May you, too, be among the survivors.

# Women I adore —
# and those I loathe

*J.J. adored women and wrote about them frequently. He admired beauty, courage, warmth, wit and compassion, and was never shy about revealing the way he felt about them.*

*He worshipped the legendary Marilyn Monroe, but the woman he wrote most about, apart from Diana, Princess of Wales, was Selina Scott. He described her as breathtaking, a vision of beauty, as well as admiring her professionally.*

*Among his favourites were the Queen Mother, Greta Garbo, Myrna Loy, Liza Minnelli, Barbara Bush, Joanna Lumley, Tiggy Legge-Bourke, Pamela Harriman, Raine Spencer, Marti Caine and Anthea Turner.*

*But, by the same token, he also gave vent to his strong feelings about the women who angered and irritated him — like Emma Nicholson, Esther Rantzen, Winnie Mandela, Glenda Jackson and Edwina Currie.*

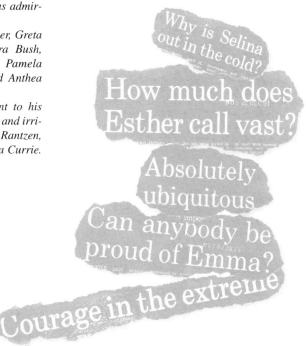

Why is Selina out in the cold?

How much does Esther call vast?

Absolutely ubiquitous

Can anybody be proud of Emma?

Courage in the extreme

**January 21, 1990**

THE other night I switched on TV and found myself watching The Seven Year Itch, the film which 35 years ago turned Marilyn Monroe into a world star.

And, having switched on, I couldn't switch off. It was magic. And so was Miss Monroe. Deliciously blonde, devastatingly desirable, it is no wonder that in 1955 she became an instant international sex symbol.

But isn't it extraordinary that 35 years later she still is one, and that hardly a week passes without a picture of her appearing somewhere?

That this should be is, of course, a tribute to her enduring greatness.

But isn't it also a reflection on all the drab, easily forgettable women film stars since her time?

**April 1, 1990**

IF Miss Glenda Jackson wins Hampstead for the Socialists at the next election, her fellow MPs are in for a nasty shock if they think how agreeable it will be to have a glamorous film star in their midst.

They are more likely to feel as if they have been hit by a tornado.

I speak from experience. Some years ago I took part in a BBC Radio 4 Any Questions? programme with Miss Jackson.

At the dinner before the show she oozed femininity, and I found myself thinking what a delightful and attractive creature she was.

It all changed dramatically the second question master David Jacobs started the show.

Miss Jackson changed from being a purring little pussy into a spitting virago, a naive blinkered Socialist who seemed to believe that nothing had changed in industrial relations since they used little boys to clean chimneys.

After it was all over I found myself reflecting how lucky it was for Miss Jackson that least in the film world she had someone else to write her scripts.

Her tragedy may be that at Westminster she will have to write her own.

April 22, 1990

■ ■ ■ ■ ■ ■ ■

**THERE** cannot have been many people who ever saw her in a film, or even saw pictures taken of her at the height of her fame, who were unmoved by the circumstances in which Greta Garbo died — old, alone, a hermit by her own choice, her only solace vodka and whisky, her only enjoyment watching Benny Hill on TV.

How could it happen? What made one of the world's most beautiful women suddenly opt out of life in 1941 at the age of just 36 and hide her face from the world for the rest of her life?

## Adoring

Could it have been that very beauty that was her downfall? The approach of middle-age must be a time of trauma for any highly attractive woman not surrounded by love and by children.

For a glamorous film star, it must seem like the end of the world.

Couldn't Garbo bear the thought of her adoring fans ever seeing on her face the ravages of age? Is that why she hid from the cameras

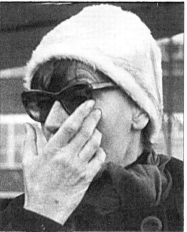

**LEGEND: *Tragic Greta Garbo***

for the next 50 years? If so, I cannot find it in my heart to blame her. For isn't it better to go out when right at the very top?

And besides, aren't there worse ways of ending your days than sitting with a full bottle of whisky in front of a TV set watching Benny Hill?

Like, for example, with an empty bottle watching Terry Wogan?

I CAN understand the South African Government's desire to handle Mr Nelson Mandela with the very gentlest of touches. He is vital to its purpose.

But is it really either necessary, or even wise, to handle his thoroughly nasty and, even among blacks, highly unpopular wife Winnie the same way?

She was, it will be remembered, a great exponent of the 'necklaces of fire' atrocities when rubber tyres filled with petrol were put around the necks of blacks suspected of collaboration with the police then set alight.

There would not seem to be reasonable doubt either that she was present at the beating-up by her bodyguard of a 14-year-old black boy, a beating-up which ended in the boy's death.

But while the man in charge of her bodyguard, the so-called

**NASTY: Winnie Mandela**

'captain' of Mandela United, Mr Jerry Richardson, has been found guilty of murder, she as yet faces no prosecution of any kind.

Why not?

Would Mr Mandela really be so upset if she were tried and did end up in jail?

Might it not, since his own release from prison, be just about the very best thing that has happened to him?

LAST Wednesday was the sort of day in London on which you could almost have fried eggs on the pavements.

Scorchingly, unbelievably hot and unpleasantly humid. No wonder so many of the young stripped to the waist and businessmen hesitated before leaving the sanctury of air-conditioned buildings.

What it must have been like for an old lady of 90 walking about in the sweltering afternoon heat is unthinkable. Yet the smile never once left the face of the Queen Mother as she made her pilgrimage to the East End.

It lasted two-and-a-half hours as she stopped to speak here, accept a bouquet there and, in general, act in a way which suggested she might be 40 years younger and it was a cool, pleasant spring afternoon. It was an incredible display of stamina and physical well being in a person so old. It left me spellbound with admiration.

It also left me wondering whether the Queen might have inherited her mother's constitution and whether she, too, might be visiting her subjects in the East End when well into her nineties. Perhaps pushing Prince Charles in a wheelchair?

**March 31, 1991**

**REATHTAKING: Myrna Loy**

**A NAME** from the past came into the news again last week when an Oscar for a lifetime's contribution to the cinema was awarded to Myrna Loy.

**Myrna Loy? Breathtakingly beautiful Myrna Loy.**

**Fifty years ago, there can hardly have been a red-blooded man alive who did not swoon at the very thought of her.**

**Now she is so old and frail that she was unable to travel from her New York home to Hollywood for the ceremony. Isn't old age tragic?**

**Was someone like Marilyn Monroe really so unlucky to have died at the very height of her fame when she will always be remembered as she was instead of the scraggy, wrinkled old-age pensioner she too would now be?**

■ ■ ■ ■ ■ ■ ■ ■

I MADE a flying visit to Aberdeen last weekend to appear on the Art Sutter show on Grampian TV with Scottish Nationalist Euro-MP Winnie Ewing; the delectable Maggie Moone, of Name That Tune fame; Scottish actor John Cairney and those great Irish singers Foster and Allen.

It was an exhilarating experience. And not just because from an entertainment point of view the show was better, in my opinion, than many of the big-name shows we see in the South.

But also becaus I love Aberdeen. There is such a wonderful buzz and vitality about the place, and its people are so warm and friendly.

On my last visit 11 years ago I had been interviewed, again on Grampian, by the then completely unknown Selina Scott.

On my return I had written about her in the most glowing terms, and shortly afterwards she was offered a job in London on ITN's News At Ten. Because of what I wrote? I do not know. Maybe. At any rate, her career took off like a rocket.

During the programme last weekend Art Sutter showed a clip of that interview 11 years ago. In it, Selina looked so completely different from the elegant, soignee, sophisticated, ultra fashion-conscious lady she now is.

## Super

Fresh complexion, a mop of fairish hair and not an iota of sophistication. But bubbling with happiness and love of life. She is still a super lady. Even so, on the flight back to London and the rat race, I found myself wondering whether, despite all the fame, fortune and no doubt wealth that have come to her in these past 11 years, she might not have been happier if she had remained undiscovered in Aberdeen.

*BUBBLY: Selina Scott before her rise to TV fame*

I DOUBT whether that thoroughly evil woman Winnie Mandela will ever serve a day of the six-year jail sentence she so richly deserves.

Clearly, she does not expect to either, judging by the arrogance of her attitude and the utter absence of remorse when she left the court which had sentenced her.

It will take months, maybe years, before her appeal is heard.

And by the time it is heard she probably reckons that even if there is not already a black militant government in South Africa, President de Klerk will be too scared of upsetting her husband actually ever to put her in prison.

And yet, has she any real cause for self-satisfaction? Perhaps the most extraordinary thing about

**APPEAL: Mandela**

her trial has been the almost entire absence of protest from the rest of the world about the sentence imposed on her.

There has been world-wide recognition that the white South African judicial system has been scrupulously fair.

Can you imagine what that judicial system is going to be like when the day comes, as I fear it soon will, and the Winnie Mandelas of South African society take over?

September 22, 1991

# Pain behind the spotlight

AT the age of 45, Liza Minnelli still looks utterly stunning — as well as being enormously talented.

Just like her mother, Judy Garland, before her.

She has an adorable, lovely elfin face. She has the legs and figure of a 20-year-old.

But underneath it all, as her fight against alcohol addiction shows, she has the same basic gnawing insecurity and inner sadness which beset her mother.

We all tend occasionally to envy the glamorous lifestyle of film stars. Shouldn't we also occasionally salute the guts and courage it must take to keep on laughing and singing and dancing when all the time, inside, you may be feeling like death?

# How much does Esther call vast?

THERE are two things which appal me about Miss Esther Rantzen's successful libel action against The People newspaper.

First the £250,000 damages awarded. It is just the latest in a long list of absurd Monopoly money amounts awarded by star-struck juries in libel cases.

For how much longer is the farce of allowing juries to decide the amount of damages to continue? Do we really want to end up with newspapers being afraid to publish anything except adulatory guff about anyone in public life?

The second thing which appals me is the fact that even if she had lost her action, it would not have cost Miss Rantzen a penny. She was in a 'heads I win, tails you lose' situation. For she was being backed by the BBC. Which meant that if the verdict had gone the other way, the £300,000 costs involved would have been picked up by TV licence payers.

I think that is an absolute scandal. If Miss Rantzen feels her good name has been smeared then she has every right to sue. She has no right at all to expect TV viewers to pay. And it is quite mon-strous that the BBC put them in a position in which they might have had to.

What is Miss Rantzen, who jumped with joy when she heard the size of the damages, going to do with the money? She announced that she would spend some of it in giving her children the Christmas of their dreams. Considering the amount of money she and her husband earn, do they really need libel damages in order to do that? With parents so astronomically well paid, couldn't they be having the Christmas of their dreams every year of their lives anyway?

She also pledged to put 'a vast proportion' of the cash into the Childline charity she heads.

Will she? And just how much is 'vast'? I will begin to believe it all when the cash has actually been paid over. Am I being too cynical? Perhaps. But in that case may we expect a public statement as to the amount of cash Childline actually receives? And perhaps even a photograph of the cheque?

If that ever happens I will frame it and hang it on the wall above my bed. To teach me in future to be more trusting.

January 12, 1992

# Mrs Bush steps into the spotlight

A NEW and formidable figure emerged on to the world stage last week, a figure whom I freely admit I had hitherto regarded as of being of no consequence at all — Mrs Barbara Bush.

It was a frightening moment when her husband collapsed in front of TV cameras at that Tokyo dinner and the whole world saw his face go blue as he began to vomit.

It could have been a moment of utter panic for the world's stock markets, too, had it not been for Mrs Bush.

Did you mark the way she took complete command of the situation? A lesser, perhaps more feminine, woman would have scurried after her husband and stayed by his side until he had recovered.

Instead, she took his place, raised her glass in a toast to the Japanese Prime Minister and, by telling a joke about her husband, had the whole banqueting room in fits of laughter.

It was not only her immediate audience that was reassured, it was the wider audience watching the event in every country in the world.

It was a remarkable achievement which set me wondering about Mrs Bush. I had always looked upon her as a grandmotherly figure interested only in her home and family. Since she looked so much older than her husband, I had even wondered how she had managed to hold on to him for so long.

Now we see her in a quite different light, as a woman of real steel with a political perception every bit as finely honed as her husband's and a character possibly a good deal stronger.

What does the future now hold for President Bush? His doctors shrug off his collapse as being of no consequence. They say it had nothing to do with his previous heart problem and that it was merely gastric flu.

That may well be true — although the uneasy

thought persists: They would say that, wouldn't they?

Either way, and even if it is only to avoid the danger of Senator Dan Quayle taking over, the hope must be that President Bush goes on for many years yet.

But if that is to be, ought he not now for all time give up the pretence of being a super-fit hero half his age? From now on, shouldn't he leave the jogging to Barbara? Maybe even the running of the country, too?

# Why is Selina out in the cold?

FASCINATING, isn't it, the difference in treatment accorded by the BBC to two of their leading women stars, Miss Esther Rantzen and Miss Selina Scott.

Miss Rantzen, whose That's Life audience figures have slumped from 15 million to 8.4 million and who many feel is long since past her sell-by date, is awarded a new four-year contract worth £1.2 million.

This on top of the fact that the BBC recently funded her successful libel action against The People newspaper.

Miss Scott, on the other hand, and despite the fact that she is Prince Charles's as well as my own favourite interviewer and that her every appearance attracts vast audiences, is shunted into inconsequential programmes.

A leaked BBC Review Board minute indicates that BBC bosses have nothing but disdain for her.

What goes on? Why should there be so much adoration of Miss Rantzen and so much favouritism extended towards her, and so much envy of the quite blameless and completely inoffensive Miss Scott?

I do not pretend to know. But I sure as hell hope that the Chairman of the BBC, Mr Marmaduke Hussey, is going to tell us.

# Currie smells a whiff of trouble

THERE can be few women in politics more thrustingly ambitious than Mrs Edwina Currie.

She has always given me the impression that to get to the top she would, to borrow Mr Alex Salmond's memorable phrase, melt her own grannie down for glue.

Yet she turns down the offer of a job in the new government from Mr John Major even though she knows that because of her refusal she may never be offered one again.

Why? I do not believe for one second it was because the job she was offered at the Home Office would have put her in charge of prisons and that that was a propect she did not relish.

Much more likely it was because the job would have involved a prospect she relished even less — working once again under the new Home Secretary Mr Kenneth Clarke who was her boss at Health when she was forced to resign over the salmonella affair.

Just what is it, I wonder, that she can't stand about Mr Clarke?

He couldn't have bad breath, could he?

**LOYAL WIFE: Judith Mellor**

■ ■ ■ ■

MRS David Mellor is quite clearly a considerable woman and a most loyal wife.

The revelations about her husband must have been a body blow to her. Yet head in air, chin up, she has stood by him. In what looks suspiciously like a professionally typed, carefully drafted letter to three newspapers, The Sun, Today and the Daily Mirror, she even calls her own father a liar.

I salute her steadfastness and her desire to save her husband's career. I just hope that in the end she will find that in terms of her own personal happiness it will all have been worthwhile. But if I were she, I wouldn't count on it.

■ ■ ■ ■

THEY say that you can always judge a man from the sort of friends he keeps.

Do you suppose that is the way Mr Mellor's closest chum Mr John Major wishes to be judged? Is that why he seems so intent on keeping Mr Mellor in the Cabinet?

THERE *was a time when the world's sex symbol was Marilyn Monroe. Gorgeous, daffy, devastatingly desirable Marilyn. There can scarcely have been a man in any country in the world who did not dream of her or whose life she did not brighten with her loveliness.*

*But today? Can her replacement as the world's sex symbol really be that ugly, shapeless, toe-sucking slut Madonna, whose book, Sex, contains 128 glossy pages of photographs depicting her exploring bondage, homosexuality, group sex, sado-masochism and posing in an unusual way with a dog? If*

*so, isn't it sad how tastes have changed with the passage of the years?*

*For isn't the difference between Marilyn Monroe and Madonna — and also perhaps the difference between 1962 and 1992 — the same difference as exists between Champagne and cat's piss?*

April 29, 1993

# Snobbery of the great ungrateful

BARONESS Helen Mary Warnock, Mistress of Girton College, Cambridge, is almost an unattractive to listen to as she is to look at.

Snobbery oozes out of every pore.

After Mrs Thatcher misguidedly sent her to the House of Lords she showed her gratitude by announcing to the world that every time she thought about Mrs Thatcher she 'felt a kind of rage'.

Not because of the Prime Minister's policies. But because Mrs Thatcher epitomises 'the worst of the lower middle class'. She savaged Mrs Thatcher's clothes and hairstyles as 'packaged together in a way that's not exactly vulgar, just low'.

She described how she once saw Mrs Thatcher on TV, choosing clothes at Marks & Spencer and 'there was something quite obscene about it, picking out yet another blouse with a tie at the neck'.

How's that for venom?

Now the Baroness is at it again.

She seriously suggests that aristocrats should be allowed to perpetuate the aristocracy by being allowed selective in-vitro fertilisation to provide male heirs and ensure that ancient titles do not die out.

She would not, of course, allow us peasants the same right and thinks that a statutory body would probably have to be set up to rule out frivolous applications for sex-selected babies.

She then adds: 'But I don't think an hereditary peerage is a frivolous thing ... if I were the Duchess of Devonshire, I would like to have a boy, and I think I should be allowed to have one.'

Has it ever occurred to her that if she were the Duchess of Devonshire, the Duke of Devonshire would probably have long since put his head in a gas oven?

# Absolutely ubiquitous

JOANNA LUMLEY, star of Absolutely Fabulous, is either sprouting a gas flame from her elegant thumb, expatiating on the brilliance of Fairy dishwasher powder or inducing us to drink Gaymer cider.

And when it is not Miss Lumley in person it would appear to be John Cleese and Ronnie Corbett dressed as lookalikes standing in for her. Miss Lumley must be making a fortune out of it all. Good luck to her. There are some, of course, who say that she is being seen too much. Nonsense. Why shouldn't she make hay while the sun still shines? For my own part, I could never see enough of her. And besides, isn't there another side to it all? I don't pretend to know how much good Miss Lumley's appearances do for the sales of British Gas or Fairy or Gaymer's. But don't they do marvels for the morale of every middle-aged lady in the land?

Isn't it wonderful for them to know that, at the age of 47, Miss Lumley is still regarded, and rightly, as the sexiest, most gorgeous bird in town?

December 9, 1993

# Courage in the extreme

MARTI CAINE was given just five years to live when, in 1988, she fell victim to the dread blood-cancer disease Lymphona.

Now, in costume and her face covered in thick theatrical make-up, she poses for pictures and talks about her forthcoming role in panto as the Red Queen in Snow White in Cardiff this winter.

Has she beaten her cancer, then? She just doesn't know. She says she is living with a time bomb. Her body is now too frail to take any more radiotherapy or chemotherapy.

She had a bone marrow transplant but it will be a week or two yet before she knows whether it has been successful.

Even if it isn't, she will still carry on with her arduous role in pantomime. Why? Why doesn't she put her feet up and take it easy?

Looking tired and gaunt under all that make-up, she says: 'I have to eat.'

There are many forms of courage. I do not think there are any which rate higher than Marti Caine's.

February 27, 1994

# The sinking of Edwina Currie

AS A general rule, the delicious Harriet Harman excepted, women politicians are not the most attractive nor feminine of creatures.

But has there ever been one quite as off-putting as that strident, loud-mouthed self-publicist Mrs Edwina Currie?

As a Junior Minister Mrs Currie was a disaster. She wreaked havoc among farmers by putting the fear of God into the nation about eating eggs.

Since then she has never been treated seriously as a politician. Which may explain why she plans to give up Westminster and try her luck in Strasbourg instead.

Recently she wrote, purely for the money of course, a torrid, steamy, no-holds-barred sex novel with the House of Commons as a background and herself thinly disguised as the heroine. What effect did the book have on her children? According to Mrs Currie, her teenage daughter told her: 'It made me feel horny.' Ugh!

Even more recently she has gone deeper into the mire by her campaign to legalise buggery at 16.

It is part of Parliamentary legend that the first woman of all to take her seat as an MP, Lady Astor, once snapped angrily at Winston Churchill: 'If I

were your wife, I would give you poison,' to which Churchill replied: 'If I were your husband, I would take it.'

If I were Mrs Currie's husband, I think I really would.

September 4, 1994

*I REJOICE that Selina Scott is to rejoin ITV in what is described as a £250,000 pay deal, and that one of her first programmes will be an exclusive interview with President Bill Clinton. Isn't that much more her style? For on Sky News doesn't the regal Miss Scott so often look as much out of place as a Duchess in a whorehouse? Always excepting, of course, perhaps one Duchess.*

## October 9, 1994

WHEN Marilyn Monroe sang Happy Birthday to US President Jack Kennedy at Madison Square Garden in 1962, she wore a dress which caused male eyebrows all over the world to rise in delighted appreciation.

Last week one of the world's top designers, Gianni Versace, sought to recreate the same dress of silver sequins and engaged one of the world's top models, Linda Evangelista, to wear it on his Milan catwalk.

What was the reaction of the critics? An almost unanimous thumbs-down. Not because there was anything wrong with the dress, but because Linda Evangelista just cannot compare to Marilyn Monroe.

But then is there any woman who can? Isn't it quite extraordinary that, although she has now been dead for more than 30 years, Marilyn Monroe still remains the world's top sex symbol?

*Linda Evangelista*

## January 29, 1995

WHEN, *during her visit to the Royal School for the Blind, 22-year-old Mr Chris Anderson, who was born without eyes, asked Princess Diana if he could touch her face, it would have been so easy for her to decline in a way which did not hurt his feelings. Instead she got down on her knees beside him and allowed his fingers to wander over her face. Afterwards Mr Anderson declared the Princess the prettiest woman he had ever 'seen'. He wouldn't have been all that wrong if he had added that she was the most compassionate, too.*

**BUBBLY: Lottery draw hostess Anthea Turner**

■ ■ ■ ■

I WAS one of the estimated 15 million people who switched on their TV for last night's National Lottery Draw.

As usual, I tore up my ticket at the end. And, as usual, I reflected on the utter dreariness and banality of the rest of the programme which precedes the actual draw.

Yet it does have one saving grace. The bubbling presence of Miss Anthea Turner.

She is not only highly attractive to look at, with quite the best figure and legs on TV. She fizzes with vitality and gives the impression that she actually enjoys what she is doing.

If there is any other woman TV presenter who does the same then I have not seen her.

I wonder then why Miss Turner attracts such hostility — especially from women critics.

Envy, perhaps?

June 4, 1995

IT was the look of triumph on the Princess of Wales's face which made the picture such a talking point.

What had she done? She had just persuaded a Kensington traffic warden not to give her a ticket for having parked her Audi convertible on a yellow line while she sipped coffee with a friend in a patisserie on the other side of the street.

How had she managed to get to the warden before he had time to record her number?

Because she had had the forethought to take a window seat in the cafe and, when she saw him approaching, had belted across the street successfully to exercise her charm on the poor man. So, instead of getting a £60 ticket, she was allowed a further five minutes to finish her coffee.

And quite right, too. What a miserable old world it would be if a traffic warden's hard heart could never be turned by the guile of a beautiful woman.

Besides, isn't it heartening to know that, instead of being chauffeured around in a plush limousine and surrounded by minders, we have a Princess who drives herself and who, in trying to park her car, suffers the same trials and tribulations as the rest of us?

**SHARP: Selina takes on Donald Trump**

■ ■ ■ ■

SELINA SCOTT has often in the past been dismissed by carping critics as a lightweight interviewer who asks marshmallow-soft questions and has nothing to commend her except her beauty.

Isn't it a turn-up for the book then that she should now be rightly acclaimed by the same critics for her devastating interview with Donald Trump — an interview which exposed Mr Trump in a way he has never been exposed before.

Mr Trump, who rarely gives interviews, could never have expected it to turn out like this. He switched on all his charm, which is considerable, on Miss Scott. He introduced her to his board as 'the legendary Selina Scott of Europe'.

He whisked her off in his private jet to the most luxurious outposts of his property empire. He surrounds her with luxury, flatters her outrageously, puts his arm around her and tells her how beautiful she is.

And what does he get in return? Such sharp, penetrating, intrusive but always icily polite questions that at one stage Mr Trump comes close to abandoning the interview.

The interview told us so much about Mr Trump. But didn't it show Selina Scott in a new light too?

ONE of the things, and there are many, which I like about the Chancellor of the Exchequer Kenneth Clarke is his obvious devotion to his wife.

Do you notice that when they are pictured together they are always hand-in-hand?

And yet — how can I put it without sounding unkind? — she is hardly a glamour girl.

However, unless I am horribly wrong, which I often am, I would not think there is a chance in a million of the News of the World or The Sun ever revealing that Mr Clarke has a girlfriend tucked away somewhere.

For, according to all I hear, the jazz-loving, beer-drinking, cigar-smoking Mr Clarke is a one-woman man and his women is the one he married and who is the mother of his children.

Might that be why Mrs Clarke, unlike the wives of some other politicians, never feels it necessary to tart herself up, slim herself down or appear in short skirts looking like mutton dressed as lamb?

# Can anybody be proud of Emma?

IN THE past seven days Emma Nicholson has achieved the sort of fame for which she has been striving desperately but unsuccessfully all her political life.

Her face has been on the front page of every newspaper in the land. There has scarcely been a TV news bulletin without her appearing on it.

She has even received what in her eyes must have been the supreme accolade of being interviewed by Jeremy Paxman on Newsnight.

After years of obscurity, in which she was rightly regarded as ambitious but talentless, does that make her feel happy?

Does she feel proud that she gave her constituency party chairman, who had served her so loyally for so long, just 45 minutes' notice of her intention to defect? Is she proud that she gave the Prime Minister exactly the same 45-minute notice and then only by faxed letter?

And is Mr Paddy Ashdown proud of his new recruit who has acted so shabbily? And who is now terrifed of fighting a by-election which she knows she would lose?

Is he proud of the knowledge that right up until almost the last moment she was writing gushily about Mr John Major's great

qualities and still trying to get a Ministerial job in the Government?

Is he proud of the knowledge that as a self-professed Europhile she was even prepared to support Euro-sceptic John Redwood's bid for the Tory leadership? So much for her devotion to principle. For my own part Miss Nicholson and Paddy Ashdown deserve each other.

Indeed, in the whole shoddy saga the only person I feel sorry for is Miss Nicholson's husband, Sir Michael Caine.

He seems such a pleasant, easy-going man. Mustn't it be awful to be married to such a bitch?

**WHEN** Raine, the former Countess Spencer, daughter of Barbara Cartland and stepmother of the Princess of Wales, married the far-from wealthy but physically attractive Count Jean-Francois de Chambrun, who was six years her junior, there were many cynics, and I was one of them, who thought that the marriage could never last.

Nor did it. Just 18 months and, in fact, it was finished long before that. But hasn't Raine, the former Countess Spencer or, as she is now called, the Comtesse de Chambrun, come out of it with enormous dignity?

For nearly two years she said nothing to anyone, not even her mother, about her divorce. She simply returned to England and took up life where she had left it. In her £2 million house in Farm Street, Mayfair. How much did the marriage cost her? Apart from the BMW she gave her husband? She does not say anything about that either.

At the age of 67 she is truly a quite remarkable lady. With indomitable spirit and apparently, according to friends, undiminished sexual libido. Doesn't that last piece of intelligence make you gasp? Wouldn't you have thought at her age she would have taken up knitting instead?

As it is, I expect that she will marry again. That is if she can find someone with an even grander title than her previous three husbands and rich enough to give her all the style and splendour to which she has so long become accustomed. How about Prince Rainier?

**RAINE: Dignified silence**

THE look of joy on little Prince Harry's face when Tiggy Legge-Bourke wrapped her arms around him and gave him an enormous hug tells its own story.

Clearly he adores her.

I have always had a high regard for Tiggy Legge-Bourke. Any criticism of her would be nonsense. She has done a marvellous job with the Royal children and especially with Prince Harry, who is so young and so vulnerable.

In the newspapers he will see almost every day pictures of his mother kissing and hugging children all over the world. But if Tiggy were not there, and with his father and mother divorced and his mother so often on her travels or busy comforting Aids sufferers, would Prince Harry have anyone else in the whole wide world to kiss and hug him?

**FLAUNTING IT: Sophie with Rena Brannan**

WHATEVER else she may be, actress Sophie Ward is not a shrinking violet.

She not only publicly declares her lesbianism, she positively flaunts it.

She even upstaged Madonna at the premiere of Evita by deliberately choosing that high-profile occasion to turn up with and show off to the world the grotesque lesbian lover frump for whom she has left her husband, taking her two children, Nathaniel, aged seven, and Joshua, four, with her.

I suppose she will glory in the publicity she has received. Paste it all in her scrapbook.

Do you suppose she thought for a moment about what her children would think when they saw the newspaper pictures, too?

Or, as long as she is all right, doesn't she give the slightest damn?

IT has been said, and with some truth, that Pamela Harriman had a more intimate knowledge of the bedroom ceilings of seriously rich men than any other society lady of her time.

But there is something else that should be said about her. And I speak from personal knowledge. She was not only devastatingly attractive, she was also the greatest of fun and a joyous companion.

She not only brought glamour and beauty to every dinner table she graced, she also brought a sparkling wit and brilliant conversation.

There are narrow-minded spinsters of both sexes who through pursed lips will say that she led a wicked, sinful, wanton life. And maybe she did.

But then wouldn't the world be a damned sight duller place if every woman in it were a Mother Teresa?

# Men I admire — and those I loathe

They came from every walk of life, from upstanding statesmen to brilliant entertainers — the men J.J. saluted.

Among his heroes were former Prime Minister Sir Alex Douglas-Home, newspaper tycoon Lord Victor Matthews and Sir Bernard Ingham — Mrs Thatcher's press secretary.

From the world of showbusiness, he enjoyed the talents of comic genius Benny Hill, Frank Sinatra, Gene Kelly, Eric Sykes and Norman Wisdom. But there were many lesser-known men whose special qualities also captured J.J.'s imagination.

Unstinting in his praise for their kind, J.J. equally turned his wrath on men who failed to measure up to the high standards he expected from those in the public gaze.

He took to task politicians John Redwood, David Mellor, Norman Lamont, John Gummer and Colin Moynihan; celebrities Chris Evans, Richard Attenborough and Richard Branson, and controversial figures Salman Rushdie, Peter Tatchell and King Hussein of Jordan.

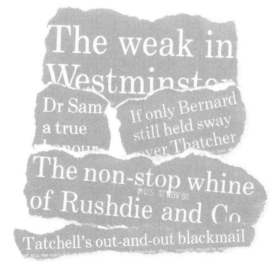

# The weak in Westminster

MR Colin Moynihan may have been, for all I know, a great cox of the Oxford boat which beat Cambridge in the University Boat Race of 1977.

But, as Minister of Sport, he fills me with dismay. I have no wish to be unkind, but the brutal truth is that, in both his bearing and in his public utterances, he has about as much impact as a butterfly alighting on a dungheap.

Nor is Mr Moynihan the only Minister who puts me on edge with the unsureness of his touch.

There is that chap with the oh-so-upper-class English accent, Mr Peter Brooke, who, for reasons I have never been able to fathom, is in charge in Northern Ireland. Why is it that every time he appears on TV he looks as if he is just about to burst into tears? Might it be because he is? Finally there is our new Home Secretary, Mr

*Colin Moynihan*

*David Waddington*

David Waddington, who on TV always seems to be waving his arms around and spluttering with righteous indignation.

Am I the only one who is beginning to suspect, especially after Strangeways, that beneath the bluster he has all the backbone of a blancmange? Or could Mr Kenneth Baker feel the same way, too? Might that be why he tried unsuccessfully to provide Mr Waddington with a minder?

*Peter Brooke*

■ ■ ■ ■ ■

IN her ITV interview with Sue Lawley, Queen Noor of Jordan showed that she was not only an outstandingly beautiful woman but also a highly intelligent and articulate one.

From beginning to end it was, of course, a public relations exercise. Her husband King Hussein backed the wrong horse during the Gulf War. He is now desperately trying to ingratiate himself again with Britain and the US.

And what better way could there be, he must have reasoned, than having his Grace Kelly look-alike wife tell Western TV audiences what a wonderful, sensitive, and much misunderstood man he is.

For my own part, I was entranced by Queen Noor. I would welcome her to Britain as an honoured guest any time. But as for the miserable little creep who is her husband and who, although his country is bitterly poor, is himself enormously rich, I hope we never again see him asked to take a passing out parade at Sandhurst or to be a house guest and intimate friend of our own Royal Family.

His proper place from now on should be the same as it was during the Gulf War. Licking Saddam Hussein's boots.

**ARTICULATE: Queen Noor**

# TV young one's poignant tribute

WHEN you think of TV stars, the name of Matthew Collins is not one that comes to mind.

In terms of fame and money he is never likely to be in the same class as Terry Wogan.

Yet, while I find it difficult remembering the contents of any Wogan programme 24 hours after I have seen it, Matthew Collins gave a performance the other night I am never likely to forget. It was on the BBC2 Travel Show. Mr Collins, who is still in his twenties, is a regular performer on the show. Each week he is sent on an off-beat, bargain-basement holiday, such as youth hostelling in Bavaria or cycling in Switzerland.

He then reports on his experiences the following week.

On the programme which captured my attention, he had been sent on a package coach tour of the battlefields of the Somme. The trip was timed to coincide with the 75th anniversary of one of the most bloody battles of the First World War, in which, on just the first 14 days alone, more than 90,000 young British soldiers were sent to their deaths.

As a holiday trip, it did not sound like a bunch of fun to me. In fact, it turned out to be riveting. The first Battle of the Somme must have taken place 50 years before Matthew Collins was even born. Yet, the atmosphere of the trenches had so clearly affected him that, as he read out poems written by teenagers who had the next day died, I was suddenly aware he was having to fight back the tears. Because it was so uncontrived, it became TV of the highest quality. The events of 75 years ago were suddenly, sharply and poignantly brought back to life.

As I watched it, I found myself reflecting. Isn't simple sincerity just about the most wonderful weapon TV has for getting at the hearts and minds of viewers?

Shame, isn't it, there is so very little of it?

# Face up to it like a man

FLANKED by eight armed security guards, Salman Rushdie emerges briefly from his hiding hole to collect an award from the Writers Guild of Great Britain.

Soon after receiving the award he scuttles out again into the night, saying as he leaves: 'I would like to apologise for the unusual manner of my appearance here.

'I would like to have been here in a more normal way. I'd have liked to have been here for the rest of the evening, but in this free country I am not a free man.'

The threat to his life, he added, was 'more real' now than ever.

Is it? I would doubt that very much indeed. The late Ayatollah Khomeini, who condemned Rushdie to death, has himself been pushing up daisies for a long time now. The last thing his successor, now desperately seeking improved relations with Britain, would want

is the assassination of Mr Rushdie. I suspect the danger to him is now mainly in his own mind. He may even have come subconsciously to enjoy the hype and drama which surrounds him and which turns his every furtive appearance into a great publicity exercise for himself and his books.

One thing is for sure. His protection, which has so far cost the British taxpayer more than £1 million, just cannot go on forever. Sooner or later it has to be ended.

Why not now, and preferably at Mr Rushdie's own request.

If I am right in my political judgment, nothing untoward will happen to him.

And if I am wrong? Well, so what?

Isn't it better to die like a man rather than endure a living death cowering behind drawn curtains?

THE MARQUESS of Blandford blames all his troubles on the fact that his parents were divorced when he was only five.

And there are many who will nod their heads in sympathy and weep into their beer with him. I am not among them.

Of course, love in childhood is important. But there are plenty of people who have been deprived of it who have gone on to make enormous successes of their lives. The reason for the Marquess of Blandford's plight is that he is a weak, miserable, whingeing character who has been spoilt rotten all his life and has had all the money in the world to indulge his every vice.

Might it not be a completely different story today if much earlier in his life, instead of people drooling over him and telling him how badly treated he had been by his parents, he had been given a few sharp kicks up the backside?

And, like every Barnardo's boy, had had to face life, not only without parental love, but also without a penny to his name.

# Dr Sam, a true honour

THEY BURIED Sam Oram in Chichester last week.

Sam who? If you are asking yourself that question, I do not blame you.

The vast majority of the British public have never heard of Sam Oram. But there are thousands who do know and revere his name.

Many of them owe their lives to him.

Sam Oram was one of the really great doctors of our time.

For many years he was director of the cardiac unit at King's College Hospital, London, and a pioneer in the treatment of heart disease.

People came from all over the world to consult him. Generations of medical students absorbed his wisdom both from his lectures and the textbooks he wrote.

If, like some other and lesser doctors, he had had as a patient a Prime Minister or some other prominent politician, he would long since have had a knighthood or even a peerage.

As it was, he died at the age of 78 without recognition of any kind.

Yet didn't he perhaps achieve the highest honour of all — the respect and affection of every student he ever taught and every patient he ever treated?

# The non-stop whine of Rushdie and Co

MR SALMAN Rushdie, with his continual whining, is fast becoming an excruciating pain in a part of the anatomy far removed from the neck. And so are his pinko supporters.

Did you see them the other night on TV at the Press conference they gave at a bookshop in Charing Cross Road, London, to protest about the way the Foreign Office seem to be giving the release of Terry Waite precedence over the need to stage a demonstration in favour of Mr Rushdie?

They were all there, the whole pompous, pontificating publicity-seeking pack of pseuds — the smug Mr Melvyn Bragg, the pretentious Mr Martin Amis, the dreary Mr Harold Pinter and his wife, better known for the size of her feet than for her political intellect, Lady Antonia. Instead of attacking the Foreign Office, shouldn't they be keeping their mouths shut? Haven't they considered the possibility that they may be adding to Mr Rushdie's danger by keeping the spotlight on him?

As for Mr Rushdie, instead of whingeing, shouldn't he be down on his knees thanking the Government for dissipating so much taxpayers' money on the apparently thankless task of protecting him?

# On the side of the Angels

I SO much admired the courage of Benny Hill as he emerged from London's Cromwell Hospital after his heart attack to face a barrage of photographers and TV cameramen.

He must have been feeling lousy. As was demonstrated by the fact that he had to return to a hospital bed within hours of getting home.

Yet, for the benefit of the cameras, 67-year-old Benny posed and jested with the nurses who had attended him during his illness.

But he had to put on an act, hadn't he? Wouldn't he have been letting down his public if he hadn't? As he was driven away, I reflected on just how brave clowns are to keep smiling in the face of personal disaster and also on just how shabbily the British Establishment treats them.

Dramatic actors like Ian McKellan, John Gielgud and Alec Guinness who bring pleasure to cultured theatregoers get knighthoods at the drop of a hat.

But comics? That is a different story.

Benny Hill is, in my view, one of the greatest comics of our generation. He has brought laughter into the lives of millions. Yet what honour has he ever received. Not a dicky bird. Two other great clowns, Eric Sykes and Frankie Howerd, have fared only slightly better. Each received an OBE. An award that puts them on roughly the same level as a good Whitehall office cleaner.

What can the Establishment have against comedians? Is it the class system operating again? Is it the official view that, while dramatic actors entertain the gentry, the only function of comics is to keep the peasants happy?

*Benny Hill*

# The sad echoes of laughter

BENNY HILL was worth probably as much as £20 million.

There was scarcely a city in the United States or Europe where his presence on the streets would not have caused a stampede of fans eager to acclaim him.

Yet he was a loner who still carried his shopping in plastic bags, used a bucket to collect drips from a leak in the roof and led such a humble, frugal, unostentatious, Chinese takeaway lifestyle that he had been dead two days before anybody even noticed he was missing.

In his shows he was always surrounded by the most beautiful of girls, all of whom he suggestively ogled.

Yet I suspect that if any of them had ever as much as raised a beckoning finger, he would have turned and run like a startled rabbit. All the evidence suggests that not since his mother died had he ever known a woman's love. Or indeed had ever seriously sought it.

His fellow clown Frankie Howerd who died, eerily, at about the same time and from the same cause, heart failure, was perhaps an even more vulnerable person.

He was such a mass of quivering insecurity that his scriptwriters even had to insert the oohs and aahs in his script.

Like Benny Hill, he was a master of sexual innuendo. Yet, the chances are that, like Benny Hill, although maybe for vastly different reasons, not once in his life did he ever have a sexual relationship with a woman.

Sad, isn't it, that it is so very often the greatest of clowns who bring so much joy and laughter into the lives of millions who have so very little to laugh about in their own?

*Frankie Howerd*

*What can be said about the OBE given to that foul-mouthed yobbo Ian Botham, save that it brings the whole honours system into disrepute and reflects scant credit on the judgment of the PM?*

**July 5, 1992**

I CANNOT understand why Socialist MP for Bolsover Mr Denis Skinner was suspended from the House of Commons for calling our gung-ho Minister of Agriculture Mr John Gummer 'a little squirt'.

Isn't it universally recognised that that is exactly what Mr Gummer is?

**October 19, 1992**

# Last of the great clowns

I WITNESSED eight minutes of sheer theatrical magic the other night. The audience which packed Leatherhead's Thorndike Theatre for the play, The Nineteenth Hole, starring Eric Sykes in the role of a downtrodden golf club secretary, ranged from yuppies with gorgeous blonde girlfriends, to middle-aged couples clutching boxes of Quality Street.

But for eight minutes they had one thing in common. For eight minutes they were convulsed in laughter and rocking in their seats as Mr Sykes metaphorically tore up his rather pedestrian script and, for eight glorious minutes, in a scene in which he was reporting to the golf club committee on his visit to the debt-ridden club's bank manager, ad-libbed and mimed in a way which had his listeners quite helpless with mirth.

I have never heard people laugh so loudly. It was clowning of the very highest order. Which is what one would expect from Eric Sykes.

I have always regarded him as being one of the few really great British clowns of this century. He ranks with people like Tony Hancock, Frankie Howerd and Benny Hill. Now he is the only one left.

Isn't it extraordinary that to see him you have to visit a provincial theatre?

When you consider the banality of our present TV programmes — and at a time when millions of pounds are being wasted on duff shows such as Eldorado — isn't it almost beyond belief that no place can be found for his genius on the box?

**May 31, 1992**

*Frank Sinatra looked a weary old man when he arrived at Heathrow Airport.*

*Yet no matter how decrepit he may look and no matter how decrepit he may be, and even though he may now have to wear a hearing aid, the fact is that from the moment he walked on to the stage of the Royal Albert Hall he held captive an enchanted audience. Which explains why, for his six-concert trip to England, he is going to earn £1.35 million. Isn't that, at the age of 76, a fantastic achievement for a singer? Do you suppose he will still be earning that sort of money when he has to go on to the stage in a Zimmer frame?*

*I don't see any reason why not. After all, aren't most of his present-day audiences likely by then to be in Zimmer frames, too?*

*THE most astonishing thing in these last few days has been the way in which Mr Arthur Scargill has become almost a folk hero in the eyes of some journalists. Not in mine. When I saw this man who has done more damage to the mining industry than all the Right-wing reactionaries in the world put together leading that march of decent miners and posturing again in the same old way, he reminded me of only one thing. An ageing, mangy rat emerging from a sewer.*

SOME people have the preconceived idea that all Hollywood sex symbols must be intellectual dumbos.

But they would have been surprised if they had watched Barry Norman's interview with Robert Redford on BBC1 last week.

Redford may be a sex symbol. He is also a highly articulate man with an intellect which I would rate a good deal higher than President Bill Clinton's — although that, of course, is not saying much.

There was much derision more than 12 years ago now when Hollywood B-film actor Ronald Reagan became President of the US.

In the event he turned out to be just as good a President as the US has ever had. From the moment he left the White House it has been

**ARTICULATE**: Redford

downhill for the US and for the world.

Could it just possibly be that there are more brains in Hollywood than there have ever been, and ever will be, among the professional politicians on Capitol Hill?

I don't know. But I tell you this. Having listened to Mr Redford, I would feel infinitely happier about the future of the world if it were he and not President Clinton who was sitting in the White House today.

# A friend Mr Major can do without

THERE is a story going the rounds that the Prime Minister is very much missing the friendship and political counsel of Mr David Mellor and that when there is a Cabinet reshuffle later in the year he plans to bring Mr Mellor back into the Government.

Is there the slightest shred of truth in the story? I very much hope not. Mr Mellor is bad news. His sordid affair with Miss Antonia de Sancha plus his acceptance of a free holiday for himself and his family from Miss Mona Bauwens left a nasty taste in the public mouth.

An even nastier taste was left by his utter lack of contrition. Instead of bowing his head in penance, as did that, by comparison, saintly figure Cecil Parkinson, Mr Mellor tried to brazen it out. He shamelessly paraded his wife and children in front of the cameras and when all that failed he ended up by bad-mouthing the Press.

Mr Major himself barely survived that crisis. He would not survive another. And the Prime Minister must surely know that. He could not possibly be so insensitive as to try to bring Mr Mellor back into his administration.

So where then is the current story coming from? From Mr Mellor himself perhaps?

June 13, 1993

# Who will want Norman now?

IT REMAINS to be seen just how much damage Mr Norman Lamont has done Mr Major by the viciousness of his resignation speech.

But one thing is already sure. By making it and by displaying such venom, Mr Lamont has gone a very long way to destroying himself.

He has certainly no future in this present Government. Nor, after his disloyalty, is he likely to have a future in any new administration either. So where does he go from here? He is far from a rich man, as was evidenced by the fact that he had to pass the begging bowl to pay the legal costs involved in the removal of that infamous whip lady from his house. He has been financially dependent on his ministerial salary, which has now gone. All that remains is his pay as an MP, and because his constituency of Kingston upon Thames is due to disappear in the redistribution of constituencies, he will no longer be able even to count on that.

And, with his record, what other safe constituency is now likely to ask him to become its candidate? How then is he going to finance the expensive lifestyle to which he and his wife have been so long accustomed.

By writing his memoirs? Maybe. But by the time they appear will there be any real interest in them? Will anyone indeed remember who he was?

How about a job in the City then? That does not seem enormously likely either. For, with his financial record, what reputable City company would want to have him on its board?

Barclaycard or Access, perhaps?

The going ahead may be tough for John Major. I suspect it is going to be a damned sight tougher for the man who has sought to destroy him.

IF there really is corruption in the Honours system and titles can be and are bought as the Socialist Party sneeringly keeps on suggesting, can anyone explain why, when Asil Nadir, who gave £400,000 to the Tories, is still a commoner, that unctuous little creep, actor Richard Attenborough, will soon be taking his seat in the Lords? He certainly hasn't given money to anyone.

He is not even a Tory. He has already announced that he will sit on the Labour benches in the Lords. Yet it was a Tory Prime Minister who made him a life Peer.

Why Mr Major did so is something I can't

**CREEP: Attenborough**

understand since I do not think that Richard Attenborough has a worthwhile contribution of any kind to make in the Upper House.

But doesn't the fact that he has been sent there give the lie to many of the Socialist sneers?

# Tatchell's out-and-out blackmail

OF ALL the nasty bits of work around there can be none nastier than Mr Peter Tatchell.

His failed attempt to blackmail the 54-year-old Bishop of London, Dr David Hope, into admitting that he is a practising homosexual was absolutely repellent. As have been his attempts to 'out' other Anglican and Roman Catholic priests.

Now he has turned his reptilian attention to the House of Commons. It is said he has written a letter to 20 MPs, including two Cabinet Ministers, urging them to be brave enough to come out and openly admit that they are homosexuals. Was the Ulster Popular Unionist MP 66-year-old bachelor Sir James Kilfedder one of the 20? Was it fear of being exposed that caused him to suffer a heart attack last Monday night on the train from Gatwick to London — a heart attack from which he died?

I do not suppose we will ever know for sure. Mr Tatchell refuses either to confirm or to deny that Sir James was one of the recipients of his letter.

What we do know and what is self-evident is that Mr Tatchell is employing a pernicious type of blackmail on people whose sexuality should be entirely their own affair.

It is said that, as the law stands, and because of the crafty way in which he drafts his letters, there is no case for bringing a criminal prosecution for blackmail against him.

If that is indeed so then all I can say is that it is time that the law was changed.

Otherwise isn't there a danger the people Mr Tatchell persecutes might exact their own revenge? By arranging for Mr Tatchell to be thrown into a cesspool? Head first?

# If only Bernard still held sway over Thatcher

AMONG the army of political commentators who day after day air their views on the Tory leadership contest on TV, one stands out like a giant among pygmies — Sir Bernard Ingham.

He knows everything there is to know about politics and the workings of Downing Street. He also idolises Margaret Thatcher. No Prime Minister has ever had a more faithful servant than she had when he was her Press Secretary.

He will not willingly say a word against her. Yet day by day he demonstrates that he is not her slave and that he has a mind and views of his own.

These views are the essence of decency and common sense.

He has no longer any influence, of course, on Lady Thatcher. That is a pity. She might sound less batty, less obvious in her envy of John Major, and not be destroying herself and her reputation in the way she is doing if he had.

*THAT king of moaners Mr Salman Rushdie complains because British Airways refuse to carry him as a passenger. But, until the fatwa against him is lifted, aren't they absolutely right to do so? And isn't Mr Rushdie being more than just a little selfish by demanding that they should allow him on board their planes? Isn't it he himself who is constantly telling us that he is in mortal danger from a terrorist bomb? Would he, in these circumstances, want perhaps 300 other innocent, fare-paying passengers to run even the slightest risk of being blown to eternity with him?*

October 8, 1995

# A PM who ought to have led longer

ALEC DOUGLAS-HOME was quite simply the most decent, most honest, most unassuming politician I have ever known.

I started with a prejudice against him. I disliked the undemocratic way he had emerged as Tory leader.

In fact, I did not meet him until after the Tories had lost the 1963 election and he was no longer Prime Minister.

Then it was a chance encounter in the street. I had been the luncheon guest at the Carlton Club of a Scottish landowner, Lord Massereene, who wrote occasional articles for the paper I was then editing.

As we left the club together we almost literally bumped into Alec walking down St James's Street towards the House of Commons.

Massereene hailed him with an 'Hello, Alec' and introduced me. I took to him immediately and I like to think that the feeling was mutual. At any rate I asked if he would like one day to lunch with me and he agreed.

Many politicians today tell journalists inviting them to lunch to just which expensive restaurant they would like to be taken. Seldom, if ever, do they put their hands into their own hip pockets.

With Alec Douglas-Home it was different. He insisted on paying for every other lunch. And our lunches became ever more frequent. He began writing leader page articles for my newspaper. They would arrive in his own squiggly handwriting and they were invariably brilliant. He had the sharpest of minds and was enormously tolerant of other people's failings.

The young South African Peter Hain, for example, now a middle-aged respectable Labour MP but at that time engaged in tearing up cricket pitches in protest against apartheid. Most Tories of that era were convinced Hain was a Communist. Not Alec. He told me he thought Hain was simply a youthful

idealist who would calm down in later life.

But of one of the most distinguished members of the Wilson and Callaghan governments — a man who is still alive and so cannot be named — he was much less sure.

'What do you think of him?' he once asked me. 'I think he is a Communist "sleeper",' I replied. 'So do I,' he said and lapsed into silence.

In my view it was a tragedy for Britain that Alec should have been Prime Minister for such a very short time. He would have made a very much better leader of the country than either Harold Wilson or Ted Heath, whom he subsequently served so loyally.

He was a 10 times bigger man than either of them.

# Regrets? Not for a moneyed yob like Liam

WHEN Noel and Liam Gallagher left school in the bleak Manchester suburb of Burnage, without a single educational qualification between them and already into thieving and drug-taking, what odds do you suppose local bookmakers would have given against their one day occupying more headlines and more front page newspaper space than President Clinton, President Yeltsin and Prime Minister John Major put together?

Yet last week they did.

The odds would have been equally astronomic against their both becoming multimillionaires.

Yet they both are.

Now, thanks to the yobbish, unbelievably bad behaviour on and off stage of cursing, spitting, foul-gesturing Liam, the bubble has come close to bursting.

Does it matter? Not a toss.

As for Liam, will he one day emerge from the haze of drink and drugs which presently appears to envelop him and regret what he has done?

I doubt it. After all, why should he?

He will still have all the money in the world and he will still have Patsy Kensit.

Could anyone with his minuscule talent ask for more?

*The death of Singing in the Rain star Gene Kelly has caused more genuine sadness among ordinary people in almost every country in the world than would have the death of any international statesman.*

*And rightly. For, by the joyous, uplifting nature of his films during almost 50 years, didn't Gene Kelly bring more happiness to the world than the whole race of politicians has ever done?*

**HOUSE DISPUTE: Loudmouth Chris Evans**

■ ■ ■ ■

THAT big-head and loud and often foul-mouthed disc jockey Mr Chris Evans has been using his air time on Radio One to moan about the plumbing in his new £600,000 home.

He told listeners: 'I paid £560,000 for the house plus agent's commission — let's say £600,000 altogether. Every time we turn on a tap the toilets overflow . . . the walls are covered with brown stains . . . the name of the developer will be revealed tomorrow unless he has done something about it by then.

'This is not blackmail.'

If it isn't blackmail then what is it?

It is bad enough that someone with as limited talent, as bad manners and as uncertain reliability as Mr Chris Evans should have made so much money in so short a time as to be able to spend £600,000 on a house.

It becomes quite appalling when he tries to use his slot on the BBC to throw his weight about on matters which are of no interest to anyone but himself.

BBC chiefs are now apparently trying to discipline Mr Evans. Wouldn't they instead be better to dump him?

I WONDER what induced Virgin owner Richard Branson to pose for pictures dressed as a bride.

Was his only aim to secure widespread publicity for his new enterprise Virgin Bride Shop? And didn't he care how much damage it might do his image in one of his other capacities as, for example, the boss of Virgin Pensions? I wonder.

Clearly he studied carefully all the pictures taken of himself before they were released. And must have liked them very much indeed.

Otherwise why should he have released them?

So what must we make of it? Does he really fancy himself dressed in drag and in particular as a woman in her wedding dress?

I don't know. But I suspect that the way in which the pictures have been hyped up tells us a great deal more about Richard Branson than any macho pictures of him twirling Ivana Trump round his shoulders ever will.

Can he blame people for wondering if he ever dresses like this in the privacy of his own bedroom?

FOR the fancy-dress party to celebrate his 50th birthday, a removal lorry had to be hired to carry Elton john the short distance from his house in Holland Park to the 600-guest party at London's Hammersmith Palais. And no wonder.

It took Elton John two hours to get into his glittering £50,000 costume, which included a 35ft dazzling-white train of ostrich feathers and was topped with a 3½ft tall wig adorned with a replica of a silver galleon.

I don't blame him for his bizarre style of dress. It is not his fault that he is a homosexual and likes dressing up. That is the way nature made him.

But it was the dress of some of the guests at his party which staggered me.

Did you see the multi-millionaire composer Andrew Lloyd Webber dressed as a football fan in Leyton Orient strip?

Mr John Major has done many good things in his time as Prime Minister. But how in the name of God did he ever come to send this buffoon to the House of Lords?

# Auchtermuchty

*Auchtermuchty's two other claims to fame pale into insignificance beside the importance accorded it by J.J. To our columnist, the small Scottish market town in Fife was the moral barometer for the wellbeing of the nation. It was a sort of Brigadoon place, bypassed by the modern world, in which old-fashioned values persisted.*

*Few will remember Auchtermuchty for its triumph in winning the Scottish Brass Band Championship in 1928. And the remake of the popular television series, Dr Finlay's Casebook, in the town in the Nineties has already been forgotten. But the pedestal on which J.J. placed Auchtermuchty leaves an indelible memory.*

*His affectionate references to its dour, upright citizens, and the values by while they lived their lives, immortalised the town forever.*

*He once described Auchtermuchty as a place where homosexuality could not happen, a town where human decency, morality and the old standards acted as a touchstone against modern life.*

*One of J.J's greatest pleasures was occasionally to visit Auchtermuchty on his way to play golf at St Andrews, and to walk through its street without anyone knowing who he was.*

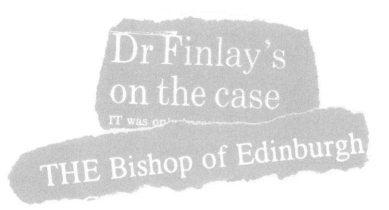

Dr Finlay's on the case

IT was on

THE Bishop of Edinburgh

MR GERALD RATNER, chairman of Ratners the jewellers, turns up at his company's annual meeting with a snazzy earring in his right lobe and tells his shareholders he is convinced men so love such adornments that they will soon become as common in the office and boardroom as a tie-clip or cuf-flinks.

And since he is an expert, I have no doubt he is right. Nor do I object. I am all for adding colour to life. I just wonder where it is all going to end.

If the fashion spreads to Scotland, as I am sure it will, could the day yet come when kilted Auchtermuchty laddies are not only wearing gold rings in their ears, but also carrying powder-puffs in their sporrans?

# Dr Finlay's on the case

IT was only because it was being filmed in my beloved Auchtermuchty — that Brigadoon where Isobel Steven bakes her scrumptious shortbread, Jimmy Shand sets the feet of kilted laddies tapping with his accordion and that upright Presbyterian, the Reverend Anne Fraser, scourges sin and Satan from the pulpit every Sabbath — that I first tuned in to the new series of Doctor Finlay's Casebook.

How does it compare with the old? Not too badly at all. As Dr Cameron, Ian Bannen may not be in quite the same class as the late Andrew Cruickshank, Annette Crosbie is perhaps a shade insipid as Janet and David Rintoul strangely dour and wooden as Dr Finlay.

But the story-line is good, the scenery enchanting, the supporting cast strong and, in the young actor Jason Flemyng, who plays Dr Neil, I suspect we are watching a great TV star in the making.

I would just like to think that on his way up he takes Auchtermuchty and its tiny tourist trade to ever-increasing riches with him.

THE Bishop of Edinburgh, the Most Rev Richard Holloway, urges the Church to accept adultery as a fact of life and forgive those who commit it. He says he believes Man was born to have many lovers and that 'for the human race to survive we must go out and sow our seeds ... God knew that when he made us. So He has given us a built-in sex drive which I believe is designed for us to go out and propagate as widely as possible.'

Is he right? I don't know. But I do know this. His views are going to go down a treat wth some kilted laddies in Auchtermuchty.

ISN'T that a terrible story from the US, where a wife was so driven to despair by her husband's sexual demands that in the middle of the night she got out of bed, found a knife and cut off his willy?

Isn't it a mercy that such a thing could never happen in my beloved Auchtermuchty? There, if ever a member of the Ladies Sewing Circle is disturbed by her husband in the middle of the night, it is never likely to be a knife she seeks.

It is infinitely more likely to be cotton wool with which to stuff her ears in order to drown the sound of the ancient kilted laddie snoring.

# Vive la France

*For Peter Mayle, it was the joys of One Year in Provence. For J.J. it was a lifetime's love of the delights of France and especially Normandy.*

*The region became a favourite holiday destination for a writer enthralled by the people he met and their undemanding way of life. His fascination for them is best summed up by the story of simple fairground stall-holder Monsieur Perrott, who epitomised their contentment.*

*France was also a retreat where he could indulge his passions for golf and swimming and enjoy its culinary delights and superb wines. It was a world of peace and simple values which drew him back time and again.*

*J.J. was a fierce patriot, but he was never able to understand the British contempt for France and the French.*

# French without tears

I WAS wrong when I said in my last column before going on holiday that you could eat like a king in Normandy for £5.

I found that for that sum this year you could only eat like a prince. To eat like a king you have to pay £2 more.

Night after night on a 70 franc menu, I found myself faced with a choice of starters, including half a dozen oysters, a whole crab, a bowl of mussels and soup.

Main courses included Dover sole, entrecote steak, canard à l'orange, coq au vin, gigot d'agneau – with the widest possible choice of desserts to follow.

Unbelievable isn't it, when for that sort of money you would hardly get a hamburger and chips in London? But it is not only the brilliance of the food which makes me warm to France. Even in the supermarkets the check-out girls invariably help you pack your purchases.

And in the gift shops, if you buy anything, you are automatically asked whether it is intended as a present. If so, it is immediately gift-wrapped without any further cost.

It all left me wondering just why, in contrast, so many shop assistants in this country, especially the younger ones in the South-East, should be so sour and sullen. Just how in Britain have we gone so wrong?

*WHEN you read this I hope to be sitting in the sun outside a cafe in a Normandy fishing village enjoying my croissants, strawberry jam and coffee and idly speculating as to whether I might have a swim or play golf before lunch. See you again in September, if it's not raining.*

September 1, 1991

# Lesson to be learnt from the French

OVER a glass of Ricard in the village café, my French friend, 62-year-old André Mauger, was complaining bitterly about the way in which the French government treated old-age pensioners.

'Do you know,' he said, 'that after having worked for 36 years from the age of 14 until I retired two years ago at the age of 60, I get a pension of only 4,500 francs a month? Not much, is it, to live on?' His voice trembled with indignation.

Meanwhile, I was doing a piece of mental arithmetic. At a little less than ten francs to the pound, that 4,500 francs a month is comfortably more than £100 a week.

And, as I afterwards discovered, André was getting less than the national average because he had been a self-employed house painter and had chosen not to enter a contributory scheme.

'What do you old-age pensioners get a week?' he demanded. His face registered total disbelief when I told him that the basic pension for a husband and wife was £83.25 a week. And that the retirement age for men was not 60, as in France, but 65. 'But the cost of living has to be a lot cheaper, hasn't it?'

He could hardly believe me when I told him that there was not all that much difference in prices in the shops and that, in fact, it was in many ways infinitely cheaper to live in France than in the South of England. Housing, for example. Where in the South of England can you buy a decent family house for £30,000? In Normandy for that money you can take your pick.

Then there is lifestyle. Where in the South of England do you get checkout girls who actually smile at you and help you pack your purchases? Where anywhere in Britain do you get shop assistants who ask if you would like even the tiniest purchase gift-wrapped? In which part of these islands can you take either your own or someone else's wife out to a first-class dinner in a good restaurant with a decent bottle of wine and still get change from £20? In Normandy you can do it almost anywhere.

Why is it that the French always seem to do things so much better than we do? Might it perhaps be because, with their insistence on never buying a foreign product if there is a French one available, they care for their country more than we do for ours?

# Hoop-la and real happiness

ALTHOUGH I have known Monsieur Perrott for more than ten years, I still do not know his first name.

Indeed, it was only this year that I learned his surname.

He and his wife – a silver-haired lady who looks like a dowager duchess – have a hoop-la stall in a French funfair which at this time of year wends its way from one Normandy seaside village to another.

I love to watch Monsieur Perrott enchanting his customers. He is especially good and gentle with children. And late at night with revellers as, with unsteady aim, they try to throw their hoop over a china dog.

Although, if the rain comes – and it comes quite often in that part of Normandy – there are times when there may be no customers at all.

It was near midnight on one such night this holiday that I got into a prolonged conversation with Monsieur Perrott. 'Where do you go from here?' I asked.

'Grandcamps,' he replied. 'And after that?' I asked. He proceeded to list a number of other towns where he and the rest of the funfair arrive at precisely the same time each year.

'When do you finish for the winter?' I asked. He looked at me in some surprise. 'We never stop. We go on right through the winter.'

'Do you never have a holiday?' I asked. He shrugged his shoulders. 'Never.' He looked at me searchingly and said: 'I expect that in England you have a house. I have no house and never have had one. I have no land. No money either. I am 73 and my wife is 74.

'Our only home is our caravan, and even that is a much smaller one than we used to have. But I wouldn't want it any other way. It's a wonderful job and I love it.'

And looking at him and his wife, who was nodding in agreement, I realised that he meant every word he said.

I got up early the next morning and sought out his caravan with a bottle of whisky which I planned to give him as a tiny gesture of thanks for the pleasure he had given me and my family over the years.

But his caravan had already gone. I hope I see him again next year. I have an instinct that he could teach the rest of us a good deal about what really constitutes human happiness.

# Tap water for French as the recession bites

IF you think that Britain is suffering from recession this Christmas, you ought to try France where the bank interest rate is some three points higher than our own.

I spent four days in Normandy and each night I went to a different restaurant.

On my first night I went to my favourite restaurant of all. The food was as brilliant as ever. And as cheap as ever.

But in the entire restaurant there were only two other diners. Both of them were men. Commercial travellers, I assumed.

Each of them was having the cheap £6 menu. One of them had a glass of wine. The other was drinking from a carafe of tap water. Something I'd never thought I'd live to see a Frenchman do.

It was much the same everywhere I went. On my final night, the only other people dining in the restaurant were the owner and his wife. And as far as I could see the shops were almost empty.

Who do the French blame for the state of the economy? Probably quite unfairly, the finger is pointed at President Mitterrand.

I don't know what would happen to John Major if, in the pre-

sent economic climate, he attended a conference of Brighton department store owners and restaurateurs unescorted.

But I have the strongest feeling that if President Mitterrand ever visited Normandy unprotected he could well end up being lynched.

# A French lesson in value

I AM aware that every time I come back from a few days in France, I go banging on about the wonders of life there.

But it is difficult to resist so doing, since it is absolutely true. The French do seem in many ways to have a far better quality of life than we have.

And, even with the pound at an artificially low rate against the franc, a holiday in France still represents wonderful value for money. Where else in the world can you eat, as I did in Normandy last week, a first-class meal in a first-class restaurant for less than £9? And an excellent one in a more modest establishment for not much more than half that?

Prices in the supermarkets are equally tempting. The same Scotch whisky I buy at home costs £2 less a bottle in Normandy and, as for wine, the shelves are full of a bewildering variety from £1 a bottle upwards.

Coffee costs half the price it does in England. And, even though prices have recently risen, so do cigarettes.

For me the final clinching point is that even in a village as small as the one in which I was staying with fewer than 600 inhabitants, there was not one but two bakers each producing the most delicious, hot, fresh, crusty bread not once but twice a day, as well as the most succulent croissants, pastries and tarts. Can you imagine that happening in any village of similar size in England?

How do the French do it? I don't know. I just wish that here in Britain we could one day find the secret, too.

# A French lesson in trust

On a quick shopping trip to Normandy the week before Christmas, I visited a small knitwear factory run by two brothers in a tiny village some two miles from Cherbourg.

I had been told by French friends that they produced high quality fashion garments which they exported exclusively to expensive stores in England. I was so impressed by their range that I bought a stylish cardigan as a Christmas present for a gorgeous TV presenter for whom I have a soft spot.

On Christmas Day it was received with much acclaim.

Last week, with another relative's birthday fast approaching, I rang the factory and asked if by any chance they remembered me. They did.

'Would it be possible,' I asked, 'for you to send me another identical cardigan, only in a different colour, to reach me within the next five days?' 'Of course it would,' was the reply. I then offered my credit card number over the telephone. But the brother who spoke to me explained that they did not deal in credit cards.

'But don't worry,' he said. 'We'll despatch the cardigan today along with the bill. Just send a cheque when you get it.'

Could you imagine any small British concern being equally trusting to someone they had met only once and whom they didn't know from Adam?

September 9, 1996

# Do the English really have to hate the French?

'WHY,' asked the gorgeous, elegant, French blonde with whom I was dining, 'do the English hate the French?'

She silenced my immediate, indignant denial by adding: 'I don't mean you. I know you are pro-French. But then you are Scottish and we French get on well with the Scots. Always have done.

'But with the English it is different. Their newspapers are always attacking us. Your tabloids call us frogs and are constantly stirring up hatred and animosity against us.

'And your middle class are just as bad. Maybe even worse. They come here, seem to enjoy our food, buy houses in Provence. But do they make friends with the French? Like hell. They always seem to keep themselves socially apart.'

I have to admit that there is some truth in what she said. In the yachting community, which is the one I suppose I know best, there is a marked reluctance on the part of the English yachtsmen to mingle with the natives. They prefer to go on board each other's boats to drink their G and Ts rather than share a Ricard and a Frenchman. Why is that?

Could part of the answer be an inferiority complex? My own theory is that the average Englishman coming to France is so thick that he barely speaks French at all even if he has studied it for years at school and that since he can't talk with the French prefers not to mix with them either.

And isn't that a tragedy? If only the English took the time to learn a little French, might they not discover that, next to the Scots and the Pakistanis, the French are perhaps the best and most civilised nation in the world?

# Charles & Diana

*Had he been alive, J.J. would have been deeply distressed at the death of Diana, Princess of Wales. For by the end of his own life he had become one of her most ardent admirers.*

*It was not always so. Some of his writings must have hurt the Princess intensely although the pair eventually became good friends. The columns which follow chart the ebb and flow of J.J.'s feelings for Diana which, as ever, mirrored perfectly the mood of the nation.*

*In the beginning, he admiringly described her as the best thing to have happened to the Royal Family in the last 20 years and said the health of the Monarchy owed more to her efforts than those of Prince Charles.*

*As rumours grew of discord within the Royal marriage J.J. refused to believe there were any real problems but urged the couple to put on a more public show of affection and togetherness. In the summer of 1991 he gave odds of 1,000-1 against divorce which, a year later, he was still describing as unthinkable.*

*It was the release of Andrew Morton's revelatory book which caused J.J.'s wrath to turn on Diana. In one of the most venomous pieces he ever wrote, he described her co-operation with Morton as "an act of the basest treachery...not just against her husband but against the whole institution of Monarchy".*

*But, in the end, the charms of Diana sweetened even J.J.'s acid-filled pen. He praised her foreign visits, raged against the paparazzi who hounded her and blamed Prince Charles as the architect of his own disasters. In one of his final Mail on Sunday columns, J.J. issued a blunt warning to the Prince on the folly of attempting to foist his mistress, Camilla Parker-Bowles onto the public.*

*Of Diana, he wrote that losing her was just about the biggest tragedy the British Monarchy has ever had to face. With hindsight, these were astonishingly prophetic words. For we now know just how great that tragedy turned out to be.*

Why did Charles stay at home?
Why did Diana turn away?
Game, set and match to Di
Is this why Charles talks to the flowers?
Is Diana on the brink?

# If Diana gets bored

I HAVE long held the view that the Princess of Wales is the only good thing that has happened to the Royal Family in the last 20 years, and if the monarchy does indeed survive into the next century it will be more because of her than her husband's dreary speeches.

I just hope she does not get too bored in the remaining 358 days of this year.

But if she does I would defend to the end her right to do as she did last autumn — dismiss her police minder and spend the next four hours until 2.30 am playing bridge in the flat of a former boyfriend, Mr James Gilbey, whose shirts it was said she once used to wash and iron.

Nothing could be more innocent than a game of bridge. I make only one point.

Next time might it not be wise and politic to tell us the names of the other people present?

*After all, doesn't it take four to make a rubber?*

# The Magic of Charles

EVEN though his brow is so often furrowed in thought, it can't be such a bad old life for Prince Charles.

There he was last week playing polo in the Florida sunshine — the first-class Concorde fares for himself and his entourage paid by the tournament's organisers — and his only real problem that of fending off all the ladies who, such is his magic, tend to come too close and, on occasion, even seek to embrace him.

This week he will be in the sunshine again, this time the mountain sunshine of Klosters on his annual skiing holiday. I grudge him not a moment of his fun. I just find it sad that once again the Princess of Wales will not be with him.

Isn't it a pity that magical though his appeal for women may well be, it so often falls short of persuading his own wife to accompany him?

But then, after nine years of marriage, couldn't the same thing be said about most husbands?

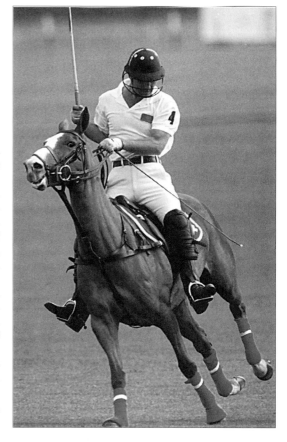

# Why did Charles stay at home?

EYEBROWS are being ever so slightly raised because the Princess of Wales along with Prince William, Prince Harry, her mother, her two sisters and children, her brother, her sister-in-law, nanny and 19 servants have decided to accept once again the hospitality of Mr Richard Branson and spend the Easter break on his Caribbean home on Necker Island.

But why ever shouldn't she?

With its sun-kissed beaches, balmy weather and turquoise blue sea, the island offers a privacy it would be difficult to obtain elsewhere. And if she is getting the house rent-free, so what?

As Britain's 17th richest man, with assets, according to the latest league table, of £488 million, which puts him only £6,212 million behind the Queen, Mr Branson hardly needs the money. And besides, any cash he might lose from giving the Princess of Wales his home rent-free will be more than made up for by the higher rent he will be able to charge subsequent tenants. It is not the fact that Princess Diana and her children are going to Necker Island which saddens me. It is the fact that Prince Charles is not going with them.

Can there be any duty which possibly matches in importance, or any pleasure which can possibly equal, that of being with one's own children on a seaside holiday?

So why didn't he go?

Could it have been because, like many another man, he just can't stand the sight of his in-laws?

# Why Charles still needs that teddy bear ...

A FEW quizzical eyebrows must have been raised at the revelation that at the advanced age of 41 Prince Charles still treasures the teddy bear he had as a child, that the teddy shares his bed at Highgrove and that the Prince insists that teddy's arms are tucked inside the sheets at night so that 'he doesn't get cold'.

It is also said that when the Prince travels abroad teddy travels with him — packed into a shirt-bag by the Prince's valet — and that the only time teddy is left behind is when Charles is visiting regiments where he is Colonel-in-Chief.

It is felt that on such occasions the teddy would not accord with his masculine image.

Nor would it. It might even make other officers wonder where he kept his powder puff.

Yet Prince Charles hardly needs to prove either his manhood or his courage. He has already done so abundantly.

He has never stopped playing Russian roulette with his wife and done things which nothing on God's earth would make me voluntarily do.

He has parachuted from aeroplanes into the sea. He has surfaced through the escape hatches of submerged submarines.

He has taken the most extraordinary chances with his life steeplechasing and on the hunting field. Indeed there have been times when he has almost seemed to be deliberately seeking a confrontation with death.

So why then the teddy bear? Might there be a clue for a psychiatrist in the fact that, according to the same source, the Prince's two brothers, Prince Andrew and Prince Edward, still treasure their teddys too. And in much the same way.

Isn't that bizarre? Have all three an effeminate streak in them? Or could there be another and sadder reason?

Life cannot be much fun for toddlers whose mother is the Queen and immersed in affairs of State and often abroad on long official tours. And whose father is also part of an official distant world. As they went to sleep at night, might the teddy bears clutched in their arms have been just about the only thing in life of whose love they were quite, quite sure?

If so, wouldn't it be good to think that at least nowadays Prince William and Prince Harry do not have to clutch to their teddy bears quite so closely?

■ ■ ■ ■ ■ ■

I AM glad for Prince William's sake that this weekend, on his half term break from school, he will see his father — the first time he will have done so for a month.

He will no doubt be thrilled that his dad is taking the trouble to fly home to Highgrove especially to see him and Prince Harry.

But the stay is not going to be a lengthy one.

Today Prince Charles goes back to Balmoral.

I wonder why. What is so wrong with Highgrove? What is so wrong with spending time with his own wife, rather than mooning about like a wounded stag in the Scottish mountains?

We keep on being assured that there is nothing wrong with the Royal marriage, that it is absolutely rock solid.

And I am sure it is. But wouldn't it be nice if just occasionally Prince Charles acted as if it were?

# But is there really cause for concern?

I HOPE they hid the newspapers from the boys at Ludgrove Preparatory School last week. At the age of eight Prince William is old enough to read, old enough to understand, insecure enough to feel desperately hurt by the banner headlines relating to his mother and father. Prince Charles and Princess Diana, Cause for Concern said the front page headline of one of the most respectable newspapers in Britain.

Would you blame Prince William, or indeed anyone else, reading that if he had thought from it that Prince Charles and Princess Diana were on the very brink of divorce? Isn't that the implication of putting it on Page One and in the sort of type usually reserved for warning the nation of impending disaster?

Yet is disaster, in fact, impending? Does anyone anywhere seriously believe that Charles and Di are actually in danger of splitting up? I would give very long odds indeed against it.

Yet Prince Charles and Princess Diana have no one else to blame save themselves for the speculation. Did it never occur to either of them the conclusions that might be drawn if they were not together on such an important birthday as her 30th? Or if there seemed even to be no plans to celebrate their tenth wedding anniversary?

As for the newspapers involved, I would defend to the end their right to examine the Royal marriage and, indeed, to discuss every aspect of the Royal Family.

And the fact that Prince Charles and his wife do nowadays certainly seem to spend a lot of their lives away from each other is worthy of comment.

But isn't the proper place for such comment the gossip column, rather than giving it the same prominence that might be devoted to the declaration of World War Three?

# Why did Diana turn away?

THE more one thinks about them, the more curious seem the stories from India about the Prince and Princess of Wales. First of all, the Taj Mahal incident. On his first visit to that famous monument, in the days when he was still a bachelor, Prince Charles was so moved by its beauty that he vowed he would one day return to share its magic with his wife. But last week he did not keep that pledge. Instead, Princess Diana went alone to see the splendour of the monument on the banks of a sacred river in Agra. And she, too, was so moved that she asked to be left alone for a few minutes.

When, after her reverie, she was asked what she thought of the Taj Mahal she replied enigmatically: 'It was very healing.'

That seemed an odd remark. What did she mean by it, she was asked? Her reply was cryptic: 'Work it out for yourself.' It was almost as if she were quite deliberately inviting speculation about the state of her marriage.

Meanwhile, where was Prince Charles? He had chosen to stay behind with the Indo-British Industrialists' Forum. A worthy but hardly vital occasion.

In his speech, he also said something most curious. He told his audience: 'A wiser prince than I would have opted for a visit to the Taj Mahal and the Red Fort in Agra, which I believe is where some of the greatest pundits of the Press seem to think I ought to be anyway, rather than make a greater fool of myself here.'

What can it all mean? Why did the Princess speak as she did? And why when, later in the trip, her husband tried publicly to peck her on the cheek did she turn her head away?

Have they really reached the stage when they don't mind the whole world knowing that all the love and romance have gone from their marriage and that nothing is left but duty?

# Game, set and match to Di

WHEN Prince Charles spurs his polo pony on to greater effort this afternoon I wonder just what is going on in his mind. Could he be reflecting perhaps on how comprehensively he has been outwitted, outmanoeuvred and completely scuppered by Princess Diana? Just a year or two ago he would have come close to being top of any public opinion popularity poll.

He might have been regarded as a little boring perhaps, maybe just a shade too earnest and certainly a little pompous.

But no one would ever have dreamed of questioning his integrity, his honour or his absolute suitability to being the next King.

But now? After Andrew Morton's book can there be anyone who looks up at him in quite the same hero-worshipping way?

Can it really be true, people are asking, that he has spurned his beautiful wife and prefers the company of Mrs Camilla Parker Bowles?

Can it really be true that he has treated Princess Diana so coldly that she has attempted suicide on five different occasions?

To the first question, the answer is probably yes.

But as far as the second question is concerned, I think that the proposition that the Princess of Wales made five suicide attempts is absolute bunkum. Where then did Mr Andrew Morton get his melodramatic facts? From Princess Diana's friends of course.

And why aren't his allegations being contradicted? Because Princess Diana does not want them to be.

After all, why should she when all the indications suggest that it was she who deliberately leaked them?

Could that be the true scenario? It begins to look very much as if it is. But what can Prince Charles do about it? Absolutely nothing.

When he married Princess Diana she was a sweet, innocent, naive girl who didn't even have a single O-level to her name. It may well be that Prince Charles patronised her and thought he was intellectually vastly her superior. He knows a good deal better now.

He is in a situation where only one partner has the whip hand in his marriage. And that is his wife.

Either he does what she wants, which you can be sure will include his giving up his relationship with Camilla Parker Bowles or she can bring down the whole House of Windsor.

In Wimbledon week isn't it game, set and match to Princess Di?

**STANDING OVATION: Diana**

■ ■ ■ ■

**THE Princess of Wales not only looked devastatingly beautiful, the picture of sophisticated elegance, when she attended the Royal Albert Hall charity tribute to Sammy Davis Jnr, she also looked radiantly happy.**

She clearly gloried in the standing ovation she received from the packed celebrity audience.

Am I the only one beginning to suspect that she is actually enjoying the crisis she has created?

If she is, I don't like it. Any more than I liked the story that she had been seen in a West End club giggling happily with some of those close friends of hers who supplied Mr Andrew Morton with his inside stories of her life with Prince Charles.

I very much hope that my suspicions are unfounded. But I do caution the Princess to take care. She has an enormous fund of public love and goodwill. But it could quickly disappear if ever the public began to feel that it was not she but Prince Charles who is the innocent victim in a marriage that has gone wrong.

# Has the Prince a death wish?

WHEN Prince Charles took that spectacular head-first tumble at high speed from his polo pony last Sunday and lay motionless on the ground after the pony had kicked him, I do not suppose I was the only person asking: 'Just why does he keep on taking such risks?'

It is only two years since he broke his arm in another almost catastrophic fall.

What is he going to break next? His neck? Just what is he trying to do? Kill himself? Perhaps that is not such a daft question.

For the last few months, perhaps even for the last few years, life must have been hell for Prince Charles.

Ever since childhood he has tried so hard, perhaps too hard, to be the perfect heir to the Crown. His life has been one of unswerving dedication to duty. But in the last year or so everything has gone sour. He is increasingly blamed for the failure of his marriage. And while Princess Diana becomes more and more popular and the halo above her head shines ever brighter, Prince Charles is ever increasingly cast in the role of villain.

He has even been depicted as not showing enough love to his own children. All utterly untrue. All desperately unfair. Yet there is nothing he can do to present his own side of the argument. He simply has to suffer in silence.

Nor, since divorce is unthinkable, does there seem to be any possible way out of his own private hell. Not ever. He could remain in that hell for the rest of his life.

Would you, in these circumstances, blame him if he more and more took the view that it no longer mattered a damn what happened to him?

*ONE of the most fascinating items in Princess Diana's taped telephone conversation was her revelation that she had dressed her Army friend Major James Hewitt 'from head to foot . . . cost me quite a bit'.*

*I'll bet it did, too. Major Hewitt's suits are said to reek of expensive tailoring. And Savile Row suits are way beyond the reach of an Army major's pay. On the tape,*

*the Princess talks about her generosity in thus treating Major Hewitt. But was it really her generosity? In the long run would it really be she who picked up the bill? Isn't it more likely to have been either her husband or, via the Civil List, the British taxpayer?*

*As for Major Hewitt. Do you suppose that at least he buys his own underpants?*

# Is this why Charles talks to the flowers?

THE person who emerges with least credit from the scandal of Princess Diana's taped telephone call is the squalid little man who did the eavesdropping — 70-year-old retired bank manager Mr Cyril Reenan.

What sort of person can he be who gets his kicks out of erecting a 30ft radio mast in his back garden and listening in to other people's private conversations?

Is he really any less loathsome than the peeping tom who trains a powerful telescope on to bedroom windows in order to watch young girls undress?

As for Princess Diana, she herself hardly comes out of the affair smelling of roses.

It is almost unbelievable that she could have been stupid enough as to speak so incautiously to a dim-witted Hooray Henry telephoning from a car when everyone has known for years that such conversations on car telephones could be overheard by almost anyone creepy enough to listen.

It is even more depressing that she should express herself in such banal, schoolgirlish, goo-goo terms and in a way which makes her sound incredibly vain.

The whole ghastly business is a mess. It leaves me with one reflection. If the taped conversations are any indication of how Princess Diana talks in private, is it really any longer any wonder why, on balance, Prince Charles prefers to chat up flowers?

September 6, 1992

# The accusation in an old lady's stare

FOR the Queen Mother, now in her 93rd year, there cannot be too many pages left in the book. All her life has been dedicated to the service of the Royal Family. I wonder how she feels now when she looks around and sees everything she has worked for, and sacrificed for, disintegrating before her eyes? One passage in that taped phone conversation between the Princess of Wales and her friend Mr James Gilbey may provide a clue.

The Princess was talking about the Queen Mother and she said: 'His grandmother is always looking at me with a strange look in her eyes. It is not hatred. It's sort of interest and pity mixed in one. I am not quite sure. I don't understand it.

'Every time I look up she's looking at me and then looks away and smiles . . . I don't know what's going on.' Would you wonder if the Queen Mother had, indeed, been looking intently and quizzically at the Princess?

In some ways their backgrounds are similar. Like Princess Diana, the Queen Mother was not of royal blood when she married into the Royal Family. Like Diana, she was a dazzling beauty. But there the similarities end. The Queen Mother had a husband who was ten times more boring than Prince Charles ever could be. A husband moreover with a nervous stammer who had never dreamed he would be King and was press-ganged into the job by the abdication of his brother.

She, and she alone, was the person who gave him the strength to succeed. Then she had to endure the wartime bombing of London. Yet never once did her devotion to her husband falter.

Would you blame her if she looked with amazement on a grand-daughter-in-law who, instead of supporting her husband, seems intent on destroying him?

# Can Diana's men resist a rich lure?

NOW that the Princess of Wales seems at least temporarily to have backed away from either divorce or separation from Prince Charles and decided instead to resume life as the dutiful wife of the heir to the Throne, there must be two men who are each asking themselves 'where do I go from here?'

I refer of course to Mr James Gilbey and dashing Captain James Hewitt. Just what does the future hold for them?

It is Mr Gilbey for whom instinctively I feel more sorry. He seems to have been genuinely besotted with the Princess. He is not a man of substantial means. Nor, judging from that taped conversation, of much intellect either. He has to work to live.

But what sort of worthwhile, well-paid employment is there going to be for a man whose only real claim to fame is that he calls the future Queen of England Squidgy and blows kisses to her down the telephone?

As for Captain Hewitt, he would not appear to be a man of substance either. How can he be when he permits the Princess of Wales to buy him Savile Row suits?

He had no doubt hoped in his career to reach the highest military echelons. But even if he had passed instead of failing his exams to become a Major, what possible future could there now be for him in the Army? The high possibility is that he could end up earning his living as a glorified stable hand teaching the wives and daughters of rich men to ride horses.

There is, of course, an alternative scenario. Both men could become very rich indeed if they chose to tell their stories on the American market.

But would either of them be tempted by the thought of earning millions of dollars? I so much hope not.

I bet that the Queen and Princess Diana are keeping their fingers crossed too

IF IT is indeed true that every picture tells a story, then what is the message we are to take from the pictures of a radiantly happy Princess Diana out on the town on not just one but two nights last week with Prince Charles?

That their problems are over and that once again they are in love with each other?

I would say 'maybe' to the first part of that question, but I would not bet as much as a brass button on the answer to the second part being 'yes'. A love that has died can never be rekindled.

Why then the look of such utter joy on the Princess's face? Is it because she is at peace with herself now that her rebellion is over?

Happy that she is once again conforming to the public perception of her role as consort to the heir to the throne? I so much hope so.

Wouldn't it be awful if the sparkle which has been restored to her eyes is there only because she has found a new friend to talk to on the telephone?

■ ■ ■ ■

THERE may be public revulsion at the Daily Mirror's action in publishing an alleged intimate telephone conversation between Prince Charles and Mrs Camilla Parker Bowles — the same sort of revulsion that there was when The Sun published its account of the alleged telephone conversation between Princess Diana and Mr James Gilbey.

But there will also be public disquiet. Did the Prince of Wales and Mrs Parker Bowles really speak in such a way as to make it clear they have been lovers for years? Did they really, as another report suggests, discuss each other's private parts on the telephone?

Prince Charles never normally issues a denial when wild untruths are published about him. I think he ought to make an exception in this case.

After all, it is not only his honour which is at stake. Isn't the honour of his best friend's wife at stake too?

# So just who is listening in?

THERE is something which puzzles me.

In the past few weeks much, possibly far too much, has been written about the taped telephone conversations which took place between Princess Diana and Mr James Gilbey, and Prince Charles and Mrs Camilla Parker Bowles.

But isn't it extraordinary that, even though such conversations have done so much damage to the monarchy, nothing is apparently being done to discover just how they ever became public knowledge at all?

At the time the Princess Diana/James Gilbey tapes exploded into the headlines, I found it difficult to believe that a retired bank manager, Mr Cyril Reenan, a radio enthusiast, had just chanced upon them while listening in from his semi-detached in Abingdon.

But all alarm bells were really set ringing with the revelation that within days of the conversations between the Princess of Wales and Mr Gilbey being taped

a conversation between Prince Charles and Mrs Parker Bowles was also being recorded. That is just too big a coincidence to be believable.

Somewhere there just has to be a highly skilled operator at work. Acting with malice.

But who? And why?

It is said that Mr Reenan, who provided The Sun newspaper with the Princess Diana/Gilbey tapes, has not so far been questioned by the police. Why not?

As for the Prince Charles/Mrs Parker Bowles tapes, has Mr Richard Stott, who was Editor of the Daily Mirror at the time the tapes were published, been questioned as to where he got them, how much money he paid and to whom? Again, if not, why not?

Who would have the ability to home in on royal telephone conversations? Certainly the Government's radio spy centre at Cheltenham could. But it is quite inconceivable that it would. It is equally inconceivable that the security services, who would also

have the capacity, could be involved. What would be the point?

So what would that leave?

The pinpointing of telephone conversations has been too precise to have been done by anyone other than professionals. But what other professionals are there save within the ranks of British Telecom, where 30,000 workers have recently been made redundant? Yet they are not likely culprits, are they?

And what is the purpose of it all? To destabilise the monarchy? Or simply to make money? There is a further question. Where is it all going to end?

The prospects of blackmail become endless. For if the Prince and Princess of Wales's telephone conversations can be intercepted, couldn't the conversations of everyone else in the land, including the Prime Minister?

Isn't this an issue far more worthy of urgent investigation than a boring, meaningless inquiry into who sold machine tools to Iraq?

**December 20, 1992**

NEARLY one in three of the letters which were waiting for me on my return from holiday asked the same question.

Why have you turned against the Princess of Wales when not so very long ago you were writing that she was just about the best thing that had ever happened to the Royal Family?

It is a good question and deserves a straight answer. I turned against the Princess of Wales because of the way she persuaded her friends to collaborate with that puffed-up, pompous and now unbelievable rich prat Mr Andrew Morton in the writing of his book.

That was an act of the basest treachery. Not just treachery against her husband but against the whole institution of Monarchy.

Princess Diana knew quite well what she was taking on when she married Prince Charles. She knew that her prime duty was to maintain the Monarchy. To act as she has done and to try, as she seems to be doing, to denigrate her husband and to set up a rival court of her own is utterly and completely unforgivable.

For my own part, I think that the sooner the divorce comes the better. That will leave the Princess free to do what she does best, holding hands with Aids sufferers, dancing with Mr Wayne Sleep or making schoolgirlish love-sick telephone calls.

As for Prince Charles, I do not pretend he is perfect. He is inclined to be pompous. But he has also enormous virtues. He has incredible courage. He also has a fantastic devotion to duty.

He could and will make a great King. I just hope the self-willed Princess of Wales is not allowed to spoil it.

**June 6, 1993**

# The joy that may spell hope

THE happiest Royal pictures for many months were surely those taken last week after the service in Liverpool Cathedral to commemorate the Battle of the Atlantic.

There was so much joy in the Princess of Wales's face and in Prince Charles's, too.

As one hardened, cynical observer said: 'If they were acting, they deserve an Oscar.'

Were they acting? Was it all put on simply because last week marked the 40th anniversary of the Coronation? Or is there the faintest chance that even after so much bitterness a reconciliation is still possible?

I would so like to think so. It would mean the ending, especially for their two children, of a Royal nightmare.

Who knows, it might even ensure the survival of the Monarchy.

# Was the Prince watching Diana?

THERE have been many critical words written in the past two years about the Princess of Wales, some of them by me and most of them justified.

But not even the most cynical critic can deny the quite spectacular success of her visit to Zimbabwe.

First of all, there was the fact that she travelled to Harare economy class. Was that a publicity gimmick worked out by a bright public relations adviser?

I doubt it. I think it was a gesture that came straight from the heart.

But, if it were otherwise, then all I can suggest is that the rest of the Royal Family would do well to employ the services of the same PR man too.

Especially the Duke of Edinburgh, who never seems to go anywhere except, at another enormous expense, by either the Royal Yacht Britannia or an aeroplane of the Queen's Flight. But it was the Princess's conduct on the ground which enchanted.

The way she hugged lepers, comforted the sick and the dying, and laughed and joked with children as she ladled out meals must have done more good for the Royal Family's image throughout Africa than ten state visits with all their pomp and panoply ever would.

I do not doubt that Prince Charles will have been following intently every single step of his estranged wife's progress. Isn't it time he did something to avoid losing her for ever?

*THEN there is the Princess of Wales.*
*Just three weeks ago she seemed to be entering into a new and more tranquil phase in her life.*
*Now with the revelation of the nuisance telephone calls to her friend Mr Oliver Hoare, who has been described by his ex-mistress, Asil Nadir's Turkish former wife Ayesha, as a 'marathon man in bed', the appearance of tranquillity has been shattered. Instead there emerges the picture of a hysterical woman, clearly teetering on the edge of a nervous breakdown. Lost and lonely and perhaps without hope for the future.*

*Who is responsible for her condition? None of us can really be sure as to what went wrong with her marriage and it may be that even if there had never been a Camilla Parker Bowles, Princess Diana would still have been difficult to live with.*

*But is Prince Charles's own conscience completely clear about what has happened to the naive, innocent 20-year-old he married 13 years ago?*

# No escape for the Princes

WHILE the whole wide world was avidly lapping up the sensational kiss-and-tell revelations of that skunk 'Major' James Hewitt, do you suppose that Prince William and Prince Harry were blissfully unconscious of what was going on?

I would like to think so. But I expect that, sadly, they would be well aware of what was happening.

No matter how much their schoolmasters at Ludgrove might have tried to shield them, there is no way in which they could have failed to learn about their mother's five-year affair with 'Major' Hewitt. And, if they hadn't read it for themselves, they would certainly have been told by sniggering schoolmates about how, once they had been put to bed at Highgrove, 'Major' Hewitt would sneak along the corridor and make love to their mother in a four-poster.

What effect is that going to have on them? Will it make them feel any better to know that simultaneously their father was having an even shoddier affair with Camilla Parker Bowles?

Poor little boys. Despite all the wealth and privilege that surround them, they don't really start off with much of a chance in life, do they? Is there really a need for a Royal divorce?

October 23, 1994

# Can Charles ever find forgiveness?

I WONDER how Prince Charles is feeling this Sunday mornng as he reads the second instalment of his biography.

Suicidal? He should be.

Never in such a short space of time can a Royal Prince have done so much to blow to smithereens his own reputation.

There is much that has happened in his life for which he can be pitied. But there are some things which he himself has done which are quite unforgiveable.

First, the fact that he married an innocent young girl whom he now says he did not love and at a time when he loved someone else.

That was wicked. It is even more wicked now to publicise the fact to the world.

The public humiliation which he has heaped upon the Princess of Wales by so doing is immense. Not to mention the humiliation he has heaped upon his own children.

Yet he has the crust to whinge about the way in which his own parents treated him.

Why did he do it? Why has he acted so much apparently out of character?

Has he, like so many of his ancestors, gone bonkers? Or has he just been incredibly, badly advised? But then, if he has, whose fault is that? Isn't it his own for not being able to keep men of quality around him?

He had a brilliant Private Secretary, Edward Adeane, whose father Sir Michael Adeane had been for many years Private Secretary to the Queen.

Edward had the same sharpness of mind as his father and was utterly and absolutely loyal to the Throne. He had spent almost his whole life being trained for the job. But suddenly it was announced that he was quitting. Why? Adeane would be far too loyal ever to say so, but I suspect it was because a stage was reached when even he could take no more.

Prince Charles was not prepared to take advice. He backed his own judgment.

He wanted around him only acolytes who would agree with everything he said. With the result that he is now surrounded by men almost as stupid as himself.

Where do we go from here? I don't know. But if anything is to be salvaged from the wreckage and if Prince Charles still has pretensions to succeed one day to the throne, then wouldn't an abject public apology to his wife, father and mother now be in order?

# Time for Charles to sack Aylard

I HAVE no idea just how much influence the Queen still has over Prince Charles.

Perhaps he now goes his own way regardless.

But if it should be otherwise, and he still does listen to Her Majesty, then, now that he has returned from his trip to the US and Far East, hasn't the moment arrived for them to have a heart-to-heart talk?

Hasn't the time come for her to say to him: 'Charles, darling. In the past few months, what with the Jonathan Dimbleby book and that extraordinary TV interview in which you confessed your adultery with Camilla Parker Bowles, you have not only harmed yourself, your wife and your children, you have also harmed the monarchy. Things just cannot go on like this. So what are we going to do about it?

'Don't you think you really need to take a closer look at the people who have been advising you? In particular, shouldn't you reassess the suitability of that private secretary of yours, Paymaster Commander Richard Aylard?'

If the Queen did tender such advice, she would be echoing the feelings of many close to the Royal Family. Prince Charles has indeed had a disastrous few months.

It would be quite wrong, of course, to put all the blame on his private secretary, although it is widely known that the two men are very close to each other and widely believed that Commander Aylard was instrumental in organising the Jonathan Dimbleby book and in urging the Prince to co-operate.

Indeed, as recently as last Wednesday, Charles went out of his way to identify himself with the book and its author by attending a literary luncheon to celebrate its publication.

It may be, of course, that even if he had been given better and more sensible advice, the Prince would still have rejected it.

Even so, I am among those who think that a change of personnel around the Prince of Wales has become a matter of some urgency.

And, if the Prince is too soft-hearted to sack his friend, might not Commander Aylard himself be prepared, in the best interests of the monarchy, to do the decent thing and quit?

# Why is Camilla divorcing now?

A QUESTION which remains totally unanswered is why Camilla Parker Bowles and her husband should have so suddenly and so completely unexpectedly decided to divorce after 21 years of marriage.

It is not as if Brigadier Parker Bowles had just discovered his wife's adultery with Prince Charles.

He has known about it and tolerated it, apparently complacently, for many years. Furthermore he is said to be a devout Roman Catholic. He presumably cannot remarry.

So what, for him, is the point of a divorce? Is it possible he has been pressured into it? Is it perhaps the last act of subservience to his future monarch?

Do Prince Charles and Mrs Parker Bowles believe that her being divorced will make their affair any less sordid? If so, I suspect they badly misjudge the temper of the nation.

In the whole ghastly business the people I feel most sorry for, apart from Prince William and Prince Harry, are the Parker Bowles children 20-year-old Tom and 16-year-old Laura.

How do you think they felt when Prince Charles unburdened his soul to Jonathan Dimbleby or at the publication of the Camillagate Tampax tapes?

Tom Parker Bowles, now an undergraduate at Oxford, is said to have asked to be known as plain Tom Bowles to avoid embarrassment.

How does he feel about his godfather Prince Charles? And what does Prince Charles feel about him?

Proud of what he has done, not only to the Parker Bowles children but to his own, too?

# Caring Princess we must not lose

IT WOULD be a very biased man indeed who would deny the success of the Princess of Wales's visit to Hong Kong.

In her three days there on what was officially described as a working visit — perhaps the last ever to be made by a British Royal before the Chinese takeover and which raised £100,000 for Red Cross, leprosy and cancer charities — she took the colony by storm.

Not only by her glamour and beauty but by something infinitely more important. That quality which is the hallmark of her character. Her compassion.

Typical was the way in which she quite deliberately chose in searingly oppressive heat to visit the island of Shek Kwu Chau, an island normally banned to women, whose population consists entirely of peacocks, snakes and 300 heroin junkies under treatment for their addiction.

She went there for the same reason she visited and comforted cancer patients in the Pamela Youde Nethersole Eastern Hospital and chatted with 31 runaway teenagers at the Youth Outreach Centre. Because she is a woman who genuinely cares. And it shows.

As one Hong Kong citizen, who had waited for hours just for a glimpse of her, said: 'She is an icon of our times. A heroine.'

Isn't it just about the biggest tragedy that the British monarchy has ever had to face that Prince Charles should have lost her?

Might is not be better in the long run if we lost him instead?

# Might Charles be trying it on?

THE action of the Prince of Wales in appearing in public with his mistress, Mrs Camilla Parker Bowles, at a London society party has been described as a high-risk strategy.

It certainly is.

The Prince must have known, and maybe even arranged, that an army of photographers would be present at the Ritz for the party to celebrate Lady Sarah Keswick's 50th birthday.

His more sensible aides were said to have advised him against attending the party in Mrs Parker Bowles's company on the grounds that it would be 'professional suicide'. And so it may well turn out to be. It is one thing for the Prince to enjoy his mistresses's company in private. It is quite another for him to flaunt her in public. Even in the presence of her ex-husband, whom for many years he has cuckolded.

Why then did he do it? And is it a one-off? A try-on to test the water? Or could it be that, after 20 years of being hidden away in the background, Mrs Parker Bowles, now that she is divorced and a free woman, is insisting on taking her place beside him in public?

If that should turn out to be the case then I think Prince Charles can say goodbye to the prospect of ever becoming King.

# Will Charles and Camilla tune in?

IT IS estimated that more than 25 million people in the UK alone will watch the Princess of Wales's sensational first ever TV interview on Panorama tomorrow night — a figure likely to be dwarfed by the vast number who will subsequently watch it overseas.

Will the Prince of Wales and Mrs Camilla Parker Bowles be among the viewers? I doubt if either of them could bear to watch.

For the Prince, the Princess's decision to give the interview at all is a devastating blow and maybe a knock-out blow.

But has he anyone except himself to blame? Didn't he start it all with his incredibly ill-advised two-hour long interview with Jonathan Dimbleby, an interview in which, po-faced, he confessed his adultery?

As for Diana giving her broadcast without the Queen's permission, didn't he do much the same himself?

How then can he criticise Diana for following his example?

He will also be dismally aware that the Princess who, from a public relations point of view, waltzes rings around him, is likely to perform brilliantly in her interview and entrench herself even deeper in the affections of the British people. While the Prince himself becomes more and more irrelevant. It is all so tragic and so unnecessary.

If only he had had a wise adviser to counsel him against committing suicide by speaking to Dimbleby.

So what will happen after the Princess's interview? Is divorce the next step? I very much hope not.

Wouldn't it be wonderful if, even at this late hour, they had the sense to stop scoring points off each other and come together again both for the sake of their children and the country?

January 14, 1996

# Is Diana on the brink?

THE picture on the front page of last Tuesday's Daily Mirror of Princess Diana weeping uncontrollably must have set alarm bells ringing in Buckingham Palace.

She had paid an early-evening visit to the home of the woman she calls her 'saviour', psychotherapist Susie Orbach. There were four photographers waiting when she emerged from Miss Orbach's Swiss Cottage home just after 6 pm.

Instead of posing as usual, she put on dark glasses, hid her face with a clipboard and raced for her car with the photographers in hot pursuit. But, before getting into the car, she stood beside it for a full minute sobbing helplessly.

What explains this extraordinary public display of emotion? It is said it was entirely due to the conduct of the photographers. Even if they behaved badly, I find it difficult to believe that they were entirely responsible. The Princess is far too old a hand at dealing with photographers for that to be the sole reason.

So what other explanation is there? Had whatever she heard from Susie Orbach anything to do with it? Or has she reached the end of her tether? Was her bizarre decision to take Prince William and Prince Harry to Centrepoint the following evening further evidence of that? Is she indeed perilously close to a complete breakdown?

It is the last question which the Queen's advisers must now be earnestly asking. She is already on record of having on several occasions sought to damage herself because, she has claimed, of postnatal depression. What if she were now to do the same again — only more seriously and more successfully?

Wouldn't that kill the House of Windsor for ever?

# Does this prove Diana's fears?

IT MAY have been Tiggy Legge-Bourke who burst into tears when the Princess of Wales, who normally ignores her, spoke those seven apparently deadly words at the royal couple's annual staff Christmas party.

But I suspect it is the Princess herself who has suffered the lasting damage.

The recent fall in the Princess's public standing has been catastrophic and has been largely her own fault. Just a few months ago there were people who almost idolised her as a lovely, warm, compassionate woman who had been badly betrayed by her husband.

Now she is almost completely isolated. First of all it was her Press Secretary Mr Geoff Crawford who resigned after having inexcusably been kept entirely in the dark about her decision to appear on that notorious Panorama programme.

Now her Private Secretary Mr Patrick Jephson also quits. His reasons have not yet been published but you can be sure they are not unconnected with the words Princess Diana spoke to Miss Tiggy Legge-Bourke.

Just what were those seven words which have caused all the commotion? We now know that they were: 'So sorry to hear about the baby'.

That was a nasty remark, implying as it did that Miss Legge-Bourke had had an abortion. But since it was also a ridiculous and demonstrably untrue remark, why did it cause Miss Legge-Bourke to collapse in tears?

Why didn't she just laugh it off? And why, above all, did Prince Charles sanction Miss Legge-Bourke's going to a lawyer with a formal complaint against the Princess?

Was it not self-evident that by so doing her complaint would inevitably become public knowledge with consequential and maybe devastating damage to the Princess? Or was that the deliberate intention?

Has the Princess been stitched up?

I have always regarded as nonsense her allegations that she had enemies at Buckingham Palace who were out to get her. Now I am not quite so sure.

*DID Prince Charles last Tuesday night switch on the TV to watch the Princess of Wales's moving account of her visit to Angola and of the time she spent among children and adults maimed by landmines? I doubt it.*

*But he should have done. If he had watched it, and even if he had thought it was all contrived, he would have a better understanding of how, unlike himself, she has captured the hearts and minds of the British people.*

# The Scum Hounding Diana

IT is said that freelance photographers Kelvin Bruce and Brendan Beirne divided an estimated payout of £8,000 from The Sun for the photographs taken by Mr Bruce of a roll of film being snatched from the bag of Mr Beirne by a casual passer-by who had come to the Princess of Wales's aid.

And that there will be thousands of pounds more to come from syndication of their work. All that cash from pictures which would have been quite valueless had the manhandling incident not occurred.

Was the whole thing a set-up? Including the intervention of Mr Kevin Duggan? I suspect it was. It can be argued that the Princess was herself partly to blame for having initially lost her cool and demanded the return of the film. But even so, isn't it utterly damnable that paparazzi should hound and profit from a young woman the way in which the paparazzi are hounding and profiting from Princess Diana?

They are the scum of the earth. Indeed, the only greater scum I can think of are the editors who pay for and publish their pictures.

# Why Charles is on a loser

I WONDER just why Mrs Camilla Parker Bowles has stepped into the public limelight by becoming patron of the National Osteoporosis Society and by allowing to be issued such a pretty, chocolate-box type picture of herself.

In memory of her beloved mother and grandmother who both suffered from the disease? I would doubt that very much. She could help the society in many ways other than by seeking publicity as its patron.

The person behind the issuing of the glamorous photograph is Prince Charles. It is all a quite deliberate attempt by him to secure public acceptance of his mistress. Possibly as a prelude to their sloping off on holiday together. He is wasting his time trying to make Mrs Parker Bowles more popular. That public acceptance will never be given. Nor will he himself be accepted if he continues to foist his mistress on the public.

# The Duchess of York

'That bloody woman...'

J.J.'s verdict on the Duchess of York reflected most people's opinion of the wayward Royal whose highly publicised misdemeanours did so much to undermine the monarchy.

J.J. was so scathing of Fergie's 'bizarre and tawdry' behaviour, he even suggested that her children, the Princesses Eugenie and Beatrice, would be better off in the care of the Queen.

Fergie's indiscretions with Texan Steve Wyatt and the toe-sucking John Bryan, her pursuit of tennis ace Thomas Muster, and her wild extravagances at a time when she was £3 million in debt, angered and exasperated the columnist. How right his prediction proved in 1992 when he warned the Queen that the Duchess wouldn't slip out of the limelight simply because her marriage to Prince Andrew had officially been declared over.

More than three years later and with Fergie continuing to heap fresh embarrassment on the monarchy, a despairing J.J. concluded: 'The sooner the Royal Family is shot of her the better.'

While grudgingly admiring the Duchess for the guts she displayed throughout her troubles, he believed that the tawdry television interview she gave Ruby Wax in 1997 was the final straw.

'Poor pathetic thing,' he wrote. 'I begin to feel for her that the end is nigh.'

Could Fergie bring down Monarchy?
Is Major Ron in on the deal? The one thing you have to
It's time to get shot of Fergie y about rgie
How long must this go on?

**January 1, 1991**

IT IS not often that one sees the publicity-loving, limelight-seeking Duchess of York with her hand to her face to hide it from the cameras.

But there it was in last Monday's Daily Mail. The caption to the picture simply said: 'A sudden attack of shyness as the skiing Duchess is caught by the camera in St Moritz yesterday.'

What was the Duchess doing in St Moritz? Apparently she left Prince Andrew at Sandringham with her two children and made a four-day private skiing trip to the Swiss resort.

Fascinating, isn't it, her penchant for making private trips?

Remember the one she made to Morocco last May accompanied only by her Special Branch minder and an unidentified man who spoke with a Texan drawl?

It was never disclosed exactly where she had been or with whom she had been staying.

In July she was off to the sun again on yet another private trip — precise destination undisclosed.

Personally, I don't give a damn where the Duchess goes. But since invariably she is accompanied at public expense by a Scotland Yard detective, I just wonder why there should be such secrecy.

**January 26, 1992**

# The odd antics of Fergie

OTHER first-class passengers were said to have been astounded by the conduct of the Duchess of York on the plane on her way home from Florida.

Astounded? They must have been goggle-eyed. One hour and two glasses of champagne out of Miami, as the Daily Mail delicately puts it, she started throwing sachets of sugar from her dinner tray at her father.

Next, she began bombarding her personal detective and her secretary with rolled-up tissues and other bits and pieces from the tray. And that was just for starters. She turned her attention again to her father, who was sitting beside her, and began to pull faces and make strange bird-like sounds. Finally, she put a bag over her head and, through a hole, poked out her tongue at Major Ferguson.

What do you make of it all, then? Her father explained to other £2,000-a-seat passengers that

his daughter was just 'letting off steam'.

But was she? I am not in the business of making excuses for the Duchess. She is a tough nut, just about as tough as they come. And she has brought her troubles on herself. Even so, I just wonder whether after all the stress and strain she has been through since the disclosure of the photographs taken on holiday with Mr Steve Wyatt and the chilling reception she knew would be waiting at home, she is not perilously close to crack-up.

Perhaps it would be a good idea if for the next few months the media gave us all a rest from reporting her activities.

Maybe the Duchess in return will do us all, and especially the Royal Family, a favour by lying low, looking after her children and, if he still wants her, her husband?

March 22, 1992

# Could Fergie bring down the Monarchy?

NOW that the marriage of the Duke and Duchess of York has been officially declared over, may we count on the Duchess slipping quietly out of the limelight?

I would not bet on it. Nor would the Queen.

It is reported that the Duchess has already been offered $2 million by an American publishing company to tell the story of her life with Prince Andrew.

And such is the worldwide interest in the affair, the report may well be true. There may even be higher offers to come.

It may be, of course, that, as part of any settlement she may receive from the Royal Family, she will have to sign an undertaking never to speak or write about the marriage. But just how big then is the settlement going to be?

Besides, and no matter how much money is given her, aren't there a million and one other ways in which, with her flamboyant lifestyle and especially if she is going to retain the title of HRH, she could be a source of continual embarrassment in the future? I so hope I am wrong.

I just fear that we have far from heard the last of Fergie and that the time may come when historians of the future point to the day she married Andrew as the day the British monarchy went down the tube.

April 19, 1992

# How long must this go on?

NOBODY can reasonably object to the Duchess of York flying off with her two daughters and their nanny to a paradise island holiday in the sun.

It is her life to do with as she pleases. And since the presumption must be that it is either her estranged husband, or maybe even some rich friend, who is paying the £22,000 which the trip is said to cost, the taxpayer has no right to complain.

What does concern me is that it is the taxpayer who is picking up the bills for the two police officers, one a chief inspector, who are accompanying the Duchess's party.

For just how much longer is that police protection to continue? Are armed, highly-paid officers going to traipse around the world with the Duchess wherever her fancy takes her? Maybe even acting as baggage carriers for her friends? That would be quite unacceptable.

In my view, both officers ought to be on the very next plane home.

# Is Major Ron in on the deal?

AS THE bizarre, tawdry and potentially monarchy-destroying saga of Fergie and the Duke of York continues to unfold, one aspect of it baffles me beyond measure. And that is the continuing presence at the royal side of Major Ron Ferguson.

For years he has been up to his neck in sleazy activities — from being caught out visiting massage parlours to writing sloppy love letters to a lady about half his age, 33-year-old divorcee Miss Lesley Player, whose fund-raising polo activities are now being investigated by the Charity Commissioners — while his long-suffering wife sits alone at home.

One would have thought that after the Miss Player episode he would have chosen to lie low for a while. But not a bit of it. There he was the other day on all the front pages, bold as brass, strutting around the Royal Windsor Horse Show with Prince Andrew.

And, of course, is still polo manager to Prince Charles.

After all that has happened it seems incredible that he should remain in that high-profile job. So why does he?

Might the state of his daughter's marriage have anything to do with it?

Clearly, as was evidenced by that cosy chat the Queen had with her in the back of a car at that same Windsor Horse Show, every possible effort is being made to keep Fergie sweet and to stop her exploding in public.

Could it just possibly be as part of that effort to keep her sweet that her father is being allowed at least temporarily to remain a member of the royal inner circle?

January 21, 1995

# It's time to get shot of Fergie

AUSTRIAN Mr Thomas Muster may be one of the best tennis players in the world.

He may have earned more than £1 million during the past year. But he is not my favourite performer on the court.

I dislike the loudness and ferocity of his grunts and the arrogance of his manner. He looks as if he would have made a perfect member of Hitler's Waffen SS. Every time I see him play I find myself willing his opponent to defeat him.

The Duchess of York clearly does not share my view of Mr Muster. She was so taken by his performance in Qatar that she talked the night away with him, drinking champagne in a disco.

And, instead of heading for London the next day to take her children back to school as had been planned, she decided instead to visit her pregnant sister in Australia where, by a lucky chance, Mr Muster would be arriving 24 hours later to play in the Australian Open. By

an equally lucky chance they ended up in the same Melbourne hotel, the Duchess in a suite costing £2,650 a night and Muster with a notice saying Do Not Disturb on his bedroom door.

Mr Muster laughs off any suggestion of an affair between them. But, knowing the Duchess's reputation for chastity, who would ever dream of suggesting that there had been?

What bugs me is the amount of money the whole escapade must have cost. Only a seriously rich woman could afford to act in the way the Duchess of York acts. I had assumed that perhaps it might all be coming from royalties and spin-offs from her Budgie the Little Helicopter books.

Now we learn that her wealth is a mirage and that, in fact, she is bust with an overdraft of £3 million; that she recently was in 'danger' of having her electricity cut off due to an unpaid bill and had the ignominy of her Access

card being rejected at a local WH Smith shop.

Who is going to save her? Not, it would appear, the Queen.

In an unusually blunt statement issued by Buckingham Palace, it was made clear that Her Majesty is fed up with bailing out the Duchess of York from her financial troubles and does not intend to lift a further finger to help.

Yet the Duchess herself looks completely unconcerned. When asked by reporters if she was on the breadline she cockily replied: 'Breadline? I don't eat bread.'

Is her lack of concern because she feels that when it comes to the crunch the Queen will once again be forced to come to her help rather than allow her to go bankrupt, or, an even greater threat, to sell for many millions of dollars her inside story of life in the Royal Family?

I don't know. What I do know is that the sooner the Royal Family is shot of her the better.

Preferably before she teams up again with Princess Diana.

# The Royal favourite with only one failing

THE DUKE of York is said to be the Queen's favourite son. And I can believe it.

The glowing pride she showed in his courage as a helicopter pilot during the Falklands War was evident to anyone who at that time ever had the privilege of talking with her. She clearly thinks the sun shines out of Prince Andrew's eyes. But then, of course. Her Majesty is biased, isn't she?

The other day I had a report on the Duke from another and completely unbiased source — a friend of mine who is a biggish name in professional golf and who recently has seen quite a lot of the Duke both on and off the golf course. Frequently as a playing partner. My friend is very far from being a royalist. Quite the opposite, in fact. Yet he becomes enthusiastic when he speaks of the Duke. Not simply because the Duke is a good golfer with a handicap of 10 — a fantastic achievement considering he took up the sport only fairly recently.

But far more important because he is, according to my friend, also a most likeable, modest and engaging character. A real man's man.

The sort of chap with whom you would happily go tiger-shooting.

And I accept that verdict to be absolutely true.

I suspect that he is, far and away, the best and most human of the Queen's children.

Isn't it a tragedy he ever married that bloody awful woman?

# The real casualties of Fergie's philandering

THE Duchess of York looked a sad, forlorn figure when she arrived by Concorde in New York —- fare paid by an anonymous well-wisher.

Gone was the fizz and the bounce and the radiant, infectious smile. This was a woman who seemed close to absolute despair. It will be said, and rightly, that she is getting no more than she deserves. Even so, I feel sorry for her. Beneath contempt was the action of that slimy toad John Bryan in publicly humiliating her by giving blow-by-blow accounts of their love-making.

Even to the extent of describing how they contin-ued making love while she was on the phone to Prince Andrew.

But I feel even sorrier for her two children, Princess Beatrice and Princess Eugenie. What is going to be the effect on them in years to come to have known and indeed to have seen that their mother was sharing a bed with Mr Bryan?

The Duchess may be as devoted to her children as she claims to be but, with her immoral lifestyle and increasing reputation as the royal bike, should she be allowed to keep them? Wouldn't they be better off in the care of the Queen?

# What's the big secret, Fergie?

I DO not suppose the organisers of the charity of which she is patron were too upset when the Duchess of York failed to turn up to launch a fund-raising trea-sure hunt to Monte Carlo.

After all, she did send a quite splendid stand-in, her husband.

So it was Prince Andrew, pre-sumably by kind permission of the Royal Navy, who last week saw off 28 cars from London's Chelsea Harbour on their four-day drive to raise funds for the Chemical Dependency Centre, a charity devoted to helping drink and drug addicts. Where was the Duchess? Occupied, per-haps, in looking after Princess Beatrice?

Not quite. It appears that for the second time in four months she had flown off with some friends in a private plane for a brief break in the sun.

On the last occasion, in May, she flew off to Morocco accom-panied by her Special Branch minder and an unidentified man who was said to have spoken with a Texan drawl. No one was saying where she went to this time. Buckingham Palace simply said: 'We never talk about private visits.'

Nor, if the Duchess were a pri-vate person, is there any reason why they should.

But she is not a private person. She and her husband are on the public payroll and they are on it for one reason only — because they damned well want to be.

Besides, why on earth should there be any secrecy about where a member of the Royal Family is going or with whom he or she is staying?

# The one thing you have to say about Fergie

NO WOMAN in recent times has received more public humiliation, more public obloquy, than the Duchess of York.

The public exposure of her sex life by her treacherous psychic healer Madam Vasso, the catalogue of her affairs with Steve Wyatt and the toe-sucking John Bryan and her pursuit of tennis player Thomas 'Raging Bull' Muster, plus the things which have been written about her, some of them by me, would have broken the spirit of most women. Perhaps even made them suicidal.

But Fergie? If she hurts inside, and she must, she takes damned good care never to show it.

Did you see the pictures of her last week celebrating her 37th birthday in New York, her second visit to that city in a fortnight?

She looked just as attractive, just as full of life and energy as ever. From the smile on her face you would not have thought that she had a care in the world.

Good for her. The Duchess may have many faults, but there is one thing for sure she does not lack. Guts.

*Steve Wyatt*

*Thomas Muster*

*John Bryan*

# Fergie finishes the job

AS I watched that extraordinary programme in which American entertainer Miss Ruby Wax made a fool and a laughing stock out of the Duchess of York I wondered if the Queen might be watching it too.

If so, she must have felt close to the point of despair.

How could the Duchess have been stupid enough to agree to the interview — and especially to allow it to take place at the Wentworth mansion she rents for £1,500 a week and with her butler, no less, meeting Miss Wax at the front door?

How could she have been naive enough to allow Ruby and her cameramen to wander at will around her house with Ruby opening drawers and cupboards and fridges, making snide comments about their contents?

How could she ever have allowed Ruby to travel with her on her trip to school to pick up her children who, mercifully at least, were not themselves filmed.

How could she ever have tried to claim that she was still Her Royal Highness?

And, even though she responded with a 'no comment', why did she submit to prying questions about her sex life and as to how good was John Bryan in bed?

Was she really stupid enough to imagine that an interview of this kind watched by 12 million people in this country alone and no doubt by hundreds of millions throughout the world would help sales of her book?

This interview will not do that. All it did do was make the Duchess look a drab, overweight, unattractive and, above all, thick-as-two-short-planks, middle-aged bag.

The Duchess recently claimed that she loved America, would like to live there because the American people loved her. After the Ruby Wax interview and subsequent interviews in America in which she made herself look almost equally stupid, I doubt very much if she would now be any more welcome in the US than she is in England.

Poor pathetic thing. I being to feel that for her the end is really nigh.

*There is a question which must exercise both the Queen and the Prime Minister. Just what is to be done about the Duchess of York?*
*And clearly something has to be done. She cannot be allowed to continue bringing the Royal Family into disrepute with her almost insane extravagance.*
*She cannot, as she has done, allow a charity to pick up the bill for a party she has thrown. She cannot be allowed to carry on accepting sums of £100,000 from casual acquaintances and then claim they were gifts not loans.*
*She cannot be allowed to be taken to court by her former lover over demands for money.*
*But just what can be done?*
*Pressurise Prince Andrew into divorcing her when clearly he doesn't want to do so?*

*Nor, I imagine, would the Queen wish the couple to divorce with the consequent hardship it would mean for her two grandchildren, Princess Beatrice and Princess Eugenie.*
*But is there an alternative to stop her going through money the way an incurable alcoholic goes through drink?*
*Short of locking her up and throwing away the key?*

# The Irish Troubles

*A hatred of the IRA and contempt for Dublin politicians who provided a safe haven for the bombers and murderers symbolised J.J.'s position on the Irish question. He did not live to witness the IRA's ceasefire in the summer of 97, but he would have remained sceptical of a lasting peace.*

*Two years earlier, he had warned of the perils of trusting the IRA. In an indictment of the men of terror he argued that anyone who trusted the IRA a single inch did so at their peril. They remained what they always had been: 'The scum of the earth'.*

*J.J. was equally scathing with the Dublin politicians and judges for their reluctance over the years, and on so many occasions, to extradite to Britain convicted IRA terrorists held in the Republic. The hypocritical Irish Premier Charles Haughey was among the worst offenders during his years in office. J.J. wondered whether such obstinacy from the Irish establishment was symptomatic of a bitter resentment of the way Ireland had been treated by the English down the centuries.*

*American President Bill Clinton's appeasement of Gerry Adams to protect and secure the Irish vote in the US elections was constantly criticised by J.J.*

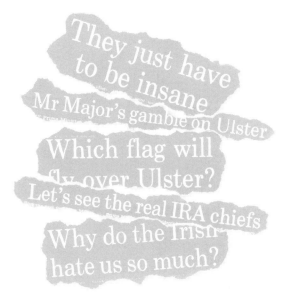

# Why do the Irish hate us so much?

WHEN five Irish Supreme Court judges, for the most insulting of reasons, refuse to extradite to Northern Ireland two convicted and indisputably guilty IRA terrorists, hasn't the time come to ask ourselves seriously what the Irish really think of the English?

None of these staid, sober, middle-aged judges could even remotely be described as supporters of the IRA. All of them, I have no doubt, absolutely abhor violence.

Why then, rather than return them to Ulster, do they, like so many other staid, sober, middle-aged Irish judges before them, release potential killers in their own midst?

Is it because deep down in the heart of even the most civilised Irishmen there still smoulders bitter resentment of the way they think their country has been treated by the English down the centuries?

I don't know. But with convicted terrorists like Dermot Finucane and James Pius Clarke now free to roam Eire, could Irish hoteliers and landladies complain if English holidaymakers were to cancel their bookings in favour of a safer and friendlier country?

And if English consumers were now adamantly to refuse to buy any Irish produce?

Starting perhaps with Guinness? And following on with cheese and butter?

Who knows — might we not even end the present idiocy of allowing Eire citizens resident in Britain to vote in British parliamentary elections?

# They just have to be insane

IN THE immediate aftermath of the murder by the IRA of the two Australian tourists in the Dutch town of Roermond, the Chief Public Prosecutor for the district, a Mr Hubert Laumen, said something on TV which seemed to me to come pretty close to the heart of our problem.

He said: 'Against murderers of this type, where a certain insanity is not far away, it is not very easy to defend yourself.'

A certain insanity?

Isn't he spot on? Freedom fighters, no matter how misguided, who risk their own lives are one thing. But who else, save the criminally insane, would go out to kill without even knowing or caring about the identity of the victims? And without giving a toss as to whether they might even include babes in arms?

Aren't they candidates for Broadmoor, rather than for prison?

Nor does the insanity stop with the men who pull the triggers?

Mr Charles Haughey may come out with all the usual claptrap about how the Irish government abhors violence, and I have no doubt it does. But if by some miracle the psychopaths involved in the Roermond murders were discovered and arrested in the Republic of Ireland, and an attempt to extradite them was turned down by the Irish courts on the grounds that they had been politically motivated, does anyone seriously doubt that there would not be hordes of well-wishers outside the courtroom eager to cheer them, treat them as heroes and whisk them to sanctuary on the backs of motorbikes?

Aren't such people psychopaths, too?

There has been recent concern over whether mad cow disease is ever going to occur in humans.

Might it not, in fact, have been present among a section of the Irish population for generations?

# A mouth full of empty words

IN A statement issued after the murder of Mr Ian Gow, Mr Charles Haughey, the Eire Prime Minister, said: 'I am shocked and stunned.

'It is almost indescribable, this sudden savagery of taking a human life in this way.'

Shocked and stunned? Really?

Why should Mr Haughey be so shocked and stunned about this one particular murder when what the IRA did in such stinking, sneaking, cowardly fashion to Mr Gow is no different from what they have done to dozens upon dozens of others from Airey Neave to Lord Mountbatten onwards?

Has Mr Haughey been shocked and stunned by all of these barbaric atrocities?

If so, why then over the years has Mr Haughey's Republic of Ireland provided the safest of havens for the murderers? Why over the years have Irish judges regularly freed IRA psychopaths rather than have them extradited to face trial in England? Why above all does Mr Haughey himself keep the nationalist pot on the boil by acting and talking as if he had some divine right to exercise suzerainty over Ulster when the truth of the matter is that, if ever Britain threatened to remove her forces from the Six Counties, Mr Haughey would be down on his knees begging us to stay rather than face the bloody civil war which would most certainly follow?

I make no great issue of the matter. But in these circumstances might not Mr Haughey have been wiser to say nothing at all about the murder of Mr Gow rather than spew out such hypocritical garbage.

# Which flag will fly over Ulster?

I HOPE the Prime Minister has marked and digested intelligence reports on the funeral last weekend in the Irish Republic of IRA terrorist Joseph McManus.

By most civilised people's standards, 21-year-old Mr McManus was a despicable and cowardly young thug.

He set off with three other IRA terrorists to murder an unsuspecting part-time member of the Ulster Defence Regiment, a dog warden by profession, whom they had lured to a lonely farm on the pretext that there was a sick dog there which required attention.

Odds of four to one in their favour hardly suggests great courage on the part of the would-be assassins. In the event, the UDR man had more guts than the four terrorists put together. He defended himself and killed McManus.

The three other terrorists took to their heels and fled for the border. It was an incident which should have caused Republican heads to hang in shame.

Yet when McManus was buried he was not only given a full-rites Roman Catholic funeral service in Sligo Cathedral of the Immaculate Conception.

His flag-decked coffin was followed to the grave by no fewer than 400 members of the local Irish community. To them Mr McManus clearly was a patriot and a hero.

How can we even begin to deal with people like that?

Politicians on both sides of the Irish Sea would have us believe that IRA sympathisers represent only a tiny minority of the Southern Irish population. But do they?

It may well be true that a majority of the Southern Irish dislike the IRA. But isn't it also true that there is something they hate even more — and that is the sight of the Union flag flying over Ulster?

Is it the present British Government's intention that sooner or later that flag is going to be pulled down and replaced by the Irish tricolor?

If so, they ought to have the guts openly to say so. But if that is not their intention and they do genuinely mean to stay loyal to the Ulster people, then why continue with an Anglo-Irish agreement which, by giving the Dublin government an advisory role in the province, conveys to both Southern Irish politicians and IRA alike the impression that if only they both continue to push hard enough Britain will in the end surrender?

# Mr Major's gamble on Ulster

THE PRIME Minister shows great courage by declaring he will take personal responsibility for conducting the negotiations to secure peace in Northern Ireland.

But is he wise to put his own reputation so clearly on the line?

If the negotiations succeed and peace is indeed achieved in Ulster, the IRA lays down its arms and the Republic of Ireland gives up its claims for sovereignty over the North, then Mr Major's personal prestige will soar. He will be the greatest of heroes. Just one thing worries me. If, as in the case of our entry into the ERM, the whole peace process turns out to be yet another shambles, who this time, now that Norman Lamont is no longer in the Cabinet, will the Prime Minister be able to blame?

*President Clinton quite deliberately, and with malice aforethought, spits in Mr Major's eye by inviting Gerry Adams to the White House and giving Sinn Fein permission to raise funds in the US.*

*How can Mr Major get his own back? I offer him this suggestion. Why doesn't he redouble the search for the picture, which is known to exist, of the young Bill Clinton, then a Rhodes Scholar at Oxford, among demonstrators on the steps of the US Embassy in London in 1969 protesting against the Vietnam War? Wouldn't the publication of that picture do draft-dodger President Clinton a power of no good with American voters?*

# Perils of trusting the IRA

THERE cannot be even the teeniest weeniest doubt that the violent protest during the Prime Minister's visit to Londonderry last week was deliberately organised and orchestrated by the IRA. That has been made crystal clear by the fact that there has been no condemnation of the violence by either Martin McGuinness or Gerry Adams.

On the contrary. Mr Adams has gone on the offensive with his condemnation of the quite blameless RUC.

But why? Are the IRA beginning to tire of the peace process?

Do they long for a return to the days of bomb and gun? I don't know the answer to these questions.

What I do know is that it underlines once again the fact that anyone who trusts the IRA a single inch does so at his peril. They remain what they always have been. The scum of the earth.

# Let's see the real IRA chiefs

FOR THE past few years Mr Gerry Adams has been treated as a figure of the greatest importance, as a man who was not only the IRA's spokesman and chief pall-bearer but was also virtually in control of the Republican movement. As such, he has been courted by Prime Ministers and Presidents. he has hobnobbed with Bill Clinton at the White House, given press conferences in the White House Rose Garden and gener-

ally been treated almost as a Head of State. And, of course, everywhere he has gone he has travelled first-class in the lap of champagne and caviar luxury.

Now we learn the painful way that it has all been a facade, a con-trick and that he controls nothing at all. So why waste time in future talking to him? Hasn't the time come for the real leaders of the IRA to step forward?

# A fitting end for IRA godfathers?

WE NOW know that while Mr Gerry Adams was talking peace, his chums in the IRA were using the ceasefire to plant terrorist cells in Britain.

That was an act of sickening hypocrisy.

Even more sickening was the fact that the new cells are believed to have consisted of young men known as 'Lilywhites' because they had no police records or any history of involvement with the IRA. When they arrived at British ports they were looked upon simply as decent young Irishmen looking for a job.

Twenty-one-year-old IRA bus bomber Ed O'Brien, whose body ended up in two black bags, was one of them.

And while his grieving parents, who had never suspected their son's involvement with terrorism, prepare to bury his shattered body in his home town of Gorey, Co. Wexford, 3,000 miles away in Washington President Clinton is deliberating on whether to grant Mr Gerry Adams another visa to attend the St Patrick's Day parade in New York.

He is also trying to decide whether to allow Irish-American aid to be sent to Sinn Fein and then funnelled to the IRA. Isn't it typical that he should even hesitate before taking these decisions.

Gerry Adams has not even now condemned the renewed terrorism.

How can he possibly be allowed to take part in the St Patrick's Day parade? And how can there be any question of Noraid being allowed to send further money to Sinn Fein?

The answer is, of course, that shoddy Mr Clinton is terrified of losing the Irish-American vote. He would do anything to prevent that happening.

That is all the more reason why we should not allow him to interfere any further in an Irish settlement.

The matter has now to be decided between the Republic of Ireland Government and the British Government.

And that must mean the most resolute action on the part of both governments against the IRA.

The identities of the seven IRA godfathers must surely be known to Irish intelligence.

Why aren't these men taken into custody?

And afterwards? Can you think of a suitable punishment for sick old men who send naive, inexperienced youngsters to do their dirty work in London?

How about putting them into a mini-van, placing a one-pound bag of Semtex on each of their laps, locking the door of the van from the outside and then, by remote control, driving the van round and round the runways of a deserted airfield?

Wouldn't it be a wonderfully happy ending if they all suffered the same fate as 21-year-old Ed O'Brien?

# Margaret Thatcher

*Margaret Thatcher was the greatest Prime Minister of the century, winning three general elections in eleven years.*

*Each time it was the will of the people that returned her to Downing Street, recognising in her a brilliance and qualities of courage, dignity and resolve that would have led to J.J. 'following her into hell'.*

*She was finally destroyed not by the voters but by the enemies within her own party. Michael Heseltine and Sir Geoffrey Howe were savaged by J.J. for the parts they played in the shameful coup leading to her resignation in the winter of 1990.*

*Following her demise, Mrs Thatcher was replaced as Prime Minister by John Major, her chosen successor.*

*But in the months which followed her downfall a bitterness set in, leading her to attack Major and in particular his policies in Europe. The lady who was never for turning had finally turned against her own, leaving a sad J.J. to mourn her loss of reputation and even to fear for her future.*

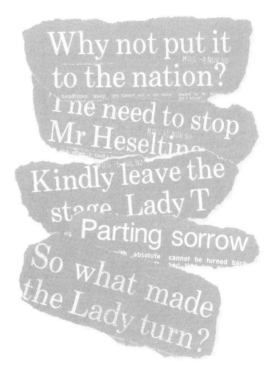

# Why not put it to the nation?

THE headlines keep blaring out that on the issue of Europe Mrs Thatcher is all on her own.

Isolated not only among the leaders of the European Community but, with the resignation of Sir Geoffrey Howe, increasingly so in her own Cabinet and in the House of Commons.

And maybe she is.

But is she on her own in the country? I think not. I think that in her stand she has the backing of the vast inarticulate majority of the people, Tories and Socialists alike. They like as little as she does the idea of handing over control of the economy of this country to a non-elected Brussels bureaucracy headed by M. Jacques Delors.

Am I wrong?

There is one way in which we could find out for sure. Why wait for a General Election? Why not have an immediate referendum on the issue? There is the strongest possible case for having one.

A political decision which could effectively mean the end of national sovereignty is not something which should be left to MPs alone.

It is a decision which must command and be seen to command the support of a clear majority of the British people.

And after the referendum on Europe, why not one on capital punishment, too?

# The need to stop Mr Heseltine

IT IS not often I find myself in agreement with Mr Neil Kinnock, Mr Roy Hattersley and Mr Paddy Ashdown.

But there is one issue on which I do.

If Mr Michael Heseltine, whom Mr Hattersley correctly describes as a 'complete second rater' and who struts around wearing a Brigade of Guards tie although he didn't even complete his six months' National Service, climaxes his successful insurrection against Mrs Thatcher by emerging from the new ballot as Prime Minister without public consent it will be a crime against the nation.

Mrs Thatcher was Prime Minister because she won three General Elections, in each of which she carried the Tory Party to victory on her coat-tails.

She was in No. 10 Downing Street by the will of the people.

She has been forced to resign not by the will of the people but as a result of a well-organised, highly-orchestrated coup by a rabble of MPs and some sections of the media without the people ever being consulted.

It stinks to high heaven that this should have been done by the Tories to a woman to whom they owe so much and who, as was demonstrated to the whole nation by the brilliance and courage and dignity of her performance in last Thursday's House of Commons debate, still stands head and shoulders above them all.

Is Mr Heseltine going to get away with it?

Are Tory MPs going to be mad enough to choose him when, even if Mrs Thatcher is not available, a decent, honourable man like John Major is? If so, I think there is an overwhelming case for the issue to be put to the people.

And if in the resulting General Election Tory MPs in marginal seats go down like ninepins, so what?

Isn't that exactly what they have been asking for by their recent quite contemptible conduct?

# Hidden friends – and foes

IN the last few bitter days before her resignation, Mrs Thatcher certainly got to know who are her true friends.

I am not talking of Cabinet colleagues.

Rather I am thinking in terms of people who are no longer in her Government, have reason even perhaps to feel bitter against her, and yet came out stoutly in her defence.

The shining examples, of course, were Norman Tebbit and Teddy Taylor. But then one would expect loyalty and decency from men of their background.

Fascinating, isn't it, how people from working-class stock are invariably so much more loyal to their chums than toffs ever are?

Much more surprising was the emergence of Lord St John of Fawsley as a ferocious supporter. As Norman St John-Stevas, he had been sacked from her Government and had every reason to feel aggrieved.

I have to tell you that I completely changed my view of him during the course of the election.

He may look foppish. But behind that red-striped Jermyn Street shirt there surely beats a heart of gold. Some of the enemies have been surprising, too. The simpering Emma ('We'll all be friends again soon') Nicholson, Tory MP for Devon West. That poisonous lady wth the poisonous tongue, Mrs Edwina Currie. That fat wheezing failure Sir Peter Emery, Tory MP for Honiton.

The gutless Peter Temple-Morris, Tory MP for Leominster, that awful creep Tony Marlow and that Bordes boudoir boy, the oleaginous editor of The Sunday Times, Mr Andrew Neil.

Haven't infinitely more attractive creatures been seen wriggling at the bottom of a dung heap?

I WONDER how that basically decent man Sir Geoffrey Howe felt as he listened to Mrs Thatcher make what was probably her farewell speech to the Commons as Prime Minister.

Proud that by his own resignation speech he had triggered off her downfall? I doubt it. Ready to join the Cabinet of her successor? I hope not. He already has an imperishable place in history as the man who caused to be consigned to the dustbin the greatest Prime Minister of the century. Wouldn't he be better to leave it at that, say farewell to politics, and spend the rest of his life in the Lords and on the board, perhaps, of a merchant bank?

**■ ■ ■ ■**

THERE is no one who admires Mrs Thatcher more than I do. No one who recognises more than I do her enormous achievements during her 11 years as Prime Minister.

But the fact remains that she is not Prime Minister now. Mr John Major is.

He was her own chosen successor. He is a decent, honourable man who played no part in her downfall but remained loyal to the end.

Shouldn't she be returning a little of that loyalty now?

Instead of giving interviews around the world, interviews which can so easily be misunderstood and misinterpreted, shouldn't she

**LOYAL: Thatcher**

be speaking out loud and clear and unequivocally in support of him.

She surely would not want to go down in history, would she, as another Edward Heath?

# Parting sorrow

I VIEW with absolute sadness Mrs Thatcher's decision to quit the House of Commons.

Especially when, as her spell-binding performance in last week's debate on Europe so clearly showed, in the Chamber she is still a giant among pygmies.

Why then is she going?

I suppose it is because she knows in her heart that the clock cannot be turned back and that her time has gone for ever.

I just hope that neither she nor the nation has cause to regret her decision. But I wouldn't count on it.

The time may yet come when the day her enemies finally succeeded in getting rid of her will be looked upon as one of the blackest in Britain's history.

# Did Mark have a hand in it?

I DO not know how much Newsweek paid Mrs Thatcher for that article in which she effectively rubbished John Major.

But I suspect it may be the costliest she has every written. Costliest, alas, only to her own reputation.

It was not only the timing of the article which was offensive, coming as it did before the dust of the Election has barely had time to settle, but also its arrogance. And especially that wounding remark: 'There is no such thing as Majorism.'

Why did she do it? No one would dispute her right, even her duty, to challenge her successor if she felt he were betraying the principles for which Conservatism stands.

But surely such criticism should await and not anticipate evidence of a betrayal.

And surely it should be made in the House of Lords to which she will soon be going — and not for a large amount of money in an American magazine.

So what explains her outburst? Could it possibly be pique because she suddenly feels she has become yesterday's woman? I do not know.

But as a long-time admirer of Mrs Thatcher, indeed someone who regards her as the greatest Prime Minister this century, I worry about her future. I can think of no more dreadful fate than for her to turn into another Ted Heath.

I also wonder just who is now advising her. Now that Sir Charles Powell has gone from the scene, might she have started taking advice from within her own family circle?

I hope not. I hate to think what we are now hearing is the new Gospel according to Mark.

# Kindly leave the stage, Lady T

I BEGIN seriously to worry about Margaret Thatcher.

From being the most highly respected, and indeed by many revered, politician in the land, isn't she in danger of becoming instead almost a figure of ridicule?

I am not thinking only of her quite baffling attacks on John Major whom she, after all, chose and groomed as her successor and who with a good deal of skill is now carrying out the European policies which she herself initiated.

I am thinking also of her quite extraordinary incursion into the world of entertainment. What on earth induced her to record Abraham Lincoln's Gettysburg Address to a background of music by Aaron Copland played by the London Symphony Orchestra?

One critic has already perceptively observed that if Lincoln had spoken with Lady Thatcher's intonations the South would have won the war. Yet the recording is said to be heading for the Top Ten and such is its curiosity value I have no doubt it will get there.

Now there are suggestions that she should follow up her Gettysburg effort with a recording of Winston Churchill's historic wartime speech: 'We shall fight in France . . . we shall defend our island whatever the cost may be . . . we shall fight on the beaches, we shall fight on the landing grounds: we shall fight on the fields and in the streets: we shall fight in the hills: we shall never surrender.'

Doesn't Lady Thatcher realise that, wonderful politician and leader though she is, she just doesn't have either the voice or the acting ability for this sort of stuff?

Isn't there anyone around her capable of advising her in the way Bernard Ingham used to do? Otherwise could we yet see the greatest Prime Minister of the age appearing on the stage of the London Palladium?

June 20, 1993

# So what made the Lady turn?

THE most curious, and most puzzling, political event of the year has to have been the appeal made by Lady Thatcher last Tuesday night on News At Ten for Tory MPs to end their sniping against Mr Major.

It comes close to defying explanation.

For isn't it a fact that most of the sniping has come from her own supporters and that, by her outspoken opposition to Maastricht and her occasional sneering reference to the B-team, she herself seems to have been actively egging them on?

So why the sudden and completely unexpected turnaround — a turnaround which took Mr Major himself by surprise?

Is it because, as has been suggested, she has become alarmed by the sudden swelling of support for Mr Kenneth Clarke, whom she dislikes almost as much as she does Mr Heseltine?

Is it because, as has also been widely suggested, she wants to delay a leadership contest until her own new blue-eyed boy, Mr Michael Portillo, is ready to take over?

I suppose that it is possible. But I wonder.

My gut feeling is that if ever Mr Portillo did get to Number Ten Downing Street, she would feel about him exactly the same way as she feels about her former blue-eyed boy, Mr Major. So why last week's intervention? Was it purely coincidental that it came so soon after the news that one woman had become Prime Minister of Canada and another Prime Minister of Turkey?

Or have these three events made Lady Thatcher restless?

Is it remotely possible that she has become bored standing on the sidelines and wants to get back into the action herself?

There is not the slightest doubt that her support, if sustained, would be enough to keep Mr Major in office.

But how can he ensure that her support will, in fact, be sustained?

By offering her a place in his Cabinet from which she could rule the roost — say, as Foreign Secretary?

July 18, 1993

# Shameless Maggie

CAN there be anything much sadder than the conduct of Margaret Thatcher?

When she was Prime Minister there are people who would have followed her to hell. I was one of them.

But isn't it, to say the least, distasteful that she is now doing to John Major what the venomous-

ly spiteful Ted Heath did to her?

Who signed the Single European Act which led us into Europe?

Margaret Thatcher did.

Who was it who turned her face against a referendum when she was Prime Minister?

Why, Margaret Thatcher did.

Doesn't she feel the slightest bit of shame that she should now be

spitting at everything in which she once believed?

As for her claim that she does not want to harm Mr Major, just who does she think she is kidding?

Wouldn't she cut a more dignified figure if she were honestly to admit that only one thing motivates her? The fact that she just cannot abide being out of office?

# The anguish on

FOR me the most abiding memory of last week's Tory Conference was not the speeches. It was the strained, gaunt face of Lady Thatcher.

She says she is proud of the Saudi arms deal which brought £20 billion worth of orders and jobs to Britain and denies that there was anything shady or underhand about it.

Do I believe her? Implicitly.

Margaret Thatcher does not lie. Nor does she act dishonourably. And she has been clearly devastated by the allegations made against the son she adores and, by implication, against herself in The Sunday Times at a time when they were carefully calculated to do most damage — on the eve of the Tory Conference.

Yet if Margaret Thatcher is innocent of wrongdoing, what about Mark?

It is true he is not the world's most pleasing personality. As his wife is now apparently in the process of finding out. He is bumptious and arrogant and, quite unlike his unpretentious and enormously likeable twin sister Carol, might be not all that unwilling to trade on his name and his connections.

But did he? It is eminently possible that without his mother having the faintest idea as to what he was up to, he engineered himself into a position where he got a cut of the commission on the arms sales.

But if he did, can his mother be blamed for that? Can she be blamed for anything except, perhaps, being over-indulgent?

Time after time in our modern society it is children who suffer because of the sins of their parents.

That is sad.

But isn't it even sadder when it is the parents who have to suffer through the deeds of their children?

# The real victim of Lady T

LADY Thatcher may not have done Mr Major much good with her speech criticising the Government as not being as Right-wing as she would wish.

But any harm she may have done him is nothing compared with the harm she has done herself. There is no one who admires more than I do the contribution Lady Thatcher has made to Britain.

She will be regarded by history as one of our greatest Prime Ministers. I just find it desperately sad that she should be so imbued with bitterness towards the successor she herself chose.

Could envy have just perhaps a little bit to do with it?

# Politics

*To the end J.J. believed the British public would not be fooled by Tony Blair.*

*In his column three weeks before the General Election and shortly before his death, the respected political commentator doubted voters would be so 'stupid' as to elect Blair.*

*Although he was racing ahead in the opinion polls, J.J. suspected the inexperienced Labour leader could hardly believe his luck would hold.*

*In an uncompromising postscript, he made a prophecy that if the people sent Blair to No 10, would they not be getting exactly what they deserved?*

*J.J.'s last political judgment was typical of the man whose illustrious career brought him into the closest contact with Prime Ministers, politicians and opinion-makers over many decades.*

*He had been a political animal from his student days at Glasgow University, and fought two unsuccessful General Election campaigns as a Liberal candidate in Scottish constituencies in 1945 and 1950. Had he been elected, J.J. believed he would have pursued a political career instead of journalism.*

*But as an astute observer of the Westminster scene, he kept his readers riveted with incisive views on the power struggles, treachery and ruthless plottings of ambitious politicians.*

Robin Cook is the real man to watch

The nasty bi of Mr Benn

The truth staring Mr Blair right in the face

The odd st of Mr Lamo

Lord Tebbit has another sta

Wrong man for Hong Kong

# The great pretender returns

ONE of the more fascinating sights of this cold but sunny spring is that of Sir Ian Gilmour, Tory MP for Chesham and Amersham, preparing to crawl out once again from the woodwork.

Ever since he was sacked from the Cabinet in 1981, Sir Ian has been one of the most assiduous and most devious of the conspirators against the Prime Minister.

If only he had had the guts he would have challenged her himself for the leadership last November. But, alas, he hadn't.

So instead he supported, and some suspect masterminded, the campaign of that ancient nonentity Sir Anthony Meyer.

When that challenge ended in fiasco, Sir Ian let it be known that he intended to retire from Parliament and would not contest the next election.

At the time that seemed a wise move since it appeared unlikely that with his record of disloyalty he would be re-selected by the local Tory association.

But now that there has been a dramatic change in the political atmosphere and Mrs Thatcher appears to be in big bad trouble, Sir Ian is letting it be known he might be prepared to reconsider his decisions to stand down.

He says: 'There is now the prospect for the first time for ten years of a challenge from a revived Labour Party. I should very much like to be the candidate and win the seat with a large majority.'

Will his local association really be daft enough to re-select him?

I do not know.

But if they are and they do, then if I were a Tory voter in Amersham and Chesham at the next election, I would unhesitatingly vote Socialist rather than for him.

For wouldn't it be better to have an MP who is in open opposition to the Tory leader rather than one who pretends to support her, and then thrusts in the knife from behind?

*ALTHOUGH he has held the job for two months now, it still comes as a slight shock to hear Mr Douglas Hurd described on the radio as Foreign Secretary. Perhaps because he had been a fixture for so long, it does not seem right to the ears that it should not still be Sir Geoffrey Howe. It does not on TV seem right to the eyes either. Mr Hurd may be, and indeed is, a great expert on foreign affairs. But on TV he still walks and talks in the tense, jerky, fashion of a Dalek robot. I wouldn't trust him to wash the dishes, far less soothe ruffled foreign feelings. It is all so different from soft, reassuring Sir Geoffrey in his crumpled suits and Hush Puppies. With Sir Geoffrey one felt that the only danger that could ever emanate from him would be that of everyone listening to him falling asleep. Can I be the only one who yearns for his return?*

# What you get if you pay peanuts

IF IT is true that Barclays Bank is to pay Nigel Lawson more than £100,000 a year as a non-executive director, then I rejoice that he will at last be going to receive a salary commensurate with his outstanding ability.

And one which, moreover, will provide both present comfort and future security for his wife and young children.

But isn't it quite wrong that he should have to go outside politics to get them? And shouldn't it be a matter of concern that in his new part-time job he will get twice as much as he ever did as Chancellor of the Exchequer.

Why do we as a nation continue to pay our senior Ministers so little — especially since, rightly, they have no security of tenure?

Is it not madness that the chairman of ICI or BP gets six times or seven times as much for running one company as the Prime Minister gets for running the country?

Why are we so mean? Is it because, subconsciously, we regard all Cabinet Ministers as rich men and women in their own right? Or is it because we grudge their being any better off than ourselves?

I don't know. What I do know is that if we go on paying third-rate salaries then we will end up with a Cabinet of third-rate duds.

Or do you take the view that that is what we already have?

# The John Major mystery

IT WASN'T just the nastiness of the attempt by some newspapers to show that Mr John Major had lied about his father's background which startled me. It was its timing.

Right on the eve of the Budget. Right at the moment when to show him to be a fraud and a liar would inflict the maximum possible damage not only on him but on the Tory Party.

Not to mention the hurt to his feelings on the eve of the most important day in his political life by the snide suggestion that his parents might never even have been married.

It is not surprising that one of the newspapers, and by far the more offensive, was the recently born and probably soon-to-die Sunday Correspondent.

But isn't it quite staggering that the other newspaper concerned was the high Tory and, some suspect, pro-Heseltine Daily Telegraph?

What on earth induced the Telegraph to cast doubts on the Chancellor's veracity at such a critical moment?

If it had wanted to explore the Chancellor's background — a quite legitimate exercise — why had it not done so months previously when he had first attained high office?

Whatever the motivation it is a relief that thanks to some intelligent research by the Daily Mail — research which could just have easily have been carried out by the other two papers — the plot, if there was one, to discredit Mr Major has blown up in the plotters' faces.

And that the Chancellor has emerged from it all not only as the decent, truthful, straightforward chap we always knew he was, but also as the proud possessor of a picture, presented to him by the Daily Mail, of his circus artist father in stage clothes — a picture which he had not even known existed.

IT IS not often that someone with aspirations to become Prime Minister commits political suicide before one's eyes.

But isn't that exactly what Mr Michael Heseltine has been doing by his continuing failure to say even one kind word in favour of Mrs Thatcher's leadership? Hasn't that disloyalty contributed at least in part to the Mid-Staffordshire by-election disaster? I hope that even after that disaster Mrs Thatcher is going to continue as Tory leader for a long time yet.

But if it should prove otherwise, isn't one thing absolutely certain?

By his far too overt display of ambition, combined with his histrionic posturing, has not Mr Michael Heseltine made himself the very last person in the world anyone, except nutters like himself, would choose to succeed her?

April 1, 1990

# The odd silence of Lord Willie

AT A time when Mrs Thatcher is in dire trouble and continues to face a barrage of hostile, niggling criticism from panicking Tory backbenchers, one would have thought that all her friends would be rushing to her aid.

In these circumstances isn't the comparative silence of Lord Willie Whitelaw, who is after all still deputy-chairman of the Tory Party, all the more extraordinary?

Normally he trumpets his views like a bull elephant. Recently it has been much more like the squeaking of a mouse.

It is true he put in an appearance at the Mid-Staffordshire by-election.

But then so did Mr Heseltine. It is also true he gave a brief supportive radio interview. What there have not been are the great clarion calls one might have expected in favour of Mrs Thatcher.

Why ever not? Wasn't he supposed by some, although never by me, to be Mrs Thatcher's most devoted, most loyal, and even, on occasion, most subservient supporter?

So why doesn't he stand up now and tell the Tories just what a wonderful leader they have?

Could it possibly be because it is not entirely distasteful to him to reflect that all the Government's troubles seem to have started from the moment he himself left the Cabinet?

Could it even be because deep down he still feels the Tory Party made a grievous mistake in choosing Mrs Thatcher and not himself to replace Mr Heath in 1975?

# Alarm bells ring for Enoch

MR ENOCH Powell could hardly be described as a friend of the Government.

He thinks that the poll tax is a disaster and that it would have been much better to stick to the old system of rates.

He is against offering British citizenship to even a limited number of Hong Kong Chinese.

And he believes that our present rising inflation is entirely due to our former Chancellor of the Exchequer, Mr Nigel Lawson, having unleashed a credit boom.

And yet despite all these things he tells us, in what has to have been a carefully calculated as well as a most unexpected intervention, that if he still had a vote in his native county he would be voting Tory in the crucial Mid-Staffordshire by-election a week on Thursday.

And for why? Because he sees Mrs Thatcher's survival as Prime Minister as being absolutely vital to the continuing independence of this country and believes that all

other issues are unimportant compared to that central one. He also clearly believes that, with Tory jackals like Mr Heseltine already yapping at her heels, if the rest of the world gets the wrong message from Mid-Staffordshire it could be for her the beginning of the end. And the start of a new and more serious challenge to her leadership of the Tory Party.

I happen to disagree with Mr Powell on at least two of the three points.

I do not regard the poll tax as a disaster. The old rating system just had to be changed. It was monstrously unfair that while 35 million people had the right to vote in high-spending Socialist councils, it was only the 18 million who actually paid rates who were left to pick up the bills.

I disagree with him too about the Hong Kong Chinese.

But my golly, isn't he right about Mrs Thatcher?

If ever she is swept from office

either by Mr Kinnock or, more likely, by some of the weak, wet, spineless Tory whingers who surround her, then this truly is going to become a wonderful country.

To get the hell out of.

# The nasty bile of Mr Benn

IN THE latest volume of his political diaries, the Right Hon. Anthony Wedgwood Benn turns his venom on the Queen.

He speaks scathingly about her intellect, says she dips only at random into the State papers she is supposed to read, and declares that she cannot even say 'good morning' without a script.

How is that for bile?

It is also the exact opposite of the truth. I am not the country's greatest royalist, but I can tell you from personal experience that the Queen is one of the wittiest, most sparkling conversationalists I have ever met and with a most impressive grasp of a wide range of subjects.

If her conversation with Mr Wedgwood Benn was indeed stilted, I wonder why.

Might it be because she despises the unctuous little toad as much as I do?

# Where will the Archer story end?

PRIME Ministers may come and Prime Ministers may go, but Mr Jeffrey Archer seems to go on for ever.

If the best-selling author were on friendly terms with Mrs Thatcher he seems to be enjoying a just as friendly, maybe even friendlier, relationship with Mr John Major.

On the last Sunday of 1990, who were the principal guests at the Cambridgeshire home of Mr Archer and his fragrant wife Mary? Why, Mr and Mrs John Major.

And on New Year's Day, who were among the guests at the Prime Minister's luncheon table at Chequers?

Why, Mr and Mrs Jeffrey Archer.

After lunch it is reported that Mr Major and some other Cabinet Ministers watched Tottenham Hotspur versus Manchester United in The Match on ITV.

But Mr Archer, who is an ardent Chelsea fan, announced in advance that he would not be joining them.

He said: 'I cannot believe that any self-respecting Chelsea fans would be prepared to watch Tottenham Hotspur. If they do, I and Norma will watch Little Dorrit on the other channel in the next room.'

I and Norma. How's that for chumminess?

I congratulate Mr Archer on the quite considerable ability he shows in keeping in with the great and the powerful.

It says a great deal not only for his charm but for

his sheer guts. Even though he was completely vindicated by a libel jury and almost canonised by the trial judge, there are not many people who would have shrugged off as quickly as he did the vile accusations made against him by the Star newspaper and prostitute Monica Coghlan. Or the subsequent and equally unfounded suggestion that he had ever used in a story of his own a plot submitted to him by an amateur writer.

So just where then is the personal Jeffrey Archer story going to end? In the House of Lords? That is for sure. Probably in the very next Honours List.

But might he not also still become a member of Mr Major's Government? Anything is possible, I suppose. But if that were to happen, then on the day it does will I really be the only one to pull the duvet over my head and turn my face against the wall?

February 24, 1991

# The star who is now an extra

IN BYGONE days a popular feature in newspapers used to be titled 'Whatever happened to...?'

If the feature were reinstituted today, wouldn't a perfect candidate for inclusion be Mr Michael Heseltine?

Just three months ago he was striding the land like a giant in his campaign to unseat Mrs Thatcher.

He contrived to give the impression that he could end the poll tax problem in a trice. He was never off TV. Everywhere he went there were cheering crowds.

And now? Completely overshadowed by Mr Major and, with the poll tax problems seemingly as far from solution as ever they were, Mr Heseltine has suddenly become a figure to whom nobody any longer pays all that much attention.

It is like an actor who had expected to play Hamlet ending up on stage as the second gravedigger.

Doesn't it all make you reflect on just what a cruel business politics are? If only, Mr Heseltine must sigh, the Tory leadership election had gone the other way it would all have been so very different. And so it would.

If he had become Prime Minister, where do you suppose Mr Heseltine would be today?

Want to bet, that wearing his flak jacket and with the world's TV cameras focused on him, he would be sitting in the turret of a British tank in Saudi Arabia?

Instead he is not even a member of the War Cabinet.

Aren't there times when it is almost possible in your heart to feel sorry for him?

April 14, 1991

*Was the Prime Minister by any chance watching Question Time on BBC1 on Thursday night? If so, was he as appalled as I was by the performance of his chum and fellow Chelsea supporter, Mr David Mellor?*

*Mr Mellor may be a whiz-kid as Chief Secretary to the Treasury, although even that I would very much doubt. As a vote-winner for the Tories, he is an unmitigated disaster. By his bumptious, arrogant, supercilious performance - it even included insulting a tolerant, moderate studio audience — he must have alienated uncommitted voters in their hundreds of thousands. It may be difficult to sack Mr Mellor from the Cabinet between now and the election. But can't it be possible to keep him off TV? PS: It wouldn't be a bad idea to put a sock in the mouth of the pompous, prissy Mrs Lynda Chalker, too.*

DURING her visit to Tehran Mrs Lynda Chalker, the Overseas Development Minister, conformed to Islamic practice by covering her hair and disguising her feminine form.

She was also warned not to proffer her hand to the Iranian Foreign Minister Ali Akbar Velayti lest she aroused his lust.

Blimey. A handshake from Mrs Lynda Chalker arousing lust. Isn't that enough to put a new spring into the step of every plump, middle-aged lady everywhere? Yet there is a serious side to it all. If concealment is so tantalising, and the sight of Mrs Chalker in a shapeless dress and with her head covered only enough to arouse such uncontrollable passion, then what in God's name might have happened to Her Majesty's Minister for Overseas Development if they had made her cover her face, too?

# With friends like David Mellor…

MR DAVID Mellor, Chief Secretary to the Treasury, seems to enjoy giving people a good dressing down. Especially when they are people in subordinate positions who cannot answer back.

No one who saw it will ever forget the way in which, when he was a junior Foreign Office Minister, he visited the Gaza Strip and gave a young Israeli officer the sharp end of his tongue in full view of the world's television cameras. It was a public humiliation of the worst and most unforgivable kind.

Now because his Ministerial box is delivered two hours late when he is weekending with friends in Yorkshire he picks up the phone and loses his temper with a village postmaster who subsequently describes him as 'probably the rudest man I've ever dealt with'.

And yet they say he is Mr John Major's very best friend. If that is indeed true then I think Mr Major ought to pick his friends more carefully.

They could end up getting him a bad name.

# Has Mr B gone round the twist?

THERE are some people who regard Mr John Biffen as an intellectual giant. For my own part I have long suspected he might be just one or two sacks short of a full lorry load.

From my one and only two-hour meeting with him years ago I cannot remember his expressing even one original thought.

What I do vividly remember, apart from his rather pedestrian waffle, were the soup stains on his waistcoat.

During the final disastrous years of the last Labour Government when the Socialists and the TUC between them were slowly strangling Britain to death, he was given a Shadow Cabinet job by Mrs Thatcher. But he did not hold it for long. He quit because, as he explained at the time, he could not stand up to the strain. Just as years earlier he had quit for exactly the same reasons when Sir Alec Douglas-Home had made him a Front Bench spokesman.

So when Mrs Thatcher became Prime Minister and offered him a real job there were many who wondered if she might be making a mistake and whether he might crack up in office. Happily he didn't, although some of the outlandish things he said lead to his being accurately described as 'semi-detached' from the Government.

Now he hands out a quite unbelievable bonus to the Labour Party. Can you imagine what they are going to make of it in every party political broadcast during the next election? Time after time after time we are going to hear Mr Biffen's words: *'I have absolutely no hesitation in saying that, when I think of Labour leaders, Neil Kinnock is outstanding.'*

No matter how straight they may keep their faces in public, that remark may be enough to make people like John Smith and Roy Hattersley in private fall off their chairs laughing.

But if it is said often enough, aren't electors going to begin to believe it?

What made Mr Biffen do it? Has he finally gone round the twist? Is he wilfully trying to destroy his own party's chances of winning the election? Or is he too dim to understand the consequences of what he was saying?

I don't know. What I do know is that with friends like Mr John Biffen around, what the hell need has Mr John Major of enemies.

# Did John Major get it wrong, too?

The Prime Minister is being much praised for his compassion and magnanimity in refusing to accept the resignation of Mr Peter Brooke, the Secretary of State for Northern Ireland.

It is not praise in which I would wish to join. Especially since it would seem that, before showing his compassion, Mr Major first tested the water to make sure the Labour Party was not going to make political capital out of the issue.

I accept that Mr Brooke is a decent, honest, if not particularly quick-witted, politician of the old school. Indeed, there are some who would say he is the only real gentleman left in the present Tory Government. Nevertheless, he showed appalling judgment in agreeing to appear at all in a late-night Dublin TV programme only hours after the IRA massacre of seven building workers.

It was then unbelievably insensitive of him, no matter how fazed he was by questions about the death of his first wife, to have compounded that misjudgment by allowing himself to be cajoled by a TV presenter into standing up and singing My Darling Clementine.

By so doing he made himself look to be a buffoon. Which, of course, is exactly what some have always thought him to be.

And what are we expected to make of the fact that instead of realising the crassness of his action and, after the broadcast, returning post haste to Northern Ireland, he instead spent the next day watching a rugby match in Dublin.

No matter how much he now apologises, no matter how many excuses are made for his acting in the way he did, how can such a man have any credibility of any kind from now on with Ulster Protestants?

Yet if Mr Brooke's judgment has been demonstrated to be almost non-existent, the fact that the Prime Minister refuses his offer of resignation and insists on his staying in office makes another question inevitable.

When it comes to Ireland, is Mr John Major's judgment all that good either?

# Wrong man for Hong Kong

It says much for the Prime Minister's generosity of spirit that he should have offered his friend Chris Patten, who lost his Bath seat in the Election, the glittering consolation prize of the Governorship of Hong Kong.

But does it say anything for his judgment?

The Governorship is more than just a plum job with a tax-free salary of £140,000 a year, a country home, a Rolls-Royce, two Daimlers and a 100ft yacht. It is also, in the next five years leading up to the handover of the colony to China, an absolutely vital post which, in the interests of both Britain and the people of Hong Kong, has to be held by the best possible man.

Is that Mr Patten? I don't think so.

He has little experience of diplomacy and no first-hand knowledge at all of either China or Hong Kong. Nor, judged by the experience of the past few weeks, is he all that brilliant a campaign organiser. There are many who believe that the General Election was won not because of him but despite him.

Are these not circumstances in which the Prime Minister should have second thoughts? If he wishes to show gratitude to a friend, would not David Owen be an infinitely better choice for the job?

# Has Major made his first mistake?

MR John Major is beginning to puzzle me.

It is far too early in his Prime Ministership to say how history will judge him. Maybe it will be highly. Maybe he will turn out to merit only a footnote.

But there is one way in which he already far outshines any of his predecessors. In his ability to sell himself.

He has a capacity for making himself instantly likeable to everyone he meets.

He is also the shrewdest of practitioners in personal public relations.

Remember how in the very first days of his Prime Ministership every newspaper in the land ran the story of how on an official visit to Scarborough he just happened to stop off at a Happy Eater and order a meal of eggs, bacon, sausage, HP sauce, toast and coffee?

That incident might have appalled nutritionists and food faddists but it endeared John Major to every bacon and egg and baked bean lover in the land.

It signalled to them that for almost the first time in history they had a Prime Minister who was 'one of us'.

At the time I wondered how, since the stop was unscheduled, all the newspapers seemed to have chronicled the event so accurately.

From that day to this the public relations surrounding the Prime Minister has been absolutely brilliant.

That this is so has to be largely his own doing.

He is on first-name terms with almost every editor in the land and almost every political writer, too.

He has also the keenest perception of what the man in the street is thinking. And indeed often reacts like a piece of litmus paper to public opinion.

I very much admire him for this ability. Which is why I am now so puzzled.

Why has he been quite so unnecessarily outspoken in his support of Mr David Mellor when he must well know that

such support could easily boomerang back against himself — and most probably still will?

The officially stated reason that he thinks Mr Mellor is far too valuable a member of the Government to lose does not ring true.

If Mr Mellor were all that valuable, why was he given such a piddling, trivial, unimportant job as Minister of Heritage?

What then is the real reason? Loyalty to an old friend?

Possibly, although I find even that difficult to believe in view of the fact that Mr Major's old friend has shown himself to be such a sleazy, unattractive character who, throughout the whole affair, has remained cockily arrogant, which is in itself curious, and shown not the slightest signs of penitence.

What then could be the real reason for Mr Major jeopardising his own position to save a man like that?

I very much hope it is not because Mr Mellor knows where the body is buried.

■ ■ ■ ■

**MICHAEL HESELTINE** clearly loves dressing up in uniform and, it has to be admitted, he looks quite splendid in one.

Still vivid in many people's minds are memories of him striding around Greenham Common in a flak jacket.

Or hair streaming behind him in the cockpit of a Challenger tank.

Last Wednesday, he was in uniform again. This time it was a pilot's flying suit and helmet he adorned as he toured the Westland helicopter factory at Yeovil. And once again it has to be said that he made a striking figure.

I just wonder, however, whether on that particular day he was in the right place and in the right uniform. Wouldn't he have looked even better in miner's clothes and helmet?

And, instead of visiting Yeovil, shouldn't he have been in a pit-head canteen, explaining to miners just why he was putting 30,000 of them on the breadline?

# The odd story of Mr Lamont

THE spectacle of the Chancellor of the Exchequer being publicly hounded for the non-payment of a comparatively trivial debt is not a pretty one to watch.

How can it have happened? The thought that Mr Norman Lamont might have personal short-term financial problems first crossed my mind a few weeks ago when the Grand Hotel in Brighton publicly complained about his failure to pay his £900 conference hotel bill on time.

Now we learn that Mr Lamont has been sent five legal warning letters by Access for failing to keep up the monthly repayments on his credit card.

It is further disclosed that he was £470 over his £2,000 spending limit and shopkeepers were being told not to accept his credit card again until he had paid some of it off.

The fascinating detail is added that when he went into a Thresher off-licence the other night and made a purchase on his card amounting to £17.47 (I wonder why he became so agitated over the suggestion that it might have been for a bottle of Champagne and packet of fags) it was only because the amount was so small that the assistant did not have to telephone Access for authorisation. If he had done so, Mr Lamont would have been turned away empty-handed.

Wouldn't that have been a quite extraordinary humiliation for the Chancellor of the Exchequer? Can you imagine the laughter it would have caused in the Bundesbank? Just what is going on with Mr Lamont? Can it all be put down to forgetfulness? Or is he skint?

Either way, the question is being asked: Can a man who is apparently such an idiot in running his own financial affairs possibly be allowed to keep on running the nation's?

But to my mind there is an even more disturbing question to be asked.

How did the details of Mr Lamont's credit card ever come to be made public? Isn't there supposed to be secrecy in banking?

Who was the person inside the National Westminster bank who, perhaps for political purposes, sold the story to The Sun?

Isn't it oddly reminiscent of the way private royal telephone conversations were listened in to and sold to the tabloids? Could we in Britain be breeding a new and nasty race of snoopers? Or is something more sinister afoot?

# People power? Not a chance!

I OFFER this thought for this last Sunday in 1992. If anyone asked you this question: 'Do we in this country live in a democracy?' I suppose your answer would be: 'Don't be silly. Of course we do. Didn't we have a General Election not that long ago?'

And so we did.

But, even so, the question remains, do we really have a democracy?

By most people's standards a democracy is a society in which, at least in the long term, the will of the majority prevails. But does it in Britain?

Take capital punishment. There is indisputable evidence that, with crime and violence again frighteningly on the increase, the overwhelming majority of the people of this country would like to see the death penalty reintroduced.

Yet every time the issue is raised in the House of Commons — and it has been raised umpteen times in the last 20 years — the anti-hanging majority gets bigger and bigger.

There is also, I would guess, a sizeable majority of people in the country who would like to see vicious young thugs who beat up old ladies given a sharp taste of their own medicine with a few strokes of the birch instead of, as now, so often being allowed to go scot free. But is there the slightest chance of the birch ever being introduced? Not a chance in hell. The will of the majority is there only to be laughed at and flouted.

It has been the same on countless other issues, including immigration.

And I have no doubt it will be exactly the same again when the time comes, as come it will,

when, after having ratified Maastricht without even ever having bothered to consult the British people, the Government announces that after due reflection it has decided to abandon the pound and adopt a German dominated European Common Currency.

There is not a chance that the people will ever be consulted about that either.

I make no great meal of it but isn't the truth of the matter the fact that apart from a three-or-four-week period during General Elections when they are down on their knees in front of us grovelling for votes, the majority of politicians don't ever really give a damn what ordinary people think?

Wouldn't it be a comfort to think that they actually do know better than the rest of us?

# Lord Tebbit has another stab

THERE was a time when no politician, Margaret Thatcher apart, stood higher in public esteem than Norman Tebbit.

The courage he showed during the Brighton bomb disaster captured the nation's heart. There was enormous respect, too, for his ability as a Cabinet Minister.

It would be a tragedy if that respect and admiration were ever to fade. But yet isn't that exactly what is happening? Even though he may always have said nice things to his face, in recent months Lord Tebbit has seldom seemed to miss a chance to stab a knife firmly in the Prime Minister's back.

As he is now doing, for example, in Newbury, where on Thursday voters go to the poll in what could be a crucial by-election. In normal times Newbury would be a safe Tory seat. With such a small parliamentary majority it is vital, especially for Mr Major's own

standing, that the Government holds it.

No one knows that better than Lord Tebbit. After all, he himself was once chairman of the Tory Party. Yet, although he goes to Newbury to speak, it is not on the platform of the offical Tory candidate, but instead to stir up anti-Maastricht feeling.

And in the London Evening Standard he writes an article under the heading 'Voters can deliver a blow to the Treaty', in which he suggests that the only important thing in Newbury is that the voters there register a massive No to Maastricht vote in The Times referendum on the issue now being conducted in the constituency. Just what sort of support is that for an official Tory candidate who is as committed to Maastricht as the Prime Minister?

So just what is Lord Tebbit up to?

There are times when I won-

der if Maastricht is the only, or even the main, cause of his present bloody-mindedness.

Might his resentment that it was Mr Major rather than himself who succeeded Margaret Thatcher not also have just perhaps the teeniest-weeniest bit to do with it?

# Is this why they hate John Major?

MY distaste for William Rees-Mogg, elevated to the peerage in 1988, God alone knows why, by Margaret Thatcher, is not based simply on the fact that he is a pompous prig who, although he has himself achieved little in life, oozes self-importance and is prepared to pontificate on almost any subject under the sun.

Even though it is a long time ago, some people have not forgotten the leading part he played with his wounding words in hounding that fine man, Alec Douglas-Home, out of the leadership of the Tory Party.

Now, 30 years later, he is at it again. This time with Mr John Major as his target. And once again he is out to destroy. In an article in The Times last week, he contemptuously dismissed the Prime Minister as someone scarcely fit to have reached even as high a post as Deputy Chief Whip.

Isn't that a quite filthy, elitist remark to make about a man who barely a year ago virtually single-handedly led the Tories to what had seemed a quite impossible victory.

Yet the Rees-Mogg outburst is typical of the hostility, and in some cases even hatred, which now surrounds the Prime Minister.

That which emanates from Margaret Thatcher and Norman Tebbit and their acolytes I can understand.

But what motivates people like Rees-Mogg, Paul Johnson, Charles Moore and all the other intellectuals and pseudo-intellectuals who write for The Spectator and the so-called quality Press, who follow each other like sheep and who have been at the Prime Minister's throat almost from the very first day he took office?

Not even they can have the crust to blame him for the world recession.

So why do they hold him in such contempt? Is it because, unlike so many of them, he comes from an unprivileged, working-class background and did not go to Oxford or Cambridge?

Might it even be because he prefers baked beans on toast to caviar? I don't know. But there is one question I would ask them.

If they do succeed in toppling him as Prime Minister, as they may well do — especially if the Christchurch by-election goes sour — just whom do they plan to put in his place?

Mr John Smith?

*William Rees Mogg*

# Might it be time to call on Enoch?

THERE is a day next month which Mr John Major and Tory Party Chairman, Sir Norman Fowler, must have circled in their diaries with utter dread — the day of the Christchurch by-election.

On paper Christchurch, with a Tory majority in the General Election of 23,000, should be one of the safest of safe seats.

But not the way things are at the moment. If today's Page One poll is any guide, the chances are that it will go exactly the same way as Newbury. And, if it does, then it could well mean the end of Mr Major's Prime Ministership and maybe even of this Tory Government.

These are circumstances in which Sir Norman Fowler must be down on his knees praying that somehow or other the local Christchurch Tory Association can pluck out of the air a strong Tory candidate, someone capable of spell-binding oratory, someone the Christchurch voters would implicitly trust as a man of truth and honour and utterly incorruptible.

Is there such a politician left in England? Just one.

He is far and away the most distinguished parliamentarian of the age.

Yet he is no longer an MP and has refused on grounds of principle to go to the Lords. It is true he is old, but not that much older than many of the Christchurch electors, 34 per cent of whom are over 60.

But he is in good health and he most certainly still has all his marbles.

So why don't Christchurch Tories invite Mr Enoch Powell to be their candidate.

Even at his great age, he might be attracted by the idea of once again having a parliamentary platform, and for him the by-election

*Sir Norman Fowler*

would be a walkover.

And, if it is argued that Mr Powell's views do not coincide on many issues with those of the Prime Minister, then so what?

Couldn't the same thing be said about half the members of the Cabinet?

# Will Major see off the jackals

AFTER the Christchurch by-election disaster, what does the future hold for Mr John Major?

Is he on his way out?

Is it only a matter of months before he is replaced — as the jackals of The Times, The Sunday Telegraph and the Spectator who, for the most contemptibly, snobbish, elitist reasons, have been at his throat almost from the moment he became Prime Minister, would have us believe?

I do not think so. On the contrary, my belief is that among the non-committed there is a growing respect for the Prime Minister and for his dogged courage and strength of character. And for his sense of humour, too.

The unguarded, off-the-record remarks he made to Michael Brunson, ITN's political editor, at a time when he thought the microphones had been switched off were initially seized upon by his detractors as yet another disastrous gaffe.

Incidentally, wasn't it quite sinister that these remarks should then have been handed over, apparently without request for payment, to Left-wing newspapers in an attempt to discredit Mr Major even further?

But far from discrediting him, they have, in fact, done him a power of good.

They have given ordinary people an insight into the difficulties of running a Cabinet with a tiny majority in Parliament and where a small splinter group of extreme Right-wingers is exerting an influence quite beyond its numbers. As for the robust language used by Mr Major, that, too, has helped rather than harmed him.

After all, if the Archbishop of Canterbury were to stand barefoot on an upturned tack on his bedroom carpet, would anyone really blame him if he came out with an expletive rather more violent than 'sugar'?

Might not even that saintly person, Mr Kelvin MacKenzie, Editor of the Sun, come out, in similar circumstances, with something rather stronger than his usual 'fiddlesticks'?

So what does it all add up to? I could be wrong. I often am. But in my view it adds up to the fact that Mr Major is going to remain in his present job for a long time to come. Maybe for longer, perhaps, than the Editors of the Spectator, The Times and The Sunday Telegraph are going to remain in theirs.

ON Tuesday Mr Tony Blair will receive the usual statutory standing ovation at the Labour Party Conference.

It would be extraordinary if he didn't. But when all the back-slapping has stopped and the cheering died down, does he really believe when he sees himself in the mirror that he is looking at the face of the next British Prime Minister?

I expect he genuinely does. And I think he is in for an almighty let-down. No matter what the opinion polls presently say, I cannot believe that, when it comes to the crunch, the British people will vote for a man who has had no Ministerial experience of any kind, whose true beliefs, since he has changed them so often, are completely unknown and whose Shadow Chancellor of the Exchequer, Mr Gordon Brown, talks such economic gobblede-gook as 'our new economic approach is rooted in ideas which stress the importance of macroeconomics, neo-classical endogenous growth theory and the symbiotic relationship between growth and investment in people and infrastructure'.

Who the hell in his right mind would want to vote for a party which talks like that? Against that, do you mark how John Major grows apace in international stature?

His standing in the opinion polls may still be low, but do you notice the way in which he is constantly scoring points, as in his visit to South Africa?

I have said it before and I'll say it again. After the next election, he is still going to be Prime Minister of this country.

And Tony Blair? With his pretty face and lustrous brown hair, wouldn't he be a sensation doing TV commercials for Vidal Sassoon's Wash and Go? With Mr John Prescott, perhaps, doing the voiceover?

# Maggie and the politics of envy

LADY Thatcher indignantly denies in her second volume of memoirs that she is seeking to encourage a leadership challenge to the Prime Minister.

She says that the meaning of a key passage in them has been 'seriously distorted' and taken out of context.

And no doubt it has. What she cannot deny is that in the new volume she has not one kind word to say about either Mr Major, the man she herself chose to succeed her, or about his policies, which he largely inherited from herself.

I find that sad. Sad for Mr Major. Sad for the Tory Party. But saddest of all for Lady Thatcher that she should apparently be so consumed with envy.

# Will Mr Major's critics ever learn?

IT IS always a joy to see so-called experts with egg all over their faces.

It is a special pleasure to see it happen to these newspapers and their political pundits who, after years of hounding Mr John Major and building up into national figures nonentities like Teresa Gorman and Tony Marlow, were predicting with utter confidence right up to last Tuesday morning the Prime Minister's humiliation in the leadership election.

How could they all have got it so wrong when it was clear to anyone with the slightest political intelligence what the result would be?

Now this same bunch of political dimwits are pontificating that the man happiest about Mr Major's re-election is Mr Tony Blair, who, according to them, is now certain to win the next General Election.

Will the idiots never learn? When will they begin to realise, as I expect Mr Tony Blair already realises, that, far from being a born loser as they label him, Mr Major, who has fought his way up from the slums of Brixton, is a born winner?

He may not have an O-level or an A-level to his name, but in his political career to date he has, in his own quiet way, seen off every single person who has challenged him.

From Michael Heseltine downwards.

In two years' time at the General Election I confidently predict he will see off little boy Blair, too.

IT has almost become impossible to switch on the radio or television without hearing the voice or seeing the face of Mr John Redwood.

_What makes him so hyperactive?

*A burning desire to help the Tories in the Election and to support the Prime Ministership of John Major?*

If you believe that then you will believe anything. Mr Redwood has only one aim. To promote his own candidacy as next Tory leader.

Would he make a good leader? That has to be a laugh.

I wouldn't trust him to lead a pack of Brownies across Dorking High Street.

*There is in my mind an abiding image of Mr Redwood. It was when he was Secretary of State for Wales and, at the finale of a Welsh Tory meeting and in full view of the TV cameras, was unable to*

**HYPERACTIVE: Redwood**

sing Land Of My Fathers because he didn't even know the words. But rather than having the sense to keep his mouth shut, he made Dalek-like grimaces instead.

He is said to have a first-class brain. All I can say is that as a politician he comes perilously close to being a gormless idiot.

*If it were to come to a choice between Mr Redwood and Mr Tony Blair then I think I would even prefer Mr Blair. And if that doesn't tell you what I think of Mr Redwood then nothing will.*

# The dangers of putting faith in Gordon Brown

IF YOUR life savings, your home, your job, your children's future depended on the ability of one man, and they may, whom would you trust more — the present Chancellor of the Exchequer or the man who earnestly seeks to supplant him?

The jazz-loving, beer-swilling, Hamlet-smoking Kenneth Clarke, who with his crumpled clothes and scuffed Hush Puppies, always looks as if he had slept in a haystack? Or that sober son of the manse Mr Gordon Brown?

As to be expected, I would go for Kenneth Clarke. Not just because he is a Tory but because I like his style. He has chutzpah. He has also a quality unique among politicians. He says exactly what he thinks, and does exactly what he believes to be right, even if at times it costs him

popularity. As, for example, it has done with his views on Europe.

Above all he has a proven track record. He has presided over the dramatic turnaround in the economy.

But Mr Gordon Brown has a good deal going for him, too. I would never dispute his honesty. I am prepared to accept that he genuinely believes, although no one else does, that he can deliver all the billions in promises Labour has made to the electors without raising income tax by as much as a penny. He has made a personal pledge to that effect.

There is just one snag. If Labour actually does win the Election and Mr Gordon Brown does indeed become Chancellor, just how long do you suppose he will last in the job?

Want to bet that after the first financial crisis, which is more likely to come in weeks rather than in months, he will be replaced as Chancellor by Left-winger Robin Cook?

And Mr Cook hasn't made any daft promises, has he?

# The truth staring Mr Blair right in the face

WAITING for the Wirral by-election result in the early hours of Friday morning will be a time of high tension for the Prime Minister.

But will it not be even more so for Mr Tony Blair?

If, even after Labour's ignominious defeat on last week's Commons censure motion and the party's farcical overnight about-turn on Tote privatisation, Labour still scores a spectacular victory, Mr Blair will be in a mood of high elation.

He will be bouncing up and down demanding an immediate General Election. But for just how long will that elation last?

For there will be a down-side to the result. Mr Blair is well aware that, far from there being an immediate election, there is now not a chance in hell of one.

He knows that, with the help of the Ulster Unionists, Mr Major will do his damnedest to hang on until his own preferred polling date of May 1. And he is more than likely to succeed.

That means a further two months of campaigning. And, if a week is a long time in politics, two months is an eternity.

Right from the moment he became leader, Mr Blair's strategy, aided and abetted by his spin-doctors, has been to force an early election while, mainly thanks to his boyish appearance and fixed smile, his popularity remains high. And, most important of all, before the voters have had a chance to find out in what, if anything, he actually believes.

For there has never been a clear statement of policy. But, if he has to struggle on until May, it means that Mr Blair will have to depend on more than sound-bites. Moreover, it is now almost certain that he will have to face TV debates with the PM — and a debate on TV is not something Mr Blair relishes.

After all, in such debates he will not have Mr Peter Mandelson or Mr Alastair Campbell sitting beside him telling him what to say. He will have to depend on himself. And these are circumstances in which the Prime Minister is likely to overwhelm him. As he so constantly does in the Commons at Prime Minister's Questions.

There is another factor. A Tory defeat in the Wirral will send a shockwave through rank-and-file Tory supporters throughout the country. It will cause Tory activists in the constituencies to redouble their efforts to get every single voter to the polls.

As for Tories who, during the present Parliament, have defected in by-elections to the Liberals, are they not now, when faced with the apparent inevitability of a Labour government, likely to return to the fold?

Who, for example, would give that awful woman Emma Nicholson a chance in hell of retaining her West Devon seat?

So what does it all add up to? Just this. No matter the Wirral result, no matter the headlines on Friday morning, everything is still left to play for.

And no one knows that better than Mr Blair.

I WONDER just how much money Lord McAlpine is getting for his memoirs, Once A Jolly Bagman, in which he does his damndest to destroy all his old friends and colleagues in the Tory Party and by so doing make a Labour election victory even more likely.

I hope it will be enough to compensate him in years to come for the fact that by his book he has revealed to the whole world that he is one of the nastiest four-letter words ever to disgrace the political scene.

# Does Blair think his luck will last

HE is 27 points ahead in one national opinion poll, 15 points in another and most of the political columnists regard Labour as certain to win.

But yet I wonder just how confident in his inner heart Mr Tony Blair feels of becoming Prime Minister on May 1.

Does he take it for granted that by May 2 he will be forming his Cabinet and delighting the trade unions by announcing that Britain is going to embrace the Social Chapter? And that a minimum wage will soon be put on the Statute book?

I doubt it. I very much doubt it. My guess is that Tony Blair can hardly believe the luck he has had so far in fooling the British people.

But he knows there are still three long weeks to go before polling day and when he goes to bed at night he must wonder if that luck can continue.

So far in his leadership of the Labour Party he has given not the slightest hint of what he actually believes in.

That is, if he actually believes in anything at all.

It has all been a succession of sound-bites, mostly written out for him by Alastair Campbell and Peter Mandelson.

That is why he is so terrified to face the Prime Minister head-to-head in a TV debate.

He knows that in such a debate he would be demolished.

But can he really go on playing cowardy-custard for a further three weeks?

And if he does, are the British people really stupid enough to elect as Prime Minister someone like him?

Someone who has not even had any experience of junior office?

If they are then can it not truly be said that they will be getting exactly what they deserve?

# Robin Cook is the real man to watch

AS Mr Robin Cook trims his beard in his bathroom mirror this Sunday morning, he must be thinking that this has to be one of the greatest weeks of his life.

Today he is just another Shadow Minister without real power of any kind. But by Friday, if the opinion polls are right, he could be Foreign Secretary. With all the power such high office brings.

Is that not in itself a dizzy prospect? But for just how long will even the job of Foreign Secretary satisfy ambitious, thrusting and exceedingly able Mr Cook?

Isn't there an even more dizzying prospect ahead? That of becoming Prime Minister in perhaps one year's time? A crazy idea? Far from it.

The fact of the matter is that intellectually Robin Cook could eat both Mr Gordon Brown and Mr Tony Blair for breakfast.

For one thing he doesn't have to have a spin-master like Alastair Campbell or Peter Mandelson to tell him what to say and how to answer questions — or rather how to avoid answering them.

Robin Cook is his own man

and says exactly what he thinks and not what he is told to say.

For another thing I suspect he has a great deal more support in the rank and file of Labour MPs than has Mr Tony Blair.

Many of them have been gagged during the Election campaign, ordered not to appear on TV or to express opinions on Europe and the single currency.

Anybody like Neil Kinnock who could prove the slightest embarrassment has been kept well out of the public eye. As has been the man who from next Friday could be our Minister of Defence, Dr David Clark, because of his past support for CND.

They all agree to being muzzled in order to win the Election but after Friday, if they do indeed win, it is going to be a different story.

Mr Blair may remain as a figurehead for perhaps a year. But after the first big financial crisis, which I suspect will not be long in coming, is he going to stay there?

Are Left-wingers like Margaret Beckett and John Prescott and Clare Short going to rush to his support and defend him fiercely?

Or instead to someone like Robin Cook who shares their own Left-wing views?

If Labour do win on Thursday and I could get the right odds, I wouldn't mind placing a bet on Mr Robin Cook being Prime Minister by this time next year.\

# John Major

*Only six months after John Major led the Conservatives to an amazing General Election victory in 1992, J.J. predicted he would be writing his political memoirs sooner rather than later. The reason was Major's extraordinary speech in Scotland in front of the TV cameras in which he gave his personal pledge that Britain would remain in the ERM.*

*Days later, billions of pounds of Britain's reserves were lost to help save sterling.*

*The Prime Minister's judgment on the monetary debacle left J.J. fearing for Major's ability to deal with future crises.*

*However, despite all the criticisms levelled at Major during that period – his remarkable capacity for policy U-turn, a 'lack of substance' and his choice of 'odd' political friends J.J. still believed he was still the country's best hope. It was a view that persisted until the General Election on May 1, 1997.*

*With his party bitterly divided on Europe and with individuals intent on political suicide, Major's belief that victory was still possible was shared by J.J. They pinned their hopes of another Tory success on Britain's healthy economy and a belief that in the run-up to the election Tony Blair would be exposed as a leader without principle. It was not to be.*

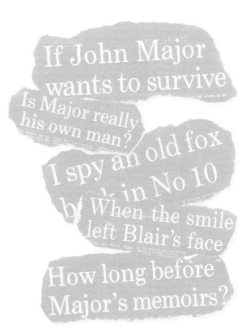

If John Major wants to survive

Is Major really his own man?

I spy an old fox in No 10

When the smile left Blair's face

How long before Major's memoirs?

# How long before Major's memoirs?

WHEN the Prime Minister comes to write his political memoirs, and I suspect that may now turn out to be sooner rather than later, I hope he will explain to us just how he came to make the mistake which has done so much to destroy his credibility.

I refer to the extraordinary speech he made to the Scottish CBI on September 10 in which, in full view of the TV cameras, he gave his personal pledge that Britain would stay in the ERM whatever happened and that, above all, there would be no devaluation of the pound. Devaluation, he said, would be 'a betrayal of Britain's future'.

Why on earth did he deliberately go out of his way to give that personal pledge when there was no need for him to do so? And when in just a few days, and after the quite unnecessary pouring down the sink of billions of pounds of Britain's reserves, he was going to be made to look so utterly foolish? Did he really believe that he could trust the Germans to help save sterling in the same way they moved in to save the franc?

Or did he actually think that simply by standing in front of the TV cameras and giving a personal pledge, he could stem the avalanche of speculation against the pound?

Either way, there has to be a nagging worry for the future. If his judgment can be so bad on such a vital matter, is it likely to be any better on anything else?

# If John Major wants to survive

FOR Margaret Thatcher it will be a moment to savour as, under the full glare of the TV cameras, she makes her appearance at the Brighton Tory Conference and delegates rise to their feet in tumultuous, rapturous acclaim.

For decent, honest Mr John Major who, to my eye, is looking stressed and perilously near the end of his tether, it will be a moment to dread.

If only the conference had taken place two months ago  it would all have been so different.

Margaret Thatcher would have been welcomed warmly and with affection. But, after his General Election victory, it would have been the Prime Minister who was the hero. Now it has all gone so sour for Mr Major. Among the Tory rank-and-file there is still gratitude to him for that April victory.

But there is also the growing suspicion that all along it has been Margaret Thatcher who was right about Europe, and especially about Germany, and that the nation is now paying heavily for having dumped her.

What can Mr Major do at Brighton this week to redress the balance? Not much.

He could try to win the conference round with a spellbinding speech. But then he is not a spellbinding speaker.

Nor is he likely to raise the conference to ecstasy by repeating that, with Socialist support, he plans to push through ratifications of Maastricht against the wishes of the British people.

So what else can he do to survive? He could, of course, simply sit back and hope that with the passage of time the present troubles will be forgotten. But he must know in his heart that there is little chance of that.

The complete cock-up he and Mr Norman Lamont have made of the economy and of devaluation is going to be remembered for a long, long time to come.

So where does that leave him? Hurtful though it may be to his pride, has he considered the possibility of inviting Margaret Thatcher to the Cabinet perhaps as Foreign Secretary?

Would she agree to do so if he made an offer?

I don't know. But if she did I tell you this. It wouldn't half take the smile off Herr Helmut Kohl's face. Off Michael Heseltine's too.

# Is Mr Major just a bit too touchy?

JUDGING by the ferocity of Downing Street's reaction, the Prime Minister has clearly been rattled by newspaper reports that he has recently been showing marked signs of stress and strain.

Yet, isn't it true that he has? Indeed, after all the policy U-turns and own-word-eating of the last few weeks, wouldn't it have been extraordinary if he hadn't?

It may be that, for the moment, the worst is over and that Mr Major will soon be his old self again. There were heartening signs of that during last week's Commons debate when, while Mr Heseltine was being knocked about at the Despatch Box, Mr Major actually seemed to be enjoying himself.

I rejoiced when I saw him occasionally smile. I so want him to survive. For although he may not be a Disraeli or a Pitt the Younger and he may have odd friends, he is still for the time being the best hope this country has.

But if he is going to survive in the long term, he will have to develop much thicker skin and be less sensitive to personal criticism.

He could make a start by not wasting his time reading every word that's written about himself. I commend to him the example of a US President, the late Lyndon Johnson. At the time of the Vietnam War, the hostility of the American Press towards Johnson was almost beyond belief.

When his personal crisis was at its peak, I had lunch with him in the White House and asked him how he managed to put up with all the abuse heaped upon him. He looked at me and said: "I know I am doing the right thing for my country. So every night, as I go to bed and pull the covers over my head, I think of my critics and say God-damn you all ‚you bastards.'

Might not Mr Major profitably follow Mr Lyndon Johnson's example? Mind you, it wouldn't half-help if, like Mr Johnson, he actually believed in something too.

# Is Major really his own man?

THERE cannot be the slightest doubt that Mr John Major is a decent, honest, well-meaning man, immensely capable of selling himself to the electorate.

But underneath the charm and the carefully combed grey thatch, just how much substance is there?

There has recently been a cruel jibe about the Prime Minister circulating in Westminster.

It is being said by his enemies that the Government's troubles stem from the fact that the brain of the Tory Party is now in Hong Kong and that only the voice is left in 10 Downing Street. When I first heard the jibe I scoffed at it – for what seemed to me then, and still do now, two very good reasons.

The first is that when it comes to political intelligence the new Governor of Hong Kong, Mr Chris Patten, has little enough between his ears to ensure his own survival, far less spread his wisdom to others.

The second is that I regarded Mr Major as, in every possible way, a much bigger man than Mr Patten.

Yet it now emerges – and I could hardly believe my eyes when I read it – that it was Mr Patten who largely crafted the Prime Minister's speech to the Brighton Tory Conference, including presumably all the platitudes and twee jokes about children wanting to wee on motorways. Mr Major had apparently called upon him for help. In God's name why? Why should a British Prime Minister go to the Governor of Hong Kong for a speech to be read off Autocue at a Brighton Tory Conference?

I have one further question. In that Brighton speech, Mr Major went out of his way to bestow lavish praise on Mr Patten and to assure him that there would be a high political post waiting for him when he finished his stint in Hong Kong.

Did Mr Patten write that bit, too? If so, I would not, if I were he, count his chickens too soon.

For the way things are going, is Mr Major going to be in a position to offer anyone anything in even five-months time, far less five years?

# I spy an old fox back in No 10

OF ALL the previous British Prime Ministers of this century, which one does Mr John Major most closely resemble?

There are some who liken him to Mr Stanley Baldwin. Mistakenly in my view.

For Mr Baldwin, who masterminded the Abdication and helped lead Britain out of the great Depression, was a man who seldom changed his mind about anything.

That is something which most certainly cannot be said about Mr Major.

How then about Mr Baldwin's successor, Mr Neville Chamberlain? In his private life Mr Chamberlain, like Mr Major, seemed the very essence of decency and integrity.

There was never, again just like Mr Major, a hint or suggestion that he even looked with lust at another woman other than his wife. The only snag was that as a Prime Minister he was a disaster.

Such was his obsession with appeasing Germany that this country by now would probably have been a German province if, after Dunkirk, he had not been replaced in the nick of time by Winston Churchill. Is there a danger that, by sucking up to Herr Kohl, Mr Major might turn out to be the Neville Chamberlain of the 1990s?

Wouldn't it be quite catastrophic if he did? For where in hell would we find another Churchill? Still, I don't think we need worry too much.

For in my own mind I cannot see Mr Major ever becoming another Baldwin or another Neville Chamberlain. Not in any respect.

With his somewhat odd choice of friends, the quickness of his parliamentary footwork and his quite remarkable capacity for making policy U-turns, isn't it beginning to look infinitely more likely that he will turn out to be another Harold Wilson?

# Stop crucifying Major's son

LIFE in modern times has never been easy for the son of a Prime Minister.

But can there ever have been one who has been treated quite as unfairly as 19-year-old James Major?

Whether or not he had an affair with 32-year-old Mrs Elaine Jordache, his boss at Marks & Spencer, is something of which I have no knowledge.

What I do find absolutely appalling is the way the alleged affair has been blown up by the tabloids.

And only, of course, for one reason. Because James Major is the Prime Minister's son.

If he had been the son of almost anyone else, except perhaps the Queen, the story would not have merited a single line of newsprint.

I know there are newspapers which do not like the Prime Minister and would seek to destroy him.

But isn't it damnable when in the process they also seek to crucify a 19-year-old boy?

# When the smile left Blair's face

WHEN Mr Tony Blair studied videos of the Prime Minister's performance at Bournemouth, and you can bet your life he did, there must have been a moment when the fixed smile left his face.

The moment when Mr Major took off his jacket.

Until last week there was almost universal agreement that Mr John Major was a decent, honest, likeable man – which is a damned sight more than can be said for most politicians.

But personal charisma? The popular perception, fostered by the media, was that he had none. That he was dull and grey and entirely lacking in leadership qualities.

Bournemouth last week was a revelation. A new John Major emerged. Relaxed, confident and very sure of himself and his audience.

The way he took and answered questions, sometimes loaded ones, from the audience was quite astonishing.

Can you imagine Mr Blair ever doing the same at a Labour conference?

No way. Not even if he had Alastair Campbell and Peter Mandelson whispering the answers in his ear. What does it all add up to? We will have to wait until the General Election to get the final answer.

But if I were Cherie Blair I would not be counting on rearranging the furniture in 10 Downing Street yet.

# Why Mr Major is toasting Blair

WHEN the clock strikes midnight on Tuesday and the Prime Minister raises his glass to toast his guests at Chequers he must surely wonder whether this will be the last Hogmanay party he will ever host there.

He knows that the odds are heavily stacked against him. It can scarcely be otherwise with a Tory Party so bitterly divided on Europe. And with individual Tory MPs like Teresa Gorman, Teddy Taylor, Bill Cash, Edwina Currie and other political morons apparently intent on committing electoral suicide.

Nor is he fooled by having been elected Today programme Personality of the Year – an honour almost certainly the result of much telephoning by party activists. And yet I have to tell you that Mr Major is far from despondent.

He still genuinely believes that providing he can postpone the Election until late April or the beginning of May, he can achieve yet another shock triumph.

Why does he think so? In the first place, he believes that the public opinion polls which give Labour such a whacking majority are hopelessly wrong.

Secondly, he believes that Paddy Ashdown is dis-credited as a leader and that seats lost in by-elections to the Liberal Democrats will, as in previous elections, return to the Tory fold.

But most of all he will depend on his secret weapon. And that secret weapon is Tony Blair.

Every day that passes, the flaws in the Labour leader's character become more apparent. In what does the Labour leader really believe? It is becoming increasingly difficult to tell. In his time Mr Blair has been both an enthusiastic supporter and an enthusiastic opponent of CND, an enthusiastic supporter and an enthusiastic opponent of the European Union. Whatever other principles he may have, adherence to principle is certainly not one of them. And the longer the election is delayed, the more that will become apparent.

Finally there is the economy, which goes from strength to strength. Come May 1997, are the people of this county going to be mad enough to entrust their prosperity to a man who has never held office of any kind and who does not seem to have held any principles for long either.

Mr Major does not think so.

Neither do I.

# Sir Edward Heath

*When Sir Edward twisted the knife into another Prime Minister, J.J. argued it should end his political career.*

*Mrs Thatcher had endured 16 years of hatred and bitterness from her jealous tormentor.*

*But a fresh attack on John Major earlier this year proved that Sir Edward, even at 81, had lost none of his old vindictiveness.*

*He threatened Major that he would defy the Party line unless the Prime Minister dropped his tough, anti-Europe stance. It had all the echoes of his attacks down the years on Mr Major's predecessor.*

*J.J. said it was time for 'the old buffer to be given the boot'.*

The night Ted lost his marbles
Time to ditch the ex-captain?

# The night Ted lost his marbles

SO PUCE and contorted was his face with rage that for a few frightening moments I genuinely thought Mr Edward Heath might be about to have a stroke in front of millions of viewers as 16 years of suppressed bile and resentment of Mrs Thatcher finally boiled over on TV last Tuesday night.

Can anyone ever have witnessed on TV such vindictive, almost insane, jealousy and hatred?

For the very first time I really began to understand what Mrs Thatcher said to me in the very first days of her Premiership some 11 years ago when I asked her why she didn't make peace with Mr Heath by inviting him to join her Cabinet. Her reply then was: 'I can't. He wouldn't want to sit there as a member of the team. All the time he would be trying to take over.

'When I look at him I don't feel that it is a man looking at a woman. More like a woman looking at another woman.'

And, as last Thursday night showed, isn't that exactly what it would have been? Indeed, isn't that exactly what it still is?

As for Mrs Thatcher herself I agreed with almost every word she said both in Chicago and New York.

And yet it is to Mr John Major that my heart goes out. The more I see of him, the more I like him. He is a transparently decent man who is so obviously doing his best not just for his party but for his country. He may be less outspoken than Mrs Thatcher but his principles are no less sound — which puts him in quite a different league from Mr Neil Kinnock, who wouldn't know what a political principle was if he tripped over one on a CND platform.

I suspect that as the months go by Mr Major's qualities are going to become ever more evident to the electorate.

And that, no matter what public opinion polls may now be indicating, when the election comes and he says to the voters 'trust me' that is exactly what they are going to do.

If I were Mrs Kinnock I wouldn't start thinking yet about getting out the Brasso to polish the Number Ten doorknobs.

*SIR Edward Heath was said to be quite comfortable in hospital after 'routine' surgery.*

*What sort of 'routine' surgery? Isn't it slightly odd that its precise nature was not disclosed? In which hospital did the operation take place? That has to remain secret, too. For security reasons, it is explained.*

*Security reasons? That has to be ridiculous. It is now nearly 20 years since Ted Heath held office. He is not even yesterday's man, he is almost last century's man.*

*Who does he imagine could possibly want to harm him now? What then is the explanation for the secrecy? Could he be getting paranoiac in his old age? Or could it just have been a desperate ploy to avoid at all costs a sick-bed visit from Maggie?*

# Time to ditch the ex-captain?

THERE is one thing that can be said for sure about Sir Edward Heath — he doesn't improve with age.

Now in his 81st year, he is almost as vindictive and bitter towards John Major as ever he was towards Margaret Thatcher.

Not so long ago he joined fellow-deadbeats Lord Whitelaw, Lord Carrington, Lord Howe, Douglas Hurd and Sir Leon Brittan in writing an anti-Government letter to The Independent in which they attacked the Government's reluctance to become 'a committed member of Europe'.

Recently he has been at it again, lambasting the Prime Minister for being too tough with Europe in a series of rows over beef and other issues. He has also made it clear that if he disagreed with a Europe policy set out in the Tory election manifesto he would defy the party line in his own election address.

And yet, in just three months' time, maybe even sooner, he will be standing again for re-election as Tory MP for Old Bexley and Sidcup. And, since it is a constituency with a massive Tory majority, he is certain to be re-elected. Nor is the presence of a candidate from the ridiculous Referendum Party likely to make any difference.

Why do the Bexley Tories keep on selecting Sir Edward as their candidate? Is it because he is so much loved? I would doubt that. Ted Heath has never been popular with the people closest to him. It has been said with a deal of truth that those who know him best love him least.

I suspect the only reason he keeps on being selected as Tory candidate is because the local Tory Association feels it would be unseemly to drop a former Tory Prime Minister. I think they are wrong. I think the old buffer should be given the boot.

But, if he isn't, why doesn't another Tory stand against him as an independent Tory candidate. Alan Clark, for example?

Mr Clark, the former Defence Minister whose outspoken diaries detailing his sexual conquests caused such a sensation, is desperate to get back into Parliament.

He has been shuffling around everywhere looking for a seat. So far unsuccessfully. And, between now and the Election, it is unlikely he will get one. So why doesn't he stand as an independent Tory candidate against Sir Edward Heath?

And, if his intervention meant that the seat was temporarily lost to either Labour or the Liberal Democrats, which I don't think it would be, wouldn't that at least be better than having it held by Sir Edward Heath?

# Is Denis the man to see off Sir Ted?

WHAT are the Tories going to do about Ted Heath? He becomes more impossible, more bloody-minded, more spiteful by the day.

Yet, as things are, and since the members of his constituency association are too embarrassed to drop him, he will be duly elected Tory MP for Old Bexley and Sidcup whenever the General Election takes place.

It goes against the grain to see that happen. A few weeks ago I suggested that Alan Clark should stand against him as an Independent Tory. But then Mr Clark managed to grab the Tory nomination in the ultra-safe Kensington and Chelsea constituency, and so is no longer a runner. But isn't there another high Tory who could take on Sir Edward and even possibly defeat him? What about Sir Denis Thatcher?

A crazy idea? Perhaps. But wouldn't it also be great fun?

It will be argued, of course, that Sir Denis has never been a parliamentary candidate and that he is too old. But then isn't Ted Heath just as old? Furthermore, as Margaret Thatcher's husband, Sir Denis has an intimate knowledge of politics.

And if he were to cause Ted Heath to lose Old Bexley and Sidcup, wouldn't it be Margaret Thatcher's ultimate revenge?

# Neil Kinnock

*Neil Kinnock was the Conservative Party's secret weapon.*

*The Socialist rantings of the leader of the Labour Party continued to guarantee the domination in the country of both Margaret Thatcher and her chosen successor John Major, even during critical times — poll tax and ERM crises — for their governments.*

*In Opposition at the beginning of the Nineties, Neil Kinnock's Left-wing views frightened the voters of Middle England to the point of making the Labour Party unelectable.*

*And after two General Election defeats, Labour replaced Kinnock with a new leader, John Smith, who tragically later died.*

*J.J.'s contempt for Kinnock, a politician he described as of low intellect, spanned Kinnock's years at Westminster and relentlessly continued when he went to Brussels to become a Commissioner with the European Parliament.*

**January 8, 1990**

IT GOES against the grain for me to give advice to Mr Neil Kinnock on how he can best ensure that his party's present lead in the opinion polls is maintained. But I do.

Between now and the next General Election he ought to do his damnedest to keep three leading Socialists off the box.

The first is Mr Gerald Kaufman. On TV he is an unmitigated disaster, with the uncanny knack of making the uncommitted viewer reach for the switch-channel button.

The second is that oozer of instant insincerity, Mr Bryan Gould.

If he were a secondhand car salesman trying to sell me an old banger, I would run a mile every time I saw him smile.

And the third? The third is Mr Kinnock himself.

If he really wants to become Prime Minister, then wouldn't he be wise between now and the election to allow the Socialist case to be presented on TV by his intellectual superiors, Mr John Smith and Mr Gordon Brown?

# Does Someone up there vote Tory?

LADBROKE'S have, it is said, installed Mr Neil Kinnock as hot favourite to become next Prime Minister at odds of 2-1 on.

Two to one on? Which means you have to wager £2 to win £1? For a man President Gorbachev doesn't even think important enought to spend ten minutes talking to?

They just have to be joking!

They could safely offer odds of ten to one against and still make a killing. For the fact of the matter is that Mr Gorbachev's assessment of the Labour leader's importance is correct, and that no matter what the polls of public opinion may say in between elections, when the real crunch comes Mr Kinnock will go down the tube. He is unelectable.

For although many of the British electorate may be not too bright, as was shown by the number who last time voted for the two Davids, not even they could be daft enough to install as Prime Minister a man who intellectually is a zero, has not the slightest experience of even the most minor office and who on top of all that has shown himself, by his change of front on nuclear disarmament, to be utterly without principles. It would be different of course if between now and the election the hand of God were to tap Mr Kinnock on the shoulder and Mr John Smith were to take his place.

I rather fancy Mr Smith would walk it. But that, I confidently predict, will not happen. Mr Kinnock will survive.

After one of his two recent and serious car crashes, he confided to reporters, rather curiously, I thought, for an atheist: 'I have the feeling that Someone up there is on my side.'

Hasn't he ever considered the possibility that the reason he survived might have been because Someone up there is on Mrs Thatcher's?

**March 4, 1990**

MR NEIL KINNOCK made a wonderful sight, mouth opened wide, tonsils on full display lustily singing his heart out in a pew behind Mrs Thatcher in St Margaret's Church, Westminster, in last Sunday's televised Songs of Praise.

Just one thing bugged me.

Isn't he an atheist?

Why then was he in a Christian church singing Christian hymns in praise of a God in whom he does not believe?

Would he have been there, do you suppose, if the event had not been televised and there had not been the votes of simple-minded old ladies to be won?

Just where did you put the sick-bag, Alice?

**April 22, 1990**

**LOOK** at this picture taken after the Mandela concert of Mr Neil Kinnock, celebrating with Left-wing comedian Ben Elton, and ask yourself: which is the bigger comic?

Isn't it the gormless Mr Kinnock by a mile?

Could anything have been electorally more stupid or more utterly unnecessary than he and Glenys repeatedly punching the air in clenched-fist Black Power salutes, when all they had to do to get the Afro-Asian vote was to sit there and look happy?

## Galling

Watching it in Washington, where he had been trying his best to make the Socialist party look respectable, Mr John Smith must have wrung his hands in despair.

It must be galling for him to

**CELEBRATING: Neil Kinnock and comedian Ben Elton**

know that, no matter how far ahead they may now be in the opinion polls, Mr Kinnock still has the infinite capacity between now and the election, with one daft action or one thoughtless speech, to make it all turn to dust and ashes.

Ironic, isn't it, that the very best card in Mrs Thatcher's hand, perhaps the ace of trumps, is still Mr Kinnock?

# The anguish of Mr John Smith

IF I had been Mr John Smith I would have felt like weeping when I saw Mr Neil Kinnock's waffling, evasive, economically illiterate performance on Panorama last Monday night.

No wonder his minders try so desperately to keep him off the box.

For Mr Smith, who the following day had to step in and sort out the mess, it must be especially galling.

The Shadow Chancellor has worked so hard, so conscientiously to secure a Socialist victory at the next Election. In the process he has so sacrificed his own health that he once came perilously close to death.

He knows that he has won the respect, and maybe even the trust, of a large section of the nation.

He believes, and I go at least half of the way to believing with him, that if only he were leader of the

Labour Party the next Election would be a walkover.

But he is not the leader of the Labour Party. Nor is he going to be.

It is the quite unelectable Mr Kinnock who is the leader and, unless the Hand of God intervenes between now and 1992, it is Mr Kinnock who is going to remain the leader. Do you wonder then at the anguish of Mr Smith? Do you wonder either why his colleague, Mr Roy Hattersley, who sees the truth as clearly as any man and must know that come the Election, and a few more gaffes from Mr Kinnock, the present Socialist lead in the opinion polls will melt like snow on a hot plate, has now started churning out novels and newsaper articles with ever greater urgency in an effort to provide himself with an alternative career?

Or why every night, when she

goes to bed, Mrs Thatcher says a little prayer: *'Dear God, please, please, please don't let anything happen to Neil — not, at least, until after 1992.'*

# This gentleman is for turning ...

IT does not bother me that the Quen should have her Civil List payment increased by 55 per cent and the amount fixed until the end of the century.

The total amount of money involved is not all that great — from £5.1 million a year to £7.9 million.

And I suppose that if we are to have a Royal Family we should treat them generously and not expect either them or the men and women who work for them to scrimp and save and suffer hardship.

Nor do I quibble all that much about the additional £2.8 million being given to individual members of the family. It can be argued that the Queen Mother is well worth her £640,000 a year, maybe even that the Duke of Edinburgh is worth his £360,000, the Duke of York and his Duchess their £250,000, Princess Margaret her £220,000, and Princess Anne her £230,500.

I will not ever, at least for the moment, raise my voice in protest against the quite extraordinary £100,000 being awarded Prince Edward.

But isn't it odd that Mr Neil Kinnock doesn't? Wasn't he once quite close to being as a republican? Didn't he once say that as a boy he felt sick watching the Coronation on TV?

Didn't he resign as Michael Foot's parliamentary secretary in 1975 because he felt bound in conscience to vote against the Civil List? Didn't he refuse an invitation to the Royal Wedding in 1981 because of a previous engagement and didn't he, when asked what that previous engagement was, laugh and reply: 'I can't remember'? And yet there he was barely two weeks ago almost curtsying in the House of Commons as he read out a sugary 90th birthday tribute to the Queen Mother. And now here he is agreeing on the nod a vast increase in the Civil List without even suggesting that in return Her Majesty, who is one of the richest people in the world, might care to start paying income tax on her quite enormous private income.

Isn't his conversion from republicanism almost as remarkable and as sudden as was his conversion from unilateral nuclear disarmament? Or, indeed, as his conversion from being anti-Common Market to being a leading pro-European?

I wonder what further fixed principle he will abandon in his bid to make himself more electorally acceptable. His atheism perhaps? Between now and the election may we expect to see him as a stand-in altar boy at High Mass ringing little bells and burning incense?

December 2, 1990

# Will Kinnock do a Captain Oates?

NOW the public spotlight switches pitilessly on to Mr Neil Kinnock.

For him this must be the loneliest weekend of his life. He knows that he is widely regarded, even by many of his parliamentary colleagues, as intellectually the most lightweight Leader of the Opposition there has ever been, a fact demonstrated to the whole nation by the pathetically inadequate performance he put up in his last Commons confrontation with Mrs Thatcher.

The public opinion polls add to his misery. In just three weeks a Labour lead of 16 points has been dramatically transformed into a Tory lead of 11. Can the Labour Party really allow him to continue as leader when it is becoming increasingly clear that Mr John Major will swamp him at the next election?

Especially when, in Mr John Smith, Labour have a champion quite capable of taking on Mr Major on his own intellectual terms — and quite capable, too, of attracting floating voters.

It will be said, of course, that the General Election is far too close and the party's selection process far too cumbersome for a change of leadership at this late date even to be considered. True. But need that cumbersome election procedure be invoked?

Might not Mr Kinnock wish to do the decent thing by standing down?

I commend to him the example of that great English hero, Captain Laurence Oates RN, who, fearing that his own physical weakness might endanger the survival of his colleagues on Captain Scott's ill-fated 1912 expedition to the South Pole, deliberately walked out of the shelter of a tent to certain death in a blizzard.

In the greatest possible service he could do the Labour Party, might he not wish to say, as Captain Oates said: 'I am going outside — I may be some time.'

NEIL Kinnock is being much ridiculed because when asked on TV if he would accept a common European currency he replied with 228 words of completely incomprehensible waffle.

Yet what else could he have done when the truth is that he simply does not have an answer to the question?

But then shouldn't Mr John Smith provide him with one? Or might it just possibly be that Mr John Smith doesn't have an answer either?

Whatever divisions may exist in the Tory Party over integration with Europe, I suspect they are as nothing compared with the explosions which are going to rock the Labour Party the moment they admit that they too are prepared to bow the knee to Brussels and scrap the pound.

# Kinnock turns on the old smarm

I COULD hardly believe my eyes when I read on holiday extracts from an interview which Mr Neil Kinnock had given to Woman's Own, in which he explained why, when Mrs Thatcher was Prime Minister, he had been so ineffective against her at the Dispatch Box.

He explained to the magazine that it had only been because of his natural deference towards older women.

'I guess it's something to do with my upbringing and the respect I have towards women,' he said, 'but it's much easier for me to challenge John Major, a man my age, than it ever was to challenge a woman nearly two decades older than myself.'

Just who does he think he is kidding? The only reason he was so ineffectual against Mrs Thatcher was because she towered over him intellectually and in every other way.

But his remarks are in keeping, I suppose, with all the other snide comments he has made about Mrs Thatcher since she left office. Instead of being generous to her, which would have cost him nothing and would indeed have improved his own image, there has scarcely been a moment in which he has not sought to disparage her.

Do you ever get the feeling that behind Mr Kinnock's smarmy smile a really nasty little man is just bursting to get out.

March 1, 1992

# Neil Kinnock's nightmare

AS the days slip past and the probable General Election polling day, April 9, draws ever nearer, there is a question that must be more and more exercising Mr Kinnock's mind and may even be giving him nightmares.

Exactly what will he be doing on April 10?

Will he be going to Buckingham Palace to see the Queen?

If so, his personal problems will be over. One way or another he will be set up financially for life. But if it should be otherwise and he loses yet again? Then his troubles really begin.

In the event of defeat he knows that he could not survive as Leader of the Opposition. He would swiftly be replaced by either Mr John Smith or Mr Gordon Brown.

He could, of course, remain as Socialist MP for Islwyn. But would he want to? Would he want to sit on the backbenches under another Socialist leader?

Yet what else could he do? He has no profession to which he could return. There is not likely to be a rush of companies eager to invite him to join their boards. Nor a stampede of publishers eager to buy his memoirs.

There was a time when I thought he would have a great future as a TV presenter. But that was when he was younger and less verbose.

It is difficult nowadays to see him as an anchorman on a programme like Panorama or Newsnight. And intellectually it would be far beyond his powers to do a Brian Walden. So what else is there for him? It is difficult to see anything.

I find it all very sad. Couldn't something be done to help Mr Kinnock? Couldn't a consortium of top businessmen set up a testimonial fund for him to give him at least a reasonable income?

After all they do owe him a lot, don't they? For won't he, by the quality of his leadership of the Labour Party, have done a damned sight more to secure a Tory victory than ever Mr John Major has?

April 5, 1992

# Will Mr K bring us to our knees?

I KNOW that Mr Neil Kinnock does not believe in God. Nor does his wife Glenys. Both are professed atheists.

I do not criticise them on that account. Indeed I rather admire their courage in being so open about their lack of belief in a party so many of whose members are devout Chapel goers.

But just suppose it were otherwise. Just suppose both Mr and Mrs Kinnock were committed Christians who every night kneeled beside their bed in silent prayer. In that event I have little doubt as to what each of them would tonight be separately asking the Almighty.

'Please let him keep on taking votes away from the Tories but please not enough to prevent an overall Labour majority, so I can get on with my task of screwing up Britain.'

And Glenys? I suspect her prayer might be 'Dear God, you have been incredibly kind to us so far. Please let it continue. Please don't let Neil say anything really stupid — at least not until after the polls close on Thursday night.'

And if both their prayers were answered? Ah, well. If they are, and on Friday Mr Kinnock becomes Prime Minister, then won't it be all the rest of us who are down on our knees praying?

In that event I just hope the response of the Almighty will not be 'You knew what he was like. If you were daft enough to make him Prime Minister, why should I help you now?'

# Thank you and goodbye, Neil

TO WHOM should credit be given for the Tory victory?

Certainly to the Prime Minister himself. His speaking voice may be more likely to send people to sleep than to have them marching down the streets. But he had two qualities more important than eloquence. Decency and integrity.

The longer the campaign went on, the more these qualities came to be recognised by the public. The brilliance of Mr Michael Heseltine's speeches and TV performances have also played a part in the victory. But isn't there someone who has contributed even more to the Tory triumph than either of them? Mr Kinnock himself.

I feel genuinely sorry for Mr Kinnock. He has fought a good campaign. He has acquitted himself well on TV and been first class at his staged rallies. He has not made a gaffe of any kind. But his past reputation for being a man who changes his princi-

ples and cannot be trusted has been a millstone round the Labour Party's neck.

The Sun newspaper savagely summed it up on Election morning when its front page was filled with a picture of Mr Kinnock and the headline 'If Kinnock wins today, will the last person to leave Britain please turn out the lights'. There can be few in any party who seriously doubt that if it had been Mr John Smith and not Mr Kinnock who had been leading the Labour Party the result would have been dramatically different.

Mr Kinnock is said to be spending the weekend talking to friends and considering his future. I hope his friends advise him wisely.

I know it will mean hardship. I know it will mean the loss of his official car, his driver and his £59,746-a-year salary as Leader of the Opposition. But if I were he, I would not wait to face the indignity of being sacked. I would be handing in my resignation now.

# The perfect job for Mr Kinnock

IN just two weeks' time Mr Neil Kinnock will hand over his job as Leader of the Opposition, and all the perks which go with it like a car and chauffeur, to Mr John Smith. It will be for him a sad and emotional moment. The end of a dream. It will also be a moment in which he must be asking himself — just what do I do with the rest of my life? Well, what does he do?

The current suggestion is that he will be given what might be termed a job for the boyo as one of Britain's Commissioners at the EC. That would be a nice, cosy little billet. Lots of expenses and other goodies and a salary of £75,000 a year.

But such a job would mean virtual retirement from the public scene. Is that what he wants?

Isn't there another job possibly coming up which would keep him in the public eye and for which he would be quite tailor-made?

Once the Maxwell pension fund chaos has been sorted out, Mirror Group Newspapers with their stridently pro-Socialist policies will be up for sale. And there will be plenty of potential buyers, one of them a management buy-out team headed by the Daily Mirror editor, Mr Richard Stott.

It will be a team committed to keeping the Mirror Group supporting the Socialist party. If Mr Stott and his management buy-out team are successful in their bid, wouldn't Mr Kinnock in these circumstances make a perfect chairman for the Group?

He put most of the blame for Labour's defeat in the last election on the tabloid Press. Wouldn't the Mirror chairmanship give him the chance to get things right for the next one? And wouldn't it also keep him at the very epicentre of British politics?

Do I hear cries of 'what a brilliant idea' from Mr Stott and his team? And if I don't, why don't I?

After all, it is only a couple of months since Mr Stott was declaring in his newspaper every day that Mr Kinnock was the very best possible man to run Britain. So shouldn't he be the best possible man to run the Daily Mirror, too?

# Sun shines on the Kinnocks

I APPLAUD the Prime Minister's decision not to stand in the way of Mr Neil Kinnock becoming one of Britain's two European Commissioners.

To have done otherwise would have been churlish.

Mr Kinnock may be a lightweight intellectually. He may have a dangerously short fuse to his temper.

But he is also a decent, warm-hearted, well-meaning man who, after all the crushing disappointments he has suffered, deserves at long last a place in the sun. But to ordinary taxpayers isn't it just a little envy-making, the exotic nature of the sunshine in which he is going to bask?

His basic salary as Commissioner will be £40,000 a year. But that is only for starters.   Perks and expenses will bring it to around £200,000 a year.

Nor, as Commissioner, will he have to put his hand too often into his own pocket.

A limousine and chaffeur will be his to command.

When he has to travel abroad on business a private jet will be at hand.

Life will be a succession of official lunches, banquets and five-star luxury hotels.

There is the added marvellous joy that he will be close again to his wife Glenys, who in pay and perks will be grossing around £140,000 a year as a Euro-MP, and their 24-year-old son Stephen, who is also on the Commission payroll as a £16,500 researcher.

With a combined income of getting on for £400,000 a year, it will mean an utter transformation in the Kinnock lifestyle. Nor does the good news end there. Even if, at the end of his five-year term, Mr Kinnock's appointment is not renewed, he will still be entitled to a pension for life of £30,000 a year.

Glenys, too, will be in line for a munificent European Parliamentary pension.

In other words, if and when the Kinnocks return to Britain with all their loot, they will do so as a rich couple set up for life.

Just one thing bugs me.

Do you suppose that, in these circumstances, and in the privacy of the polling booth, they will still want to vote Socialist?

*Neil & Glenys Kinnock*

# Family values

*The importance of the family was central to J.J.'s whole outlook on life. A dedicated father of two, his simple belief was that no child needed more than the love of its parents.*

*His pen was quick to praise those who put their children's happiness and welfare above their own, and to condemn totally those who failed to follow such a simple creed.*

*He would excuse even the greatest villains, like Robert Maxwell, who plundered millions from pension funds, if he could see evidence of parental love. He was generally dismissive of movie stars but Robert Redford came in for high praise for the love and care he lavished on his sick son as he recovered from a liver transplant.*

*And he was constantly touched by the love Diana, Princess of Wales, demonstrated towards her sons when traditionally royal children have been brought up by nannies.*

A selfish pregnancy

First love of a good man

Tribute to a mother's love

The First Lady who puts herself second

Silver spoonful of despair

# Great actor's saddest role

SIR REX HARRISON, now in his eighties but still currently starring on Broadway, is one of theatre's all-time greats.

There are some who still genuflect when they remember his performance in My Fair Lady. I wonder whether they include members of his own family.

His actor grandson Simon, aged 28, is off with his guitar to the US for two months in search of fame and fortune.

Will he be seeing his grandfather? Apparently not. A friend says: 'They are not close and have little to do with each other.'

Isn't that sad? Not only for the grandson. Surely even more for the grandfather. I wonder why this man who has in his time captured the hearts of so many beautiful women should have such cool relations with a grandson.

Might it be because, like so many other great men, the only person he has ever really loved in life has been himself?

# What comes first with Princess Di

WHEN eight-year-old Prince William made what for him had to have been that terrifying journey in an ambulance from the Royal Berkshire Hospital in Reading to London's Great Ormond Street, it must have been a wonderful comfort to him to have his mother by his side, her hand in his.

It must have been enormously reassuring for him, too, to have his mother sleeping in the room next to his after his operation. Just the very same way any doting suburban mother would have done.

Far cry, isn't it, from the days of not so long ago when the only shoulder on which a Royal child could sob would be that of a nanny?

But then did anyone really expect Princess Diana to do anything else? In the ten years she has been Princess of Wales the British public have learned one thing for sure about her.

It is that when she fusses around her children it is not part of a public relations gimmick.

It is because, maybe unlike some other Royal mothers, she puts their interests before her own personal pleasures.

The day before Prince William's accident, she had taken six-year-old Prince Harry to a gymkhana at Highgrove where, bursting with pride at appearing before Mother, he performed valiantly and won two trophies and a rosette.

A sharp-eyed photographer spotted that in between events the Princess was reading a £3.95 paperback entitled The Game Of Life And How To Play It. Judged by the way she treats her children, Princess Diana does not really need any guidance on how to play the game of life.

She is already a four-star winner.

# A sight to light up my day

AT THE wheel of my car on my way to work of a morning I occasionally see such wonderful things.

Last Friday morning there was this mother, still in her thirties I would guess, with her two children, a boy aged perhaps 13 and a girl aged about ten, standing on the pavement in London's Hammersmith Broadway, waiting for the lights to go green at a pedestrian crossing.

There was so much laughter and love among them as they crossed the road, mother in the middle and a child clutching her hand on either side, that it lit up my whole day. That evening as I passed back along the same road, there, coming out of the West London Hospital at Hammersmith, was a young white mother clutching in her arms a baby in a shawl. With her, carrying a shabby suitcase, was a young black man in jeans who I assumed was the baby's father.

It seemed probable to me that the infant had been born only a day or two previously and that mother and child were now making their way home after her confinement.

There was neither car nor taxi waiting for them. And the evening air was chill. But again there was such a look of happiness on the mother's face that I knew that, whatever happened, in at least one way that baby was going to be all right.

It might not have much else in life but it would have its mother's love. Does any child need more than that?

Or can there be any greater reward in life for any woman than that of her own child's hand being thrust trustingly and unquestioningly into her own?

Pity, isn't it, that with the passing of the years it all so often turns to tears?

IT is said that Freddie Trueman is picking up the whole bill for the marriage blessing in Yorkshire, above, of his daughter Rebecca and Raquel Welch's son Damon — some £50,000.

That includes Miss Welch's first-class air-fares from America and her £250-a-night suite in a local luxury hotel and even the carefully steamed, pureed green beans and poached chicken, which were the only things she would eat. Miss Welch says that she offered to contribute, but Mr Trueman wouldn't let her. Quite right too. It was his daughter's marriage and he was going to do her proud in a proper Yorkshire way, even if it bust him financially.

I salute him. I tell you something else. He may never have been in the same earnings class as her, but, with 2,304 first-class wickets to his credit, in the real world isn't he still a bigger celebrity than Raquel Welch ever was?

October 27, 1991

# Tribute to a mother's love

THE LATE Jean Rook was fiercely proud of her Yorkshire background and of her title First Lady of Fleet Street.

But her pride in both faded into nothing compared with her pride in her son and only child Gresby. From the moment he was born she seldom stopped talking about him. Within minutes of my first ever meeting with her she had fished into her handbag and produced photographs of him as the baby he then was.

As Gresby grew older she continued to do the same to almost everyone she met.

At her memorial service in St Bride's, London, last week the congregation was told how, during an interview with President Ronald Reagan in The White House, she had secured an autograph for her son written on White House notepaper and in the handwriting of the President himself.

It read: *'Gresby, you don't know me. But I sure as hell know a lot about you. Signed Ronald Reagan.'* But perhaps her greatest pride of all was in the fact that her son had gone to Eton and that after Eton had had the distinction of being accepted for training at the Royal Academy of Dramatic Art.

This explains why one of the readings at the memorial service was given by a drama coach from RADA and consisted of a stirring passage from Shakespeare's Henry V – the very same excerpt which Gresby himself had declaimed during his successful audition for RADA.

It appears that on her deathbed that brave woman Jean had discussed her own memorial service and had chosen that reading herself. Just as she had also chosen the song with which the quite brilliant St Bride's choir ended the service.

As they sang I turned to my next-door neighbour, a former Mail On Sunday editor, and hissed: 'What's that they're singing?' He hissed back: 'It's the Eton Boating Song.' And my God it was, too. Isn't it enormously touching that even on the point of death Jean Rook was thinking only of her son and had, in fact, turned her own memorial service into a service of thanksgiving for him?

Gresby gives the impression of being a fine young man. And, if he has his mother's talent, he may well reach the top of the acting profession.

If so, then many, many years from now there may even be a memorial service to him. If so, may I suggest that in tribute to that mother who loved him so much, he arranges in advance that the choir end the service by singing On Ilkley Moor Baht 'At?

# The secret that was lost at sea

THE DEATH of Robert Maxwell takes a lot of the fizz out of Fleet Street.

His enemies, of whom there were many, regarded him as a monster who sadistically destroyed executives by deliberately humiliating them in front of their subordinates.

And he did, too. Often.

Outside his inner circle, and maybe inside it too, there were few who would trust him in business dealing further than they could throw him. And at 20 stone, that was not far. Yet it was almost impossible not to like him. For if he had great failings, he had great qualities, too. How else could he ever have emerged from his background of poverty and illiteracy and racial persecution to reach the heights he did?

His courage and energy and zest for life bordered on the unbelievable. His personality and charisma were such as to light up every room he ever entered. But perhaps his greatest and least-recognised achievement was the way in which, despite his blustering brutality towards others – and perhaps, on occasion, towards them, too – he retained the love of his own wife and children. Nor was there any play-acting about it.

To anyone who ever saw them

together, it was clear beyond doubt that his sons and daughter adored him.

As did his wife, who had estranged herself from her own rich French Christian family when she had declared her intention of marrying a then virtually penniless Jew all those years ago.

No matter what else he may have done in his life, can a man be wholly bad who can retain the love and affection of his own wife and children over such a long period of time? Can you think of all that many respected

pillars of our society who have managed to do the same?

Now to his death. Was it suicide? Or did he *really* die from natural causes? Precious few sophisticated observers are ever going to accept the Spanish coroner's report that he had a massive heart attack before falling overboard.

They may accept that he had a massive heart attack. What they will doubt for evermore is that it took place before and not after he jumped.

But if he did take his own life, then why? Of one thing I am sure. It had nothing to do with the ridiculous accusation that he had been an undercover agent of the Israeli secret service.

Nor am I convinced that the financial pressure of his huge debts was a decisive factor. He had faced up to, and survived, that sort of problem many times before.

So where do we go from there? Perhaps the answer to the whole mystery of Robert Maxwell's life and death may lie in that closed vault in Liechtenstein.

It should be opened now and the world told just who were the true beneficial owners of the crumbling Maxwell Empire.

# Gary strikes at the heart

IT IS said that for the sake of his ten-week-old baby son, now being treated for leukaemia in Great Ormond Street Hospital, Gary Lineker may turn his back on the £6 million he would have earned playing in Japan.

His transfer there is not due to take place until February 1993 and the hope is that by that time the baby will be out of danger. But even so, the probability is that he will still need treatment at Great Ormond Street for up to five years.

If that should be so then, according to friends, there is no way in which Mr Lineker would risk the child's health by taking him to Japan.

Nor is there any way in which he himself would leave this country if his child's life were still at risk.

But would Mr Lineker be serving any purpose staying here? Especially since with the marvels of modern communication he could keep in constant touch and in an emergency be home within hours?

I do not know the answer to that question. All I do know is that the more I see and hear of Gary Lineker, and of the way he puts his child above all other things, the more I like and respect him.

May 25, 1992

# Silver spoonful of despair

SIR ANTHONY PARSONS reached the most glittering heights of diplomacy.

He was our Ambassador in Iran. He was special adviser to Mrs Thatcher during the Falklands War. He was at the very centre of the Establishment.

It seemed that his son Simon would be equally brilliant, equally successful. He started off well: head prefect of his school, excellent at sport as well as academic.

But then somewhere along the line something went wrong. He opted out.

Although he still loved his family he detached himself from them. And although he still wrote long, loving letters to his mother and father, he visited the family only for one week twice a year and even then stipulated that there should be no other visitors while he was there.

He took a humble, £140-a-week job as a hospital porter and lived alone in a London bedsitter where he would spend his leisure time writing poetry.

It was in that bedsitter that tragically two years later he was found dead at the age of just 40. The autopsy report said he suffered a heart attack. What went wrong with Simon Parsons? Why did he become a recluse and a loner? I don't expect anyone will ever know.

At a cost of some £1,500 to himself, his father is now publishing privately a volume of Simon's poetry which he discovered when he visited the bedsitter where his son had died.

According to a brilliant profile in the London Evening Standard, Sir Anthony discovered something else. He discovered drafts of letters which Simon had written home. He clearly had spent hours over every apparently casual letter to his mother and father.

It is a heart-rending story. But perhaps the saddest part of all is, as the Evening Standard tells us, that Sir Anthony, now retired, spends hours poring over his son's poetry.

He says: 'Not an hour passes when I don't think of him. I've just been through the notebooks again for the 50th time. Somehow, while I'm working on the poems, we're together again.'

Does he ever blame himself for what happened? Does he ever reflect that if he had read the poetry and the notebooks earlier Simon might still be alive?

I hope not. All the evidence suggests that no son could have had a more loving father. Yet isn't it strange the number of the children of prominent politicians and other high flyers who do go tragically wrong?

Do you, like me, ever wonder if there can be any greater handicap in life then being born the child of a famous parent?

# No way to treat your mother

WHEN she was 18, young blades of the aristocracy swooned over Margaret, Duchess of Argyll.

She was not only beautiful, she was also enormously rich.

But that was long, long ago. Now the beauty has gone and so has the money.

Next week she celebrates her 80th birthday in an old people's home in London's Pimlico.

Celebrates? It is hardly the right word. There will be no children and grandchildren around to hug her.

She has not been on speaking terms with her daughter, Frances, now the Duchess of Rutland, since 1970. She is never invited to her daughter's home.

Nor will there be any reconciliation on her 80th birthday. Her son-in-law, the Duke of Rutland, explains to the London Evening Standard why he is disinclined to celebrate her anniversary. 'She is very old and ga-ga,' he says.

And maybe she is. But is that any reason to be quite so unforgiving?

Margaret, Duchess of Argyll, may or may not have been a very good and loving mother. She may have been an absolute bitch. I just do not know.

Either way, I feel sorry for her in her old age and loneliness. But I feel even sorrier for a daughter and son-in-law apparently so imbued with hatred as to be willing to pursue hostility to the grave.

Wouldn't it be nice to think that when their turn comes to be old they will be treated rather better by their own children?

February 28, 1993

# The First Lady who puts herself second

THERE are not too many Prime Ministers' wives who would pass up the chance to accompany their husbands on a state visit to Washington.

The glamour and the glitter of it all, the chance of queening it in front of the world's TV cameras as a world personality almost in one's own right is difficult to resist. But Mrs Major is so wise to do so. I have always doubted the wisdom of international politicians taking their wives with them wherever they go.

We are only now beginning to learn how destructive Raisa Gorbachev was to her husband's peace of mind on trips to foreign countries. Of how, on a visit to London, she became hysterically jealous of Margaret Thatcher — because of her husband's admiration for the Prime Minister — and of how she ranted and raved at him before an important meeting because she thought his socks did not match his suit.

She must have been a real millstone round Gorby's neck. Norma Major is not, of course, like that. She is simply a charming, delightful, unpretentious person who does not like the bright lights, who loves her husband and puts her home and her children first. I am all for that.

And I bet that when that unhappy, miserable-looking 13-year-old Chelsea Clinton grows up she will be wishing that her mother had done the same.

July 25, 1993

# First love of a good man

ACTOR Robert Redford is said to be frantic with worry about his 31-year-old son Jamie, now recovering from his second liver transplant in five months.

Jamie, a scriptwriter, suffers from a disease which attacks the liver's bile ducts and has been in and out of hospital since he was a teenager. His first transplant, carried out in March, failed because of clotting.

After that first unsuccessful transplant a nurse said: 'Jamie is still weak and pale but Redford looks as though he's been through almost as much of an ordeal as his son.'

Mr Redford, who has been maintaining a vigil at Jamie's bedside, has told friends that the most important thing to him in life is not his career but the well being of his children and the health of his son.

I believe that. I have always had a gut instinct that Robert Redford is a good man. His present conduct confirms me in that impression.

But isn't he a rarity among film stars? Can there be many top stars in that narcissistic profession who love their children even half as much as they love themselves?

# A selfish pregnancy

WHEN a woman reaches the age of 58, is unmarried and childless and has not had an elderly parent to look after, it can be for only one of two reasons.

Either no one has ever fancied her enough to want to marry her. Or she has set out quite deliberately to put her career before all other considerations.

In the case of the anonymous lady who, helped by an Italian doctor, is now to have twins by artificial insemination from her 43-year-old lover, it would appear to be the latter.

She is said to be blonde, attractive, rich and to look much younger than her years.

And maybe she does. She also has to be selfish beyond measure.

It was presumably by her own selfish choice that she put her career first.

It was by her own selfish choice that she put the making of money before both marriage and children.

Isn't she acting equally selfishly now by, entirely for her own gratification, giving birth to children who will be denied the joys of a normal childhood?

It may be too late now to stop the process. I just pity her two babes in the hard and lonely years ahead.

If one of them should happen to be a girl, could she, in turn, end up deprived of both marriage and children because she has had to spend the best part of her life looking after an elderly invalid mother.

IF and when Mr Peter Malkin, who kidnapped his 12-year-old son from his ex-wife a month ago, ever returns to England, the probability is he will be clapped in jail.

Fair enough. It is the fourth time in six years that Mr Malkin, in defiance of court orders, has snatched the son he loves so much from his ex-wife, a cancer sufferer, who now lives with her new husband in France.

And people who break the law have to be punished.

Threats are also being made that all his wealth will be sequestrated.

I suppose that on legal grounds that can be justified, too. But isn't it wrong that, at a time when the callousness of men who walk out on their wives and children without giving a damn is costing the welfare state so much, we should actually want to put in jail a father who does the opposite?

# Why her eyes stopped shining

THE sign outside the cottage offered hanging baskets for sale and the one on display was full of such gorgeous colours that I stopped to look.

The hanging-basket seller was a ruddy-faced man in his mid-sixties.

We chatted about this and that while he prepared my purchase. Then he looked at me searchingly. 'You're Scottish, aren't you? My wife and I just love Scotland. We go there every year for our holiday. We would love to sell up here and go and live there.'

'Well, why don't you?' I asked. He explained: 'We couldn't do that. We couldn't leave our son.'

By this time his wife had joined us. 'You see,' he continued, 'he is in an institution. He has been there since the age of three but we get him home every weekend and we couldn't do that if we lived in Scotland.'

'How old is he?' I asked.

'He is 32,' was the answer. 'And how long is he likely to live?' I asked.

'We hope for a long time,' they answered in unison. 'You see, he is both the light and the linchpin of our lives. We couldn't exist without him.'

There was so much happiness in their eyes as they spoke that I knew for sure that what they said was true. I drove away wondering whether I had just met the unluckiest or the luckiest parents in the world.

That was nearly three years ago. I went back there again last week in search of a holly ring to hang on my front door. This time it was only the wife I saw.

'How is your son?' I asked. This time I thought her eyes did not shine quite so brightly.

'He is fine,' she said. 'But due to cutbacks, they are closing down the hospital in which he lives. It would be impossible for us to look after him full time and we are afraid he may have to go to another too far away for him to come home or for us to visit him.'

This time I drove away praying to God that they and their son would have as happy a Christmas as Virginia Bottomley and the rest of us.

# Such a tribute to her father

DID you immediately recognise the girl in my picture? I certainly didn't.

Although the face looked vaguely familiar, I thought it might belong to a model or an emerging film star. Except for the fact that models and emerging film stars don't usually look as happy as this girl does.

The picture was, in fact, of the Prime Minister's daughter, 23-year-old veterinary nurse Elizabeth Major, and she was on duty at the racecourse in her father's Huntingdon constituency. It was one of the rare occasions in which her photograph has appeared in a newspaper. It is the same with her brother.

He, too, is seldom in the news and when he is it is for the most healthy of reasons, either playing football or chasing a girl.

It is a tribute to both the Major children that they should be such normal, happy, healthy youngsters, content to stay in the background. But isn't it also a tribute to both their parents that they should be as they are?

Mr Major may not be the best Prime Minister we have ever had. But doesn't he just have to be a damned good father?

NEVER can a child have so quickly and completely captured the heart of the nation as has 11-year-old Jaymee Bowen. She is so spunky, so vital, so self-possessed and with a courage and a wisdom quite unbelievable for her years.

Who can forget her words: 'Never give up, because if you give up, you will just end with nothing left. I'd rather have gone through more suffering to live than not to go through anything and die.'

Of her father she has said: 'He's trying to look after me. What he doesn't realise is that it's me who is looking after him.'

And what a father he is who, instead of giving up, has fought so hard to save his child.

Jaymee is not only a girl in a million. But hasn't she a dad who is one in a million too?

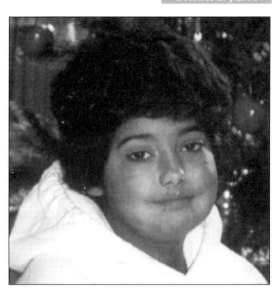

MISS Julia Somerville is a lady of the highest quality. I understand her indignation at the suggestion that her seven-year-old daughter might have been the subject of pornographic picture-taking. I hope and expect that if it ever comes to court she will be cleared completely.

In the meantime, I admire her courage in continuing to front an ITN news programme. I just wonder whether she might not be better at home looking after that child.

There cannot be many seven-year-olds who in their short lives have had no fewer than three fathers, the last one, the one who took the pictures, simply a live-in lover of little more than 12 months standing.

Are these circumstances in which Miss Somerville should be allowing him to take nude pictures of her child at all?

# Sporting Heroes

*The unfashionable footballers of Partick Thistle were J.J.'s first sporting heroes. He supported the team from boyhood, and no matter where he was in the world, theirs was the first result he looked for on Saturdays.*

*He pondered on what might have been Thistle's fate if only the great Alex Ferguson had stayed in Scotland to control their destiny.*

*From early days in Scotland cheering his favourites from the terraces, J.J moved into the big league enjoying a grandstand view of the finest sporting personalities in the country.*

*Many were invited into his personal hall of fame: great footballers like Danny Blanchflower and Gary Lineker, golf stars Ian Woosnam and Tony Jacklin, tennis ace Jimmy Connors, and a particular favourite, world snooker champion, the Scottish-born Stephen Hendry.*

*Others were excluded on the grounds they lacked the qualities of true sportsmen. Paul Gascoigne, for example, came in for fierce criticism despite J.J's initial hopes for him.*

Folly of Botham and Lamb

. . . and lay off Gazza, too!

Stop pointing the finger at Clough

. . . know what I mean, Frank?

Woosie just loves to laugh

# Don't they owe him something?

DANNY BLANCHFLOWER, captain of Tottenham Hotspur's great double-winning team of the Sixties, was everything you would want a top football star to be.

Joyous to watch on the field, modest and unassuming off it.

Impeccable in his sportsmanship, and honest in a way that has gone out of fashion, he set a wonderful example to the young.

He had a rapier-like brain, too.

On a TV programme I once saw him run rings round Henry Fairlie, then one of the country's leading intellectuals, who was rather patronisingly trying to interview him. I had further experience of his brilliance when he later became a journalistic friend and colleague.

Now, 30 years later, it is all turning to dust.

His mind is not what it was, he is crippled with arthritis and he is living on just £20 a week.

Yet he is still so fiercely independent that he refuses to accept charity from either the state or anyone else.

But would it be charity if, with a really glamorous testimonial match, football were to pay back just a little of what it owes him?

# Know what I mean, Frank?

THAT immensely likeable man Mr Frank Bruno tells us that he is itching to get back into the ring again with Mr Mike Tyson.

And I can understand why.

Even if he were massacred, an open-air fight in front of 55,000 sepctators at Wembley in September could, with TV fees, easily bring him in a further million pounds.

But would it be worth it? Didn't he make enough out of his last fight with Tyson to keep him comfortably for the rest of his life?

And on top of that, isn't he now with his modelling, TV commercials, personal appearances and panto performances making a very rich living indeed?

Why run the risk of losing all that and of incurring brain damage in an ill-matched fight?

Besides, ought he not to face up to the fact that, although he may be the cuddliest heavyweight boxer in the world, he is very far from being the best?

If he wants so much to get into the boxing ring again, wouldn't he be wise to pick an opponent against whom he has a better chance of winning?

Like, say, Terry Wogan?

**January 8, 1991**

# Guts maketh the man

WHEN he was young I was not the only one who desperately wanted to see Jimmy Connors beaten on the tennis court.

He was looked upon as a foul-mouthed, big-headed grunting yobbo. He still is. But haven't the rest of us changed in our attitude towards him? Last week in the US Open Tennis Championship at Flushing Meadows I found myself passionately on his side as, at the age of 39, he took on players 15 years his junior and knocked the hell out of them.

And when finally he himself was beaten, as of course in the end I expect he had to be, it was a moment of real sadness for me and, I suspect, for millions of others. Why have we changed? Could it be because we have come to realise that Connors has qualities perhaps more important and more enduring than manners? Character, and courage and guts?

Besides, by doing what he has done, hasn't he put a new spring into the step today of every pot-bellied middle-aged tennis-playing father in the land?

**January 13, 1991**

# ...and lay off Gazza, too!

THERE is one other person I think the Press ought to lay off — Mr Paul Gascoigne, the Tottenham Hotspur and England football star.

During the World Cup, Mr Gascoigne was turned into a great national hero by the media.

Now they seem determined to turn him into a great national villain.

They lambast him because, in the heat of the moment, he allegedly swore at a referee. But what if he did? How do they expect a virile young man to behave on the football field? As if he were President of the Band of Hope?

They sneer at him also because he is not all that literate. But what do they expect of a professional footballer? A potential Poet Laureate?

Above all, they are angry because, in a moment of utter exasperation, he swung his hold-all at a photographer trying to get a close-up picture of his anguish after having been sent off. And that, I agree, was naughty.

But how would you feel if you had photographers snapping at you all day every day? Might there not be times when even a vicar might lose his temper?

My own view is that Gazza is a likeable young man, in addition to being a quite outstanding footballer.

Why the hell don't they just leave him alone for a while?

# Woosie just loves to laugh

IAN WOOSNAM tells us that he is not going to allow winning the Augusta Masters' Golf Championship and the £3 million which it will be worth to him to alter his life in any way.

'Anybody who knows me also knows this won't make any difference to me. I'll booze, smoke and bloody well enjoy myself.'

And he will, too. I tell you something else. He will also go on winning. He is that sort of man.

The first time I met him was at a British Caledonian Airways Golf Pro-Am at Gleneagles.

Many of the leading tournament professionals at the time, including Brian Barnes, Sam Torrance, Tommy Horton, Gordon Brand, Martin Poxon, Ewen Murray and of course Ian Woosnam, were taking part. Neil Armstrong, the first man on the moon, fellow astronaut Alan Shepard, Sir Adam Thomson, Bobby Charlton and myself were among the amateurs.

We were all staying in the Gleneagles Hotel. It was a huge fun party of which little Woosie was the life and soul.

On the last night of our stay we were all conscious of the fact that we had to be up very early in the morning for the coach which was arriving at 6.30 am to take us to Glasgow Airport for the flight back to London.

But instead of going to bed at all, Brian Barnes, a keen fisherman, persuaded Ian Woosnam to spend the night fishing on the nearby River Earn. John Stark, the golf club professional at Crieff, was going to lead them to the best pools.

They took with them on the expedition a plentiful supply of whisky and sausages, which they planned to cook on a camp fire, which they hoped would also keep off the ferocious local midges.

In the morning all three of them staggered into the hotel looking like death, ravaged by midges, and not one fish among them.

When dawn came Ian Woosnam had discovered that even if there had been sea trout in the river he never could have caught one because his tackle had slipped off his line and he had been fishing all night

without either fly or hook.

I remember still the laughter which shook his frame as he told us before passing out in the coach into a deep sleep from which he did not stir until we reached Glasgow.

Ian Woosnam may never become a patron saint of the Band of Hope.

But isn't it refreshing, just for a change, to have a champion who doesn't take life too seriously but treats it for what it really is — a splendid, if sometimes cruel, joke?

# On cue as a Major asset

THERE cannot be a mother in the land, forced perhaps against her will to watch the Embassy World Snooker championship on TV, who does not fall for Stephen Hendry.

He looks so young, so vulnerable, so innocent and so transparently decent and honest, the sort of young man any woman would be proud to have as a son.

He is just about the best sporting ambassador Scotland has ever had. But where, I wonder, does he go from here? He is already a milllionaire, probably a multi-millionaire.

What is he going to do when, as happened to Steve Davis, a younger man comes along and eclipses him, too? Surely, he will not want to keep on playing at a lower level. Might his mind, then, just possibly turn to politics — as other sportsmen like Chris Chataway and Sebastian Coe have already done?

If so, for what party? With all that cash in the bank, surely not the Socialists. Nor can I imagine someone who travels the world as widely as he does being attracted to the Scottish Nationalists.

But might the Tories not appeal to him? Maybe not. I just do not know.

But what does occur to me is that our sports-loving Prime Minister, Mr John Major, has already had in his short spell as PM such sporting heroes of his as Jimmy Greaves, Alec Bedser and the great West Indian cricketer Clive Lloyd at Chequers.

Might he not now think about inviting Stephen Hendry, too?

Even if it did nothing else, wouldn't pictures of Mr Hendry having the best of three frames with Mr Major do the Tories a power of good in Scotland?

**IT was shameful that the international career of England soccer captain Gary Lineker should have ended in the way it did.**

He needed only one more goal to equal Bobby Charlton's all-time English goal scoring record in internationals when, 28 minutes before the end of time in Stockholm, he suffered the humiliation of being substituted.

Yet he showed no petulance, no dissent. Instead he took his place on the bench and watched his team crash to ignominious defeat. Afterwards his only comment on having failed to equal Bobby Charlton's record was: 'Bobby is a far better player than me. He scored greater goals. When the disappointment has died down in a week or two's time I'll be able to look back and realise that you always get hiccups in your career. Unfortunately I had to finish on one. I didn't want to come off but Graham Taylor decided I had to.'

I salute the sportsmanship of Gary Lineker. As for the man who substituted him and who, before the tournament, cockily told us 'Just sit back in front of your TV and enjoy yourselves', what can I say about him and his ham-handed handling of the English side? Or about his unlimited capacity when things go wrong to blame everyone except himself? Only one thing. Hasn't the time come for another substitution?

*Mr Paul Gascoigne is an ill-mannered oaf and I have no sympathy for him. He richly deserved being disciplined for having deliberately burped into the face of an Italian TV reporter when asked how he felt about being left out of the Lazio team for the match against Juventus. But £9,000? Isn't that a bit steep? Just how much do you suppose they would have fined him if he had used another orifice to express his feelings?*

# Stop pointing the finger at Clough

I DO NOT care for Mr Brian Clough's politics. Nor for the fact that at times he can be a quirky, irascible bighead.

But there is one thing that no one can take away from him. He is outstandingly the best football club manager of our times.

He seems to have qualities as a father, too. His son Nigel, himself one of the most talented footballers in England, could have become a very rich young man indeed if he had transferred to another and bigger club.

Instead he has chosen to stay with his father at Nottingham Forest. You don't get loyalty like that from a son unless there is a lot of love and respect there, too.

Now Nottingham Forest is in trouble, at the wrong end of the table and fighting for survival in the Premier League. And there are some supporters who are taking it out on the Cloughs.

Last Sunday when the club failed to win a vital league match against Leeds United a section of the crowd shouted abusive comments. One reporter suggested they were directed at Nigel.

It was too much for Brian Clough to take. He turned in his seat in the dug-out and gave a two-fingered salute to the people who had done the jeering.

Now he may be in trouble for the gesture. There is the suggestion that he may be charged by the

Football Association with bringing the game into disrepute. Could anything be dafter?

If I had been Mr Clough I would have done exactly the same. As for bringing the game into disrepute, isn't it the disgruntled Nottingham Forest supporters who are doing that?

IT is said that the Newcastle United and England striker Alan Shearer, in addition to his enormous wages, might easily pick up a £10 million bonanza in sponsorship deals.

Advertisers like Braun shavers, Jaguar cars, Umbro sportswear and Lucozade are keen to cash in on his clean-cut image.

I do not begrudge him a penny of it.

He is a wonderful player and an inspiration to the young.

I just wonder how someone like Sir Stanley Matthews, who spent most of his playing life on a maximum wage of £12 a week, feels about it.

# Why Jacklin is forced to swing for his supper

IN HIS DAY Tony Jacklin was just as great a golfer and just as world-famous as Nick Faldo now is. At the age of only 25, he won the British Open at Royal Lytham in 1969. The following year he achieved what had been regarded as the impossible for a British player and won the US Open too.

Overnight he became just about the greatest golf hero Britain had ever had. The wealth flowed in. He acquired a magnificent white Rolls-Royce. He was invited to lunch with the Queen at Buckingham Palace.

I met Tony Jacklin again last week. He was giving a golf clinic at the new splendid golfing complex, Slinfold Park, near Horsham in West Sussex. He confessed to feeling like a zombie. He had been on Sky TV until midnight the previous night and, after a sleepless night in an overheated London hotel room, had risen at 5.30 that morning and driven to Sussex to give the clinic.

There was yet another clinic he had to give at yet another golf course later that day. And he was doing it, unashamedly, because he needs to earn money. Not that he is completely skint. But he was a name at Lloyd's with devastating consequences. There have been other disastrous investments. And at the time he made his money, the tax rate was 83 per cent. So the millions have gone up in smoke. He has to work for a crust again.

But he doesn't whinge about it. He is the same modest, likeable, approachable person he always was. And, instead of moaning about the past, he talks eagerly about the future and about 1995 when he will be 50 and eligible to play in the Seniors Tour which provides such huge money prizes in the US.

As I listened, I found myself wondering. Nick Faldo is now, as Tony Jacklin once was, an enormously wealthy man. But wealth, like fame, can be so transistory. Could the day yet come when Nick Faldo, too, is at the wheel of his car driving on a Sunday morning to give a golf clinic?

# Take a tip, young Stephen

STEPHEN HENDRY is, to my mind, just about the best sporting ambassador Scotland has ever had.

He looks so clear-eyed and clean-cut. He never seems to lose his temper. His manners are impeccable.

And, as a fellow Scot, I so much wanted him to win the Embassy World Snooker Championship.

And yet, in that final played over 35 frames, I found both my sympathy and, at least temporarily, my support straying from Stephen to his opponent Jimmy White as in front of millions of TV viewers Hendry pitilessly destroyed him.

There was such anguish in White's face, the bags under his eyes seemed to get bigger by the minute, his hair more unkempt, his suit even more crumpled: such desperation, too, in the way he drew so heavily on his cigarette as Hendry made huge break after break that he must have captured the hearts of everyone watching.

Nothing, of course, can detract from Stephen Hendry's triumph, but might he not be even more likeable if occasionally he showed, like Jimmy White, just a touch of human weakness, too?

Has he ever considered changing the public perception of him by doing something really wild and out of character?

Like, perhaps, whistling on the Sabbath?

# Quiet Kenny's endless pursuit

WHEN I saw the tension on the face of Kenny Dalglish last Wednesday night as he watched his team Blackburn Rovers, reduced for almost the entire match to 10 men, struggle to hold off Leeds United in a critical Premiership game, I found myself wondering about his future.

As a footballer for Glasgow Celtic and later Liverpool, he reached the highest pinnacles of the game. And when he gave up playing and took up management instead he was equally successful.

He succeeded in doing what many people would have thought impossible — keeping Liverpool at the top. Then suddenly, after six years as manager, he quit. Why? No one ever really knew quite why. Mr Dalglish is a man of few words and does not go in for lengthy explanations. It

seemed as if he might have turned his back on football for ever.

He was eight months out of football before he was tempted back to become manager of Blackburn Rovers.

And what a brilliant success he has made of that job.

His team leads the Premiership and plays the most exciting football in the land. The chances are that they will end up champions. I hope they do. But, if so, will a relaxed Kenny Dalglish then settle down to years of contented managership at Blackburn?

I would like to think so but I doubt it. In Kenny Dalglish there is, I sense, a restlessness that is never going to be satisfied and when one mountain has been conquered he will be looking for yet another to climb.

*MR Will Carling calls the men who run the Rugby Football Union '57 old farts'.*

*I don't know what the effect of his offensive remark will have on the '57 old farts' — one of whom is 35-year-old history don Mark Bailey, who won four of his seven England caps in the same three-quarter line as Mr Carling.*

*What I do know is that it certainly has not done Mr Carling himself — rightly sacked yesterday as England captain — much good. For didn't it demonstrae that he himself is a particularly offensive young fart?*

■ ■ ■ ■

ONE defeated British rugby captain comes back from South Africa with enormously increased prestige — Scotland's skipper Gavin Hastings.

The Scottish team performed brilliantly and none more so than their captain. He led by personal example. Never bragged. Never boasted. Never even called the Scottish selectors 'a bunch of old farts' even though, for all I know, he may *think they are.*

He has scored a record number of World Cup points — a record which may never be equalled. In the end Scotland were defeated by New Zealand but only after an enthralling struggle.

After the game the New Zealand captain Sean Fitzpatrick said of him: 'He has been a fantastic ambassador for the game . . . a great credit to Scotland and Rugby Union.'

These are sentiments with which I absolutely agree.

*If, in the next Honours List, there are to be more awards to rugby players, shouldn't Mr Hastings, who already has an OBE, be ahead of anyone else, including Will Carling, on the list for something grander?*

THAT DECENT and enormously likeable man Frank Bruno is clearly, and rightly, overjoyed at having confounded his critics by becoming world heavyweight boxing champion.

Yet are there not two people who have even greater cause for joy? Mr Frank Warren, who manages Bruno, and US fight promoter, the all-powerful Don King, who manages the man Bruno beat, previous champion Oliver McCall. They will now be able to go ahead and arrange a match in London between Bruno and Mike Tyson whom Don King also manages. Such a match would excite worldwide attention and generate wealth beyond measure.

It is said that Frank Bruno himself could get £7 million out of it. But that, I guess, would be peanuts compared with what Tyson and the promoters would make.

But wouldn't it all have been very different if McCall had held on to his title as he was confidently expected to do? He would probably have had a match against Tyson but it is a fight that would have attracted little interest outside the US and certainly nothing like the money that Tyson versus Bruno will fetch.

So isn't it lucky for both Mr Don King and Mr Frank Warren that the Bruno-McCall fight turned out the way it did? It is lucky of course for Frank Bruno, too. But if I were he I wouldn't push that luck. He is already a very rich man. Instead of risking being knocked senseless by Mike Tyson, would he not be wiser not to enjoy his wealth and retire as undefeated world champion?

# Mean streak of a sporting hero

BY THIS evening, if Britain has won back the Ryder Cup, Nick Faldo may be a national hero.

Even so, he is not and never will be my favourite golfer. There has always been a hardness, a toughness, a meanness about him which I do not like.

My prejudice against him started 12 years ago during the Suntory World Match-Play Championship at Wentworth. His opponent was an Australian called Graham Marsh and their match had reached a critical stage. At the 16th hole, when they were all square, Nick Faldo was saved from defeat when, after his recovery shot from a wooded area had sailed over the green, it was thrown back on to the putting surface by a partisan Faldo supporter in the crowd.

It was not Faldo's fault. No one admitted to having thrown the ball back on to the green. But March, already safely on the green in two shots, was clearly unhappy. He was unhappier still when Faldo putted to the edge of the hole for a knock-in while March himself putted three feet short. Everyone expected Faldo to concede the putt, but he didn't and an upset March missed it.

There are some who will acclaim what he did as showing his killer instinct. And maybe it did. I just looked upon it as showing an appalling lack of sportsmanship.

I did not care very much either for the way he told his first wife Melanie after five years of marriage that they were divorcing — in a telephone call from Hawaii.

Now there is a mystery as to whether he has been cautiously costing out how much a divorce from his present wife Gill, who is also his business manager, would reduce his fortune. And has found it could be as much as £10 million. There is a ring of truth about the story, although both he and Gill deny that

they have divorce in mind. But their denials are couched in words that are short of convincing.

Will the publicity affect his performance today in the Ryder Cup? I wouldn't think so for a minute. He is too much of a cold fish for that.

But if he does win, and once again is lionised, I for one will be restrained in my rejoicing

It is said that following the ignominious departure of former England team manager Graham Taylor from the managership of Wolverhampton Wanderers, Mr Brian Clough, the former Derby County and Nottingham Forest manager, has applied for the job. Brian Clough? At the age of 60? Isn't that a bit of a laugh?

Doesn't he have a drink problem and hasn't he, on occasion, even spent the night in a field?
And yet if I were the millionaire chairman of Wolverhampton Wanderers I would not be laughing.
Mr Clough, drunk or sober, has a rare genius for managing football teams. If, long years ago, he had been appointed, as

he should have been, manager of the England International team instead of the long line of duds who did get the job, then I suspect that our international soccer standing would be a good deal higher than it now is. Even at the age of 60 might he not do for Wolverhampton Wanderers what Kenny Dalglish did for Blackburn Rovers?

# Man who lets a good side down

FOR THE millions who watched the match on TV between West Ham and Chelsea on September 11 there is not much doubt that West Ham hard man Julian Dicks deliberately stamped on Chelsea's John Spencer's head.

The referee did not see the incident. John Spencer, who required eight stitches in the wound, publicly accepted Dick's assertion that it was an accident.

The FA thought otherwise and Dicks, who has been sent off nine times and booked 54 times in his bruising career, and who, according to what I have heard from friends who have met him, is just about as charming off the field as he is on it, was summoned

to appear before an FA disciplinary committee.

In the event and because John Spencer did not give evidence against him Mr Dicks got off virtually scot-free. Just a derisory three-match suspension. Yet even that is regarded as excessive by West Ham manager Mr Harry Redknapp, who looks upon Dicks as a pivotal team member.

But should he be? West Ham have a long tradition for playing subtle, skilful and sporting football. They may not win many trophies but wherever they go, they win friends. Do they really want their fine name tarnished by having in their side a nasty thug like Julian Dicks?

# The moaning ways of yesterday's hero

There was a time when Damon Hill was a hero, a god-like figure to every youngster in Britain — and many an adult, too. Everyone wanted him to win.

Everyone groaned when he lost. But that was last year and the year before that. But now? Can the same thing really be said? Hasn't he become a moaner?

**BANNED: Matthew Simmons**

IF anyone had ever doubted the extreme provocation Eric Cantona was under when he launched that infamous kung-fu kick at Crystal Palace fan Matthew Simmons, then these doubts were surely dispelled last Thursday in Croydon Magistrates' Court when, after having been found guilty of screaming racist obscenities at Mr Cantona, Simmons threw himself over the table and tried to throttle the prosecuting lawyer and kicked and punched at the six policemen and two security guards who sought to overpower him.

In so doing he was acting entirely in character. He is a racist thug and potentially an extremely dangerous one at that. We now learn that four years ago when he was only 17 he was convicted of attacking a petrol station attendant with a spanner. He had pleaded guilty to assault with intent to rob. And what was his sentence for that violent deed? Just two years' probation.

For the foul words he hurled at Cantona he is banned from all football grounds for one year, a ban which will be almost impossible to enforce, and fined £500 plus £200 costs, which will almost certainly end up coming, one way or another, from Social Security. And what punishment does he receive for his violent conduct in court? Just seven days in jail, of which he serves only one night.

Isn't that anger-making? Or should we count our blessings that at least the magistrates didn't send him away with a consoling pat on the back and £5 from the poor box?

# Folly of Botham and Lamb

THERE is only one question in my mind after the catastrophic failure of Ian Botham and Allan Lamb's libel action against Imran Khan.

What on earth induced them ever to bring it? Right from the beginning they were on a hiding to nothing.

The article in which Imran Khan was said to have accused Botham of cheating and suggesting that both men were racists and lower class appeared in an obscure Indian cricket magazine more than two years ago. Nobody paid any serious attention to it then. Had it not been for the libel action it would have been long since forgotten.

So why then did Mr Botham and Mr Lamb elect to go to law?

Was it because they thought they could make a good deal of money out of it?

If so, they know a damned sight better now.

With costs totalling half a million pounds against them, they could face total financial ruin.

How do they hope to raise the money?

Mr Botham brushes the problem aside by saying he will just have to do a few more road shows. I find that difficult to believe.

I think the judgment will be a crippling financial blow to him and an even bigger one to Allan Lamb, who says it is going to bankrupt him.

So who is going to help them? Do they expect a flood of cash from cricketing fans eager to rush to their aid?

If they do, then I think they are going to be sadly disappointed. They would certainly not get a penny from me.

My view is that anyone stupid enough to make lawyers rich by embarking on a libel action deserves everything he or she gets.

*Ian Botham*

*Allan Lamb*

**December 5, 1996**

*Alex Ferguson may have the irritating habit of endlessly chewing gum during a match but hasn't he other great qualities to compensate?*
*Hasn't United's victory at Wembley yesterday shown him to be the greatest, bar none, football manager of our time?*
*To have achieved the 'double' of FA Cup and Premiership title twice in three years is a fantastic achievement. Yet it has been the same wherever Alex Ferguson has gone. In Scotland with St Mirren and then Aberdeen, he achieved enormous and almost instantaneous success.*

*And that success has multiplied immeasurably in England. So many of yesterday's winning Cup team were youngsters he has schooled and trained.*
*In his triumph I have only one regret. If only he had stayed in Scotland, mightn't he have done wonders for one football club which has commanded by loyalty all my life? Partick Thistle? A club which is now in such sad decline that the cruel Glasgow joke is that, when a visitor to the City rings up to book a stand seat at Firhill and inquires the kick-off time, he receives the reply 'What time would suit you best, sir?'.*

THERE are few people I have met in my life whom I liked more than I did Denis Compton.
He was a lovely man.

As a sporting legend idolised by millions, he could have been big-headed, arrogant and full of his own self-importance. Instead he was almost unbelievably modest and unassuming. He treated everyone from dustmen to dukes in the same friendly way and, above all, he was fun and a joyous companion.

There cannot be anyone who ever knew him who has not been immeasurably saddened by his death

# Greed

*A canny Scot, J.J. believed in just rewards, often argu-
ing that the pay of senior politicians, for example,
failed to reflect their responsibilities.*

*But with the growth of privatisations in the Nineties,
and the emergence of the fat-cat syndrome where bosses were awarded astronomic salaries, J.J. protested
loudly.*

*He condemned as plain guzzling greed the awards
which were an affront to the man in the street.*

*He was also quick to round on many other examples
of excess.*

The lady and the
£20,000 kitchen
The one innocent

Is he even worth a
Green Shield stamp?

Why wasn't the poor man told?

# The one innocent

THE reunion of 20-year-old Dawn Griffiths with her abducted baby Alexandra should have been such a joyous occasion. Instead, the public has been left with the sourest of tastes in its mouth.

Doesn't it stink that after everything had been done for them and all the help and support they had been so freely given, Miss Griffiths and her boyfriend should use the facilities of a Health Service hospital to set up a squalid auction for the sale of their story to the highest and sleaziest bidder?

Nor is the revulsion lessened by the revelation that the baby's father has a police record as long as your arm, including convictions for violence, and had a spell in jail for beating up a previous girlfriend — a beating in which the lady's leg was broken.

In the whole miserable affair there is only one person to whom my heart goes out — the baby.

I would just like to think that with her natural parents she has more happiness for the rest of her life than she would have had with the misguided, but apparently caring, woman who abducted her.

# If this were not the Sabbath

THERE may be very good arguments why the chairman of Marks & Spencer, Lord Rayner, should be awarded a 48 per cent pay rise to £619,961 a year and British Telecom's Mr Iain Vallance a 32 per cent rise to £374,000 a year.

There always are.

They are just two more in a long line of company bosses who have had quite astronomical pay rises — and almost invariably the excuses are the same, that the chairmen themselves are quite innocent in the matter, that the increases have been recommended by an impartial committee of high-minded non-executive directors who usually point out that the increase only brings the chairman's pay into line with comparable rates in other countries.

If I were not a Presbyterian and this were not the Sabbath, I would be sorely tempted to say: Ballocks!

Most often it is just plain guzzling greed that is at the back of it all. And as far as pay rates in other countries are concerned, I say to hell with other countries. It is this country which matters.

Don't the bosses who pocket such rises care what they are doing to Britain, after they themselves have had enormous tax concessions and at a time when there is an urgent Government plea for moderation in wage demands?

Aren't they aware of the bitterness being created among ordinary wage earners by the sight of so many fat snouts in the trough or what the electoral consequences might be?

Or as long as they themselves are all right, Jack, don't they give the slightest damn about anyone else?

NO-ONE would wish to deny the Defence Secretary, Mr Tom King, and his family protection against terrorism.

There has already been one IRA plot to kill him. There may well be others.

The arrest of suspected IRA terrorists near Stonehenge last week and less than 20 miles from his home will not exactly strengthen his sense of security.

So I am entirely in favour of the massive security operation in force at Mr King's Wiltshire home.

But one thing does stick just a little in the throat. That is the fact that Mr King is

*SKINT? Tom King*

charging the police £40-a-week rent for the cottage on his Castle Combe estate which they use as an operation room and to store surveillance and communication equipment.

Can he really be that skint that he could not afford to let them have it for free?

# The lady and the £20,000 kitchen

WHEN the Chancellor of the Exchequer's wife, Mrs Rosemary Lamont, first saw the kitchen of her new home at 11 Downing Street, the Daily Mail tells us she did not like it the slightest little bit.

It was too gloomy she thought.

So she complained and asked instead for a new-style German one of the type that costs around £20,000.

This despite the fact that the old one had been installed barely five years ago. It is further reported that the Government Property Services unit gave Mrs Lamont a dusty answer. Good for them.

But isn't it extraordinary that she should have asked for it at all?

At a time when VAT is going up from 15 to 17½ per cent and the Government is trying so desperately to cut down on all unnecessary public expenditure, shouldn't the Chancellor of the Exchequer's wife be setting a better example?

Nor was Mrs Lamont the only Downing Street wife to want a new kitchen. Mrs John Major did so too. And in her case, perhaps because the kitchen at Number Ten is more than 25 years old, her request has been granted.

But should it have been? Mrs Major is a gentle, unassuming lady whom I much respect and admire. But even so, wouldn't it be better to postpone all such expenditure until after the General Election?

For after the votes have been counted, can either lady be quite, quite sure that she will still be in Downing Street at all?

Except, perhaps, if Glenys ever invites them in for tea?

# Mucky money in the Kitty

AMERICAN author Kitty Kelley has already made a mint of money out of the muck-spreading books she has written on public figures in the United States.

But it looks as though she has really hit the jackpot with her book on Nancy Reagan.

No wonder there is such a vast demand for it when it contains such juicy scandal as the fact that during Ronald Reagan's presidency on almost every occasion he was out of town his wife was getting into bed in the White House with Frank Sinatra.

Can that possibly be true? It sounds improbable. But since their combined ages at the time must have been nudging 145, would it really matter anyway?

For my own part, I do not give a damn what Nancy did or did not do.

I just find it distasteful the way in which some authors make money out of destroying the images of our heroes.

I also bitterly resent the hurt inflicted on that decent old man Ronald Reagan who, during his presidency and in his own kindly, bumbling way, transformed all of our futures by extending the hand of friendship to Russia and bringing to an end the Cold War.

The one consolation is that for this alone his name will live in history. Whereas trash like Miss Kitty Kelley will be forgotten the day after tomorrow.

■ ■ ■ ■

IF it were possible for one man, single-handed, to ensure that the Socialists win the next election then I guess that Mr Ian Vallance, Chairman of British Telecom, will come pretty close to being that very fellow.

His staggering 43 per cent pay rise to over £500,000 a year would be controversial enough if it had been achieved through his managerial brilliance in a highly competitive economy.

*It stinks to high heaven* when it comes from running a recently privatised telephone service which is still to all intents and purposes a monopoly.

It is not only the greed behind the pay rise which is offensive. It is also the mind-blowing insensitivity of it all.

Wasn't Mr Vallance aware of the political uproar his increase would cause?

Didn't it ever occur to him that it would infuriate not only working-class voters in their millions but middle-class voters, too?

## Blame

Or, as long as he was all right, didn't he bloody well care?

With people like Mr Vallance around, would you really blame Mr John Major if sometimes he felt like putting his head in his hands and sobbing?

# Is he even worth a Green Shield stamp?

THERE has been much discussion as to what can be done about people like Mr Roger Evans, chairman of British Gas, who lifts two fingers to us all by grabbing a pay rise of 60 per cent and pushing his salary up to £370,000 a year.

In his greed he joins Mr Iain Vallance, chairman of another recently privatised near monopoly British Telecom, who helps himself to a 43 per cent pay rise, taking his pay to a quite ridiculous £536,000 a year, and the Governor of the Bank of England who, while preaching pay restraint on others, takes a 17 per cent rise for himself — something akin to an archbishop being caught in a whorehouse.

I will tell you one thing that could be done for starters. We could end the potentially corrupt system whereby the pay of company chairmen is decided by a so-called independent remuneration committee consisting of non-executive directors each of whom is usually dependent for his continued place on the board on the chairman's goodwill.

If company chairmen want more money then they ought to be made by law publicly to ask for it in front of shareholders at the company's annual general meeting. Secondly, company chairmen who display anti-social greed at a time when they are imposing pay restraint on their workforce should all be debarred from ever appearing in an Honours List.

Normally the Governor of the Bank of England is almost automatically given a knighthood or maybe a peerage.

I wouldn't even give Mr Robin Leigh-Pemberton a book of Green Shield stamps.

I would also make sure that even if Mr Iain Vallance and Mr Roger Evans live to 100 they stay plain misters to their dying day.

Might not the threat of exclusion from the Honours List be a wonderful deterrent to any other company chairmen who have wives who are social climbers?

And can there be many company chairmen who haven't?

*Iain Vallance*

# Why wasn't the poor man told?

MR Francis Reynolds, aged 54, of Shovell Road, Moston, Manchester, drowned himself in a canal just hours before he was due to appear at Manchester Crown Court on a charge of having twice raped a schoolgirl.

He died unnecessarily. If he had appeared in court he would have learned that the Crown intended to offer no evidence against him because police had confirmed that his alleged victim had been lying. She was in fact a virgin who had made false rape allegations against other men too.

It is sad that Mr Reynolds should have died as a result of her fabrications.

It is also anger-making in the extreme.

For the fact is that the decision to drop the rape charge against him had been made 16 days earlier.

Why wasn't Mr Reynolds immediately told of that decision? The excuse given by the Crown Prosecution Service is that it did not tell him because it first wanted to explain the decision to the unstable girl who had made the allegation.

What about his own lawyers then? A spokesman for the late Mr Reynolds' solicitors said that they had been given 'informal indications' of the Crown's intentions but this had been insufficient information to pass on to him.

Insufficient information? Wasn't there anyone in the whole cold legal process with enough sensitivity to understand the enormous pressure Mr Reynolds must have been under?

Wasn't there one single person with enough compassion to pick up a telephone and at least hint to the poor wretch that his nightmare would soon be over?

Do you suppose they even bothered to send flowers to his funeral? And would it surprise you at all if they hadn't?

# Greedy face of Mr Roache

WHEN I saw the pictures on TV news of Coronation Street actor Bill Roache emerging from the High Court with his wife to face an army of photographers after having been awarded £50,000 libel damages against The Sun newspaper, I couldn't for the life of me understand why Mr Roache was almost in tears and clearly on the point of hysteria.

Shouldn't he, instead, have been singing and dancing with joy?

I couldn't understand either why Mrs Roache had burst into tears when she heard the jury's verdict and the sum of damages awarded. It was not long before we had the answer. Mr Roache need not have proceeded with the High Court case at all. The Sun, it transpired, had already offered him a £50,000 out of court settlement — an extraordinarily generous sum for a comparatively trivial libel.

Yet Mr Roache and his lawyers had contemptuously turned it down and, according to The Sun, had said: 'Give us £200,000 or else we go on with the action.'

The fact that the jury had awarded Mr Roache only £50,000 meant that normally he would have had to pick up all the legal costs from the time the offer was made. Do you still wonder, then, why Mr Roache went a ghastly shade of white and his wife started blubbing? In his wisdom, the judge in the case decided The Sun should still pick up Mr Roache's £100,000 legal costs.

I think that was a lamentable decision, and I hope and expect it is going to be overturned on appeal. Which will leave Mr Roache with egg all over his greedy face. And quite rightly, too.

Might it not also have the marvellous side-effect of deterring other litigants from using the libel courts, as Mr Roache clearly did, simply to enrich themselves?

■ ■ ■ ■

IT is splendid that Mr Anthony Hopkins should have won a Hollywood Oscar as Best Actor of the Year for his performance in The Silence Of The Lambs.

But should we also rejoice about the film itself, named as the Best Film of the Year, in which Mr Hopkins plays a serial killer with an insatiable appetite for eating the livers of his victims?

Cosy little subject, isn't it, for family viewing? And it is only one of many similar ghoulish movies now making

**SPLENDID: Hopkins**

millions at the box office since Hollywood discovered that the sicker the subject the bigger the profits.

Can I be the only one who yearns for a return to the good old days of Gary Cooper in High Noon?

SACKED in disgrace by Arsenal and suspended from all football for 12 months by the FA after allegedly accepting bungs totalling £160,000, Mr George Graham is back in the big time again. Looking like a cat which has swallowed the cream, he emerges as the new manager of Leeds United on a reputed salary of £350,000 a year and with £10 million at his disposal to buy new players and complete freedom as to how he spends it.
Does he show any contrition for the past? Not the slightest. But then why should he?
In our modern society aren't honesty and decency and straightforward dealing old-fashioned fuddy-duddy values?
As for Leed United, do they show any hesitation about employing a manager with his financial record? Not the slightest. But then why should they? Football is now big business. Mr Graham is a brilliant manager who could well win the League title for Leeds. And in our modern society isn't winning the only thing that matters?
I wish both Leeds United and Mr Graham luck. It sounds as if they might be well suited to each other.

# The Church

*There was precious little charity shown towards the leaders of the Church of England by J.J. He feared the Church was terminally sick.*

*He rated George Carey an even bigger disaster as Archbishop of Canterbury than his predecessor, Dr Robert Runcie.*

*Runcie was a 'deadbeat' at the heart of a Church in decline, plagued by falling congregations, homosexual priests and trendy political bishops who didn't believe in its dogma.*

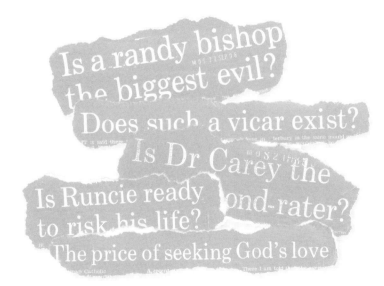

# Is Runcie ready to risk his life?

IF, after his six-day visit to Ethiopia, the Archbishop of Canterbury is wondering which country he should visit next, may I make a suggestion?

How about the Lebanon?

It is now more than three years since he despatched Mr Terry Waite there on a special mission.

He did so in a rather off-handed way.

So off-handed, in fact, that Mr Waite was not even provided with a car to take him to London airport, but had to travel there by Tube. For more than three years — that is, if he is still alive — he has been kept captive in the most horrifying of conditions.

Almost certainly blindfolded for much of the time. Almost certainly in solitary confinement.

Dr Runcie, who surely must feel a deep sense of personal guilt, has lit a candle in Lambeth Palace for Mr Waite.

Might he not now think of carrying that candle personally into the Lebanon in an attempt to secure Mr Waite's freedom? I accept that it would be a hazardous mission. But it is also one which would excite the imagination and admiration of the world.

In these circumstances, and with all the attendant publicity, I find it difficult to believe that the Archbishop would fall victim to a terrorist bullet.

But even if he did, would there not be for him the enormous personal consolation of knowing that in death he was achieving more, much more, for the Anglican faith than ever he has done in life?

*Dr Runcie*

# Does such a vicar exist?

IT IS said there is going to be a great battle to decide who succeeds Dr Robert Runcie as Archbishop of Canterbury.

Yet when you examine the credentials of the candidate so far named, does it matter a damn which of them does?

With its dwindling congregation, its homosexual priests and, its trendy political bishops, some of whom do not even believe in the Resurrection, the Church of England is sick unto the point of death. What possible good can come from choosing yet another deadbeat?

If it is ever to stage a miraculous recovery and capture once again the hearts and minds of the people, then instead of seeking another Archbishop of Canterbury in the same mould as Dr Runcie, wouldn't it be better by far to pick a simple parish priest, who just happens to believe that the prime and indeed only purpose of the Church should be not to play politics but to preach the word of God?

Do you suppose there still is such a cleric left in the Church of England?

*Dr Robert Runcie is said to be worried that when he steps down next week as Archbishop of Canterbury, the Church of England will be left without a leader until Dr George Carey takes over in April. The anxious cry is that the Church will be left 'rudderless'. Rudderless? What will be so new about that? Isn't that exactly the way it has been ever since Dr Runcie became Archbishop 11 years ago?*

# Is Dr Carey the only second-rater?

I READ the other day in one of our allegedly more serious newspapers that, because they have so little in common, disagree about the Ordination of women and small talk is difficult, the Queen does not always relish the frequent visits to her homes by the Archbishop of Canterbury, Dr George Carey.

On what authority the report was based, I do not know. Certainly the information would not have come from the Queen herself.

Her Majesty is far too correct ever to betray, even by the flicker of an eye, her distaste for a house guest. Not that I would blame her if she did, indeed, feel she had not too much in common with the Archbishop. Dr Carey is not everyone's cup of cocoa. He is certainly not mine. Indeed, is he anyone's? There is only one positive thing that can be said about him. And that is the dismal fact that, in the comparatively short time he has been Archbishop of Canterbury, he has demonstrated that he is an even bigger disaster than his predecessor, Dr Robert Runcie.

At a time when the country cries out for spiritual leadership, he puts on an idiotic baseball cap and gives absolutely none.

Yet, to be fair, cannot the same thing be said about the leaders of all the Christian churches throughout the world — including, alas, even the Church of Rome?

There was a time when I thought Pope John Paul was going to be one of the greatest Popes of all time.

Alas, his light has been dimmed by increasing age and the devastating after-effects on his health of that so-nearly successful attempt to assassinate him in 1981. Now his candle barely flickers.

But it is not only in spiritual matters that the world lacks leadership. The international political scene is equally barren. Everywhere one looks, one sees only second-raters.

In France, President Mitterrand is old and ailing. In Germany, Herr Helmut Kohl is a burst balloon.

In Russia, their only potentially great leader, Mikhail Gorbachev, is washed up.

In the US, the saxophone-playing President Clinton demonstrates more and more his utter inadequacy.

And here in Britain, we have that super, decent, well-meaning Prime Minister, Mr John Major.

But as a leader? In a time of real crisis would anyone trust him to lead even a Salvation Army band — although wouldn't he look just marvellous in the uniform?

Yet, since nature abhors a vacuum, leadership will come. It always has throughout history. It always will.

But from where? And in what country? And in what form?

Wouldn't it be comforting to think that, when it does come, it will be from another Churchill or Roosevelt or De Gaulle — and not from another Hitler?

March 12, 1995

# Is this bishop a hero or a creep?

THE Rt Rev Derek Rawcliffe, 73-year-old Assistant Bishop of Ripon and former Bishop of Glasgow and Galloway, is being acclaimed in some quarters as a hero because he has openly confessed that he is homosexual.

Hero? Is that really the right word for a man who admits that when he was over 50 years old and serving in the Solomon Islands before becoming Bishop of Southern Melanesia he took a young man, presumably a native, as his lover?

Did he confess his homosexualism to his wife Susan whom he married in 1977 and who, suffering from severe diabetes and confined to a wheelchair, died ten years later? He certainly didn't tell his father-in-law into whose house he moved after his wife's death.

His 95-year-old father-in-law, Wing Commander William Speight, says of his son-in-law's homosexuality: 'It became obvious within a few weeks of him living here. He was more interested in a certain type of man and his younger male friends who stayed here with him.'

At the age of 73, is the Assistant Bishop of Ripon still a practising homosexual? 'That's my affair,' he replies.

His equivocal reply suggests that even at his age he may still lust after younger men.

In these circumstances would you really call the Rt Rev Rawcliffe a hero?

Wouldn't a slimy, unctuous old creep be an infinitely more accurate description?

# So will the Dean keep on jogging?

THE DEAN of Lincoln, the Very Rev Brandon Jackson, must be bitterly regretting the day when out jogging in training for the London Marathon, and by chance carrying with him a bottle of wine, he dropped in at the house of his verger Verity Freestone.

He must also be bitterly regretting that when Miss Freestone said to him that she was desperate for sex he did not start jogging fast in the other direction. For even though the 60-year-old Dean has been found not guilty by a consistory court of 'conduct unbecoming the office and work of a clerk in holy orders', and even though he has subsequently suggested on TV that there has been a conspiracy of the local Church hierarchy against him, the blaze of publicity attending the hearing will have cast a long shadow over his future Church career. And it may have ended all hope of any future advancement.

That would probably be a pity. The Dean may have acted foolishly in getting entangled at all with such an obsessive and, as it has turned out, clearly emotionally disturbed lady.

But does that make him a bad priest? Did it justify his being dragged into a public court?

Isn't there something terribly and sadly wrong with a Church which, while quietly condoning and forgiving homosexual clergy, still takes to court and, if found guilty, deprives of his living a priest who has been ensnared by a woman and is suspected of having sex with her?

# The price of seeking God's love

The Roman Catholic Archbishop of Birmingham, the Most Reverend Maurice Couve of Murville, urges RC churchgoers to dig deeper in their pockets when the collection plate comes around.

He says: 'It has been worked out that each Catholic on average gives £1.13 each Sunday . . . this is less than other denominations.' How much less?

A recent statistical report from the Church of England shows that in Birmingham, Church of England parishioners outgive their Catholic counterparts with an average weekly donation of £3.50 per adult. For England as a whole the average weekly donation by C of E members was £4.42.

And north of the border? What about the Church of Scotland?

There I am told that the average amount slipped surreptitiously into the collecting bag by my kilted compatriots is a measly £1.14.

Isn't that extraordinary? Why should Presbyterians and Roman Catholics be so much meaner than Anglicans?

Might it be because they are so much nearer to God they don't feel a need to impress Him?

# Sanctimonious Runcie simply beggars belief

LORD Runcie, the former Archbishop of Canterbury, tells us that he tried his best to die before the publication of the sensational biography of him which has been making such headlines.

Did he really? I doubt it.

He suggests that the biography's author Mr Humphrey Carpenter was guilty of a breach of faith in publishing the book before his death.

I doubt that too.

What Lord Runcie does not deny is that every single word that appears in the book came from his own lips as he chatted to Mr Carpenter while a tape recorder was recording everything he said. He makes no attempt to deny, either, the fact that he was paid £1,000 by Mr Carpenter for the taped material he provided.

From it all Runcie emerges as a vain, arrogant, indecisive man who has no fixed principle of any kind, who although oddly going out of his way to deny that he himself had ever been homosexual was suspicious of the homosexual priests who surrounded him, feared that they would stab him in the back and yet not only tolerated but even ordained one.

He could be cold and ungenerous too, as in his treatment of Cannon Gareth Bennett of New College, Oxford, who after receiving hints that he might be given ecclesiastical preferment, wrote most of Runcie's sermons for him and who, when he realised he was being strung along by the Archbishop, ended up by attacking Runcie in an annonymous foreword to Crockford's Clerical Directory and then, when his authorship was discovered, committed suicide.

Runcie also emerges as both indiscreet and two-faced. Blabbing about the Royal marriage and betraying Royal secrets to his biographer. Allowing the Princess of Wales to believe that he was her friend and supporter while in private he was describing her as a scheming actress.

He even had the crust to accuse Prince Charles of not believing in the Church of England. But who could believe in the Church of England with someone like Lord Runcie as Archbishop of Canterbury? And yet I suppose that in it all there is one consolation for the sanctimonious old creep. And that is that, with all his faults and all his blemishes, can't it be argued that at least he was better than his successor?

# Churchmen beyond belief?

WHEN the Archbishop of Canterbury, the Most Reverend George Leonard Carey, bows his head in prayer this Easter morning I wonder if he will have the humility to reflect on what a failure he has been as leader of the Church of England.

He has been Archbishop for five years now. Can anyone recall any moving declaration he has made of his faith in that time?

Today, on this special day, Anglican churches throughout the country may be full.

But next Sunday and all the Sundays after? They will be mostly empty.

And can anyone blame the masses for staying away when there is so little leadership from the top? How can humble Anglican parishioners be expect-ed to believe in the Resurrection when clearly so many of their leaders do not?

It is unfair, of course, to put all the blame on Dr Carey.

He is merely the last in a long line of disastrous Archbishops of Canterbury.

Nor is it the Anglican Church alone.

There is no inspired leadership in the Church of Scotland or the Methodist Church either.

As for the Roman Catholic Church in England, Cardinal Basil Hume is a good deal less than inspiring.

Even in Ireland there is the scandal of homosexual priests meeting and even dying in gay clubs and of child abuse which the Church has done its best to conceal from the public.

*Dr George Carey*

Only 50 years ago there was a general belief in God, in the divinity of Christ and in the sanctity of marriage.

Can anyone say that this island is a happier place now that that belief has gone?

September 22, 1996

# Is a randy bishop the biggest evil?

The Roman Catholic Bishop of Argyll and the Isles, the Right Reverend Roderick Wright, must be quite a character.

And not a very pleasant one at that.

When he first went missing there were some innocents who feared the worst and thought that the stresses of his job coupled with the recent death of his much-loved younger sister might have caused him to commit suicide.

It was, of course, only hours before the truth emerged. That far from putting his head in a gas oven, he has it between the boobs of a 40-year-old divorcee — and an attractive-looking one at that.

Then came the revelation that, far from this being his first lapse from grace, he has a 15-year-old son from a previous liaison. Now the question is being asked: how many more affairs has he had? His disgraceful conduct has caused all hell to be let loose in the Roman Catholic Church and there is renewed controversy as to whether the Church is right to demand celibacy in its clergy.

Even that strict traditionalist Cardinal Basil Hume initially conceded that there might be a case for ending it and for allowing priests to marry.

For my own part, I think that to do so would be utterly wrong. There will always be sexual scandals in the priesthood. There always have been.

But no matter how many scandals there are, it should not mean an end to the principle of celibacy which has endured for nearly 1,000 years and which means that a priest has consciously dedicated his life entirely to the service of God.

Besides, what good would it do? There is no celibacy in either the Church of England or the Church of Scotland. Yet that has never prevented the occasional high Anglican dignitary or sober-sided Presbyterian minister from creating a national scandal by being found in bed with another man's wife.

Why should it be any different in the RC Church?

Meanwhile, as far as the Bishop of Argyll and the Isles and his stinking conduct is concerned, cannot it at least be argued that it is a damned sight less sinful to have heterosexual affairs than to have been found guilty, as so many priests have, of sexually abusing young children? Or having been found, as one Irish RC priest recently was, dead in a male brothel?

The ending of the celibacy rule would not affect homosexual priests. So why change a principle almost 1,000 years old for those, who, although they might have to suppress their natural desires in the service of the Church, would never, in any circumstances, think of turning to sick perversion?

CARDINAL WINNING, the leader of the Roman Catholic Church in Scotland, is not everyone's hero.

Not many supporters of Glasgow Rangers, for example, would be likely to have his photograph on their mantelpieces.

There are members of the Scottish Labour Party, too, who resent his recent criticism of Mr Tony Blair. Criticism which suggested that Mr Blair might be guilty of just the teeniest touch of hypocrisy in his attitude towards religion.

But can there be any who doubt the Cardinal's own shining sincerity on the issue of abortion? Or his love for children. When he cradles a baby in his arms there is a look in his eyes which says more than words.

By his outspokenness he has angered Pro-Choice groups throughout the country. Feminists and Guardian readers are up on their soapboxes denouncing him. Their denunciations have no effect on him. He goes on proclaiming what he believes to be the true faith.

I do not go along with everything Cardinal Winning says. But wouldn't it be wonderful for the Church of England if they had even just one bishop like him? A bishop who actually believed in God?

# Has the Bishop a top job in mind?

THERE may be more pompous, self-satisfied, self-righteous men than the Right Reverend David Sheppard, the Anglican Bishop of Liverpool.

But if there are, then so far it has been my good fortune never to have met one.

The Right Reverend Sheppard's self-righteousness and self-satisfaction have not come simply with advancing years. He has always been like that. When he played cricket for England he was very far from being the most popular member of the team. I remember my old friend Denis Compton telling me exactly what he thought of him, but this is not something I would wish to repeat on the Sabbath.

Certainly that side of David Sheppard's character has not impeded his progress in the Church. He has constantly championed what he would term the 'poor and oppressed' and unemployed in Liverpool even when many of them have brought their unemployment on themselves. Now he chooses the middle of a General Election campaign to launch in the name of the Council of Churches for Britain and Ireland a policy statement which, although they deny it, is clearly an attack on the Government.

Why? Why at this precise moment when it will do the maximum damage to the Tories?

*David Sheppard*

Does the Right Reverend David Sheppard have aspirations to become Archbishop of Canterbury? And believe he will have a much better chance of securing that post from Mr Tony Blair as Prime Minister than ever he would have from Mr John Major?

# The Press

*J.J. had a disarmingly simple and mischievious answer to one of the great newspaper debates of the Nineties. Millions of words were written speculating how Rupert Murdoch's worldwide newspaper dynasty had set out systematically to destroy the British monarchy.*

*Flames were fanned by the Sun's publication of the sexually explicit taped telephone conversation between Prince Charles and Mrs Camilla Parker Bowles, followed by the serialisation in the Sunday Times of Andrew Morton's book on the disastrous marriage of Charles and Diana. The newspaper's editor Andrew Neil was accused by J.J. of conducting an unremitting campaign to rubbish the entire Royal Family.*

*Despite nagging doubts, J.J. was never convinced of the conspiracy theory. Murdoch's motive, he suspected, was more likely to be the maximisation of his sales and profits.*

*He doubted Mr Murdoch cared one way or the other what happened to the Royal Family. After all, the Australian tycoon had NO allegiance to Britain.*

*And herein lay the simple solution to sideline Mr Murdoch's activities in the UK.*

*The idea would be for Britain to follow the example of France where the law makes it impossible for anyone other than a French citizen to own and control a newspaper. Such an eminently sensible law said J.J!*

*Casting an eye across the Fleet Street he graced with such style for more than 50 years, he looked at the qualities of some of its better-known characters. He examined the courage of Kelvin MacKenzie, the naivety of Donald Trelford, the hypocrisy of Andrew Neil and Peter Stothard, the loyalty of Charles Wilson and the special talents of Nigel Dempster.*

Has Bordes boy lost his marbles?

Man with loyalty at all Times

Sums to put the wind up Kelvin

How to deal with Rupert

What's so special about the Mirror?

# Man with loyalty at all Times

Mr CHARLES WILSON did not conform to the traditional image as Editor of The Times.

His scholastic background was not public school, followed by Oxford or Cambridge.

It was a tough Glasgow secondary, followed by having to get up off his backside when his parents' marriage folded and go out to work at a newspaper office by at the age of 16.

Without help from anyone, he has reached the very top. And despite some snobbish sneers about his intellectual background, not the least of his achievements has been at The Times, which he has turned from a dull, wordy sheet into a tight, readable newspaper.

Now, at the age of 54, he is relieved of his command and pushed sideways into another job.

The hurt to his pride must be enormous. Yet he

*Charles Wilson*

shows no bitterness, throws no tantrums, cannot be induced to say an angry word even in private about the proprietor who made the change.

Mr Rupert Murdoch may find that his new Editor has infinitely more style and savoir faire than Mr Wilson.

I just hope for his own sake he also finds that the new Editor has even half Charlie Wilson's loyalty.

# The one innocent

I DEPLORE as much as anyone the brutal execution in Iraq of Observer reporter Farzad Bazoft.

Nor do I doubt the genuineness of Observer Editor Mr Donald Trelford's grief. He was clearly finding it impossible to keep back tears the morning of the execution.

But barbaric although President Saddam Hussein may be, is Mr Trelford himself completely a holy innocent, even though he is now back-pedalling like mad from responsibility?

Although Mr Bazoft was a British resident and Mr Trelford says he was unaware he had a criminal record, the fact remains that he was an Iranian.

In the aftermath of the Iran-Iraq war, was it really the greatest idea to have an Iranian reporter — especially one whose background had not been checked — investigate an explosion at a secret Iraqi weapons factory?

Isn't perhaps the most damnable result of the whole lamentable cock-up the fact that an entirely innocent English woman, Mrs Daphne Parish, now faces 15 years in an Iraqi jail?

*Donald Trelford*

# A review that made me sad

WHEN you publish a controversial book, as I did last week, you expect to get a few knocks from reviewers.

Especially those working for newspapers which might have a few past scores to settle with you.

Fair enough.

If you dish it out, you also have to learn to take it.

But there was one review of my book which saddened me. It appeared in a newspaper which I myself edited for more than 30 years, the Sunday Express.

It was written by a man to whom many years ago I had given his first chance in journalism.

It suggested that my book had not been written by myself, but had been ghosted. It even hinted that my columns were not all my own work.

The man who wrote it must have known that what he wrote was utterly untrue. He must have known that nothing that has ever appeared in print under my name has ever been written by anyone except myself. Yet he still wrote as he did.

Why? Anger because I now write for The Mail on Sunday? I neither know, nor care.

What I do deplore is that a once great newspaper should have sunk so low as to be so mean and spiteful.

The Sunday Express once bore the proud legend: Founded by Lord Beaverbrook.

Is its epitaph going to be: Killed by Lord Stevens?

# How Nigel scooped the honours

NEITHER of the principal characters in the Viscount Althorp affair comes out of it smelling of Chanel Number 5.

The way in which Lord Althorp went blubbering to the other woman, seeking solace and sexual reassurance when he thought his marriage of less than six months was already over, is not so much the mark of a randy young man-about-town as it is of a weak, wet wimp. As for the other woman, Miss Sally Anne Lasson, she emerges from it all as a really nasty bitch.

But there is actually one person who does come out of the story with increased prestige — The Mail on Sunday and Daily Mail gossip columnist Mr Nigel Dempster. He has had an extraordinary coup.

It was he who first broke the story, and in the most sensational fashion. He left his pedestrian rivals on other newspapers light years behind, frantically trying to create stories of their own by lifting chunks of his. Yet all the time there was a halo around his head.

Why? Because he was on the side of the angels. He was not guilty of intrusion. He wrote his story at the personal request of Lord Althorp, who when in trouble sought his old friend Mr Dempster's counsel.

How much grander can you get than to have the Princess of Wales's young brother as a friend pouring out his heart to you? Do you really wonder why, then, his rivals are spitting green with envy?

It may be, of course, that Mr Dempster will have to pay a price for his triumph. After the enormous publicity fall-out which has engulfed Lord Althorp, how many more young aristocrats will pour out their hearts in future to their old chum Nigel?

Might they not think, on reflection, that it would be safer by far to make their confessions to their parish priest?

February 17, 1991

# Has Bordes boy lost his marbles?

I WONDER just why Mr Andrew Neil, editor of the Sunday Times, made his quite extraordinary and way-over-the-top attack on the Royal Family in general and the young royals in particular?

The sort of language he used about their 'parading a mixture of upper-class decadence and insensitivity which disgusts the public and demeans the monarchy' would have been astonishing enough if it had come from a Wee Free minister preaching from the moral high ground of a West Highland Presbyterian pulpit.

It is hypocritical cant coming from the former lover of Miss Pamella Bordes. And reads almost as if he had lost his marbles. For his onslaught had not even the semblance of being fair. One of the main targets of his spleen, Lord Linley, the Queen's nephew, was criticised for jetting off to Mustique for a sunshine holiday during the Gulf War.

But why on earth shouldn't he? Lord Linley is not in the Armed Services and never has been. He does not receive any money from the Civil List. And never has. He earns his own living, and in the most honourable way.

He has never sought to use his rank and privilege to advance himself. So why shouldn't he go on holiday?

Prince Andrew is attacked because when his ship, HMS Campbeltown, docked in Spain, he spent a couple of days playing golf with shipmates.

But, again, why shouldn't he? Does a helicopter pilot who fought in the Falklands need to take lessons in courage from someone like Mr Neil who has never faced anything more dangerous in his life than a cork popping from a champagne bottle in some sleazy West End nightclub? What would Mr Neil expect him to do while his ship is docked in Spain. Sit in the wardroom wearing a black armband?

Even Prince Philip, who is now nudging 70, and

*Andrew Neil*

Prince Charles have their conduct labelled as 'hardly faultless'. Apparently because they went pheasant shooting when, presumably, they should have been watching the war on TV. Can you beat it?

Yet Mr Neil is no fool. He must have been quite aware that his remarks would raise the same sort of storm as attended his violent and vicious atack on his proprietor Mr Rupert Murdoch's friend, Mrs Thatcher, during the last days of her premiership.

So why did he make them? Might it be because he does not want to remain as editor of The Sunday Times for very much longer?

# Why not simply pull the plug?

I CAN understand the anger of the Prime Minister and Mr Chris Patten at the chronic Left-wing bias of the BBC.

And especially at the way in which the Corporation has handled the NHS issue.

What I cannot understand is the fatuity of the corrective action they propose taking.

What is the point in urging listeners and viewers to jam BBC switchboards after every biased broadcast? What good will that do, except increase the profits of British Telecom? And make the producers of the offending programmes themselves fall about laughing? Surely, the time has come to examine seriously whether the BBC should have any future at all. After all, what useful purpose does the Corporation any longer serve?

Fifty years ago the BBC was a vital institution. Now, apart possibly from the World Service, which could be separately funded, it wouldn't matter a row of beans if it vanished altogether.

In the new technological age, and with a multi-plicity of TV channels available, it has become as much an anachronism as the Beefeaters in the Tower of London.

The independent and satellite companies not only provide a better and less biased news service than the BBC. Because they have to answer to shareholders, they are infinitely less wasteful of resources. Compare the 270 cameramen, technicians, reporters, commentators and other personnel the BBC used to cover the Blackpool Tory Conference with the 50 used by ITN. How can that sort of extravagance be justified?

As for TV entertainment, if the BBC were to go, there would be a stampede of commercial companies eager to take its place and produce programmes every bit as good and maybe even better. And at no cost to the public.

Might it not also be electorally atttractive to be able to promise that, instead of being raised, the quite unnecessary £78 TV licence fee will soon be scrapped altogether?

# What's so special about the Mirror?

A GREAT play is being made of the fact that whoever buys the Daily Mirror must covenant to keep it a Socialist newspaper.

I cannot for the life of me see why.

I regard as utterly specious the argument, which we will no doubt soon be hearing from the likes of Mr Gerald Kaufman and Mr Roy Hattersley, that it is vital for the political health of the nation that the Daily and Sunday Mirror continue to support the Labour Party.

And that even if the successful bidder is a Right-wing group, like the Pearson Company which also owns the Financial Times, then the chairman of that company should stand aside and agree never to interfere with the newspaper's policy.

That seems to me to be a recipe for utter disaster. For if the proprietors of a newspaper do not control the policy of that newspaper, then who is going to do so? The editor?

If so, to whom then is the editor going to be accountable?

And what if he turns out to be incompetent, his newspaper's circulation starts haemorrhaging and the financial losses become unacceptable? Can he be sacked?

And if so, who appoints his successor? The controlling boards of directors? Or a committee of committed Socialists? Whichever way, it is nonsense.

The facts are that the Daily Mirror is up for grabs. If there are Socialist supporters who want to buy it, and are rich enough to do so, then they ought to go ahead and take control. I would support that.

But if they are not willing to come forward or cannot raise the wind, they ought to pipe down. Whoever buys the Daily Mirror should have control of that newspaper's policy.

And if that means the newspaper abandoning Socialism, then so what? After all, hasn't Mr Neil Kinnock already done so?

# A priceless loyalty

IN his book Maxwell's Fall, Mr Roy Greenslade, who was for a brief but highly lucrative period Editor of the Daily Mirror when the late Robert Maxwell was its owner, tells how once, in his presence, Maxwell barked at his secretary: 'Get me Kelvin MacKenzie, Editor of The Sun, on the telephone' and waited expectantly to be connected.

He waited in vain. His secretary explained to him: 'I'm sorry, Mr Maxwell, Mr MacKenzie will not accept your call.'

Maxwell apparently could hardly believe his ears. He demanded she relate in full her conversation with Mr MacKenzie. The secretary looked flustered and said she would prefer not to. 'Come on!' screamed Maxwell. 'You will not get into any trouble. But if you refuse, you will. Tell me his exact words.' The secretary took a deep breath and blurted out: 'He said: "I don't want to speak to that fat Czech bastard".' A few days later, according to Mr Greenslade, the secretary was out on her neck.

Mr Greenslade tells the story to illustrate how cruel and merciless Mr Maxwell could be to his underlings. And that may be so. But isn't there another side to the story? Doesn't it also indicate just how tough and independent a character Mr Kelvin MacKenzie is?

At the time of that incident Robert Maxwell was still a great power in Fleet Street. He appeared to have limitless amounts of money. He could and did pay vast salaries to journalists, including Mr Greenslade, whom he wanted to employ.

There could hardly be a journalist in the land who out of hand would have turned down an invitation to talk to him. Yet Kelvin MacKenzie did. For all he knew, Maxwell might have been about to offer him a king's ransom to join the Mirror Group. He still didn't want to know.

The more I hear of Mr MacKenzie, the more I respect his courage, if not his style.

There is no journalist who did more to win the Election for John Major than Kelvin

*Kelvin MacKenzie*

MacKenzie did. There is no journalist who has done more to make money for Mr Rupert Murdoch than Mr MacKenzie has.

I would just like to think that Mr Murdoch will be as loyal to Mr MacKenzie as Mr MacKenzie has been to him.

September 6, 1992

# When all the riches will never buy talent

THE first Lord Beaverbrook started life as Maxwell Aitken with absolutely nothing.

By the age of 30 he was a millionaire. By the time he died he was not only one of the world's richest and most famous men — he controlled and owned perhaps the greatest newspaper empire the world had ever known.

His grandson, also christened Maxwell Aitken, started life with almost everything.

Now at the age of 40 he is so financially bust that he cannot even keep up the payments on his car. He blames the recession for his difficulties.

And I am sure that the recession did play its part. But hasn't the real villain in the downfall of this immensely likeable young man, and indeed of his brave, loveable, war hero father before him, been Nature?

Isn't one of the cruellest things in life the fact that although a rich man can leave money to his descendants, the one thing he can never be sure of leaving is the talent to handle it?

January 17, 1993

# In the court of King Rupert

IT will have surprised no one that the Australian magazine New Idea, which published in full the taped, and explicitly sexual, three-year-old telephone conversation between Prince Charles and Mrs Camilla Parker Bowles, is owned by Mr Rupert Murdoch.

If the publication had been deliberately designed to cause the maximum damage to the Prince at the very moment public opinion at last seemed to be swinging his way, it could not have been better or more carefully timed.

In London another of Mr Murdoch's newspapers, The Sun, put the boot in further by devoting its front page to the story under the shrieking headlines 'Another Royal Scandal — How Much More Can We Take? Six Minute Love Tape Could Cost Charles The Throne.'

And I expect it could. Is that perhaps the objective of the whole exercise — an exercise which has been going on right from the moment yet another of Mr Murdoch's newspapers, The Sunday Times, serialised Mr Andrew Morton's book?

It all makes me wonder just what Mr Murdoch's overall purpose is. Simply to sell more newspapers? Or to destroy the House of Windsor completely? If the latter is his objective, and since we are assured that he is not a republican, I wonder with which Royal dynasty he would wish to replace it.

Perhaps with that of King Rupert and Queen Anna?

# Sums to put the wind up Kelvin

I AM a reluctant admirer of Mr Kelvin MacKenzie, Editor of The Sun — and not simply for his taste in girlfriends. He and his newspaper may have been guilty from time to time of gross and maybe unforgiveable invasion of privacy.

But they have done good things too, uncovered many scandals, and secured many brilliant scoops.

Printing the Queen's Christmas broadcast two days before she made it was not one of them. That action was contemptible and cheapjack.

It was for the convenience of newspapers and TV and radio stations throughout the world, many of them owned by Mr Rupert Murdoch, that advance copies of the speech had been circulated with the strict embargo that nothing should be published before the Queen had actually spoken.

No matter how The Sun received its copy, to break that embargo was the journalistic equivalent of stealing from a blind orphan's money box.

Now, when the Queen announces that she will sue for breach of copyright, The Sun's defiant response is to spit in her face with a tasteless Page One presentation of her complaint and to jeer 'See you in court'.

Do they really mean that? If so, then so be it. But in that event I would expect the court to award the Queen very large damages indeed. How large? What about a sum amounting to last year's total profit of the Sun's parent company News International?

Might that not teach both Mr MacKenzie and his proprietor Mr Rupert Murdoch not to break wind in public.

# How to deal with Rupert

I HAVE long been aware that some people very close indeed to Buckingham Palace are convinced that Mr Murdoch is a committed republican whose prime purpose in life is to destroy the monarchy.

When they express their fears to me, I laughed them to scorn.

'Rupert Murdoch has only one prime purpose,' I told them, 'and that is to sell even more newspapers and make even more money. Besides, why should he try to destroy the Royal Family when they are so effectively doing that for themselves?'

Now I am not quite so sure that they were wrong and I was right.

It is the unremitting ferocity of the attacks, and from every corner of the Murdoch empire, which makes me wonder. There has been no newspaper more anti-Royal than Mr Murdoch's Sunday Times except, perhaps, and in an even more brutish way, Mr Murdoch's Sun.

They both go on and on and on seizing every possible chance to spit at all the members of the Royal Family and from time to time at the Queen herself.

Now tonight Mr Murdoch's Sky TV company joins the onslaught with the much-hyped so-called 'world TV premiere' of the dramatisation of Andrew Morton's book. I have only so far seen the trailers to the film but in them Prince Charles appears to be depicted in a peevish, pompous, petulant and most disagreeable light.

So what is the end purpose of it all? Is Mr Murdoch still concerned simply with maximising the sales and profits of his newspapers? Or could he really be out to destroy the monarchy?

I still doubt the latter motive. I suspect the truth is that Mr Murdoch doesn't give a toss either way about the future of the Royal Family. After all, he is not a citizen of this country and owes no allegiance of any kind to it. So why should he give a damn either way as to what happens to it?

But doesn't that fact in itself pose another, and perhaps greater, problem? In France they have what seems to me an eminently sensible law which ensures that only a French citizen can own or control a French newspaper.

Wouldn't that be a good rule to follow in Britain too?

# Come clean over this conspiracy

I COULD hardly believe my ears when I heard the Editor of The Times, Mr Peter Stothard, deny, albeit stumblingly, on the Today programme last Friday morning that there was a Press conspiracy against Mr John Major.

Or that his own newspaper was doing anything other than treat the Prime Minister objectively.

How can he tell such a whopper? Of course there has been a sustained campaign in certain sections of the Press to do down and belittle Mr Major at every opportunity. And The Times has been right at the forefront of it. Nor, when it is not doing its damndest to destroy the Royal Family, has its sister and rather better newspaper, The Sun, been all that far behind.

Mr Stothard has been The Times editor only a short time. I wish him success and long tenure in his job. But I will respect him more if next time he is on the Today programme he has the guts to tell the truth. Which is that he and his newspaper group want to get rid of Mr Major at all costs. And after him, maybe the Royal Family, too.

MR ANDREW Neil, who perhaps reached the apogee of his fame as Pamella Bordes's lover, does not seem to have done all that badly for himself during the years he has spent working for Mr Rupert Murdoch.

He owns a house in the South of France, an expensive flat in the West End of London and an apartment in New York.

And, if the reports are true, he has had a pay-off of somewhere near £1 million.

And, of course, he will claim that he is worth every penny. He could point out that during his time as editor of The Sunday Times he did perhaps more than any one single person to bring down his employer's friend, Margaret Thatcher, and, by serialising the Andrew Morton book, to destroy the marriage of the Prince and Princess of Wales.

He also conducted an unremitting campaign to rubbish the entire Royal Family. He then did his damndest, so far unsuccessfully, to bring down John Major.

He can also fairly claim single-handedly to have brought all Britain's trade with Malaysia to an end for six months after implying that that country's Prime Minister might have accepted bribes.

It was always something of a puzzle why he acted so outrageously, sometimes spitting, it seemed, in the face of his own employer Mr Murdoch.

There were some who suspected that he might even have been deliberately provoking Mr Murdoch into sacking him, knowing that such a sacking would be accompanied by a large pay-off.

In the end he was not sacked. He was simply and adroitly shunted sideways — to a TV job in New York which has turned out to be a non-starter after the bosses of Fox TV, which is controlled by Mr Murdoch, decided that neither his appearance nor his personality would go down well with American audiences. So now he is back in England, still brimming with energy, his ego as huge as ever, and still only 45 years old.

Where does he go from here?

He tells us that he plans to write a book and also a column for The Sunday Times. I should not think the latter will last long. If it is as bad as his last one, it will be unreadable.

But his real aim is to become a big name as a TV political chat show host, although I don't hold out high hopes of that happening either, since Mr Neil on TV has all the charisma of a tin of Brasso.

But apart from TV what else is there? Plenty. Why doesn't he go into politics?

Why doesn't he join the Labour Party and become a parliamentary candidate? With his anti-establishment, anti-Royalist, anti-John Major views, wouldn't he be welcomed with open arms? Wouldn't his dynamism add enormous strength to the Parliamentary Labour Party?

And if it is argued that he cannot do that because he does not believe in Socialism, would that really matter?

After all, wouldn't that put him in exactly the same boat as Tony Blair?

# Will Murdoch rue the day?

FOR the past two weeks the Independent has had a new editor, Charles Wilson. Until Mr Rupert Murdoch sacked him, there was a time when Mr Wilson was editor of The Times.

Was he a good Editor? In my view, a splendid one. And that despite the fact that he had left school at 16 and started in newspapers as an office boy.

But there are some snooty members of the Times' staff who were appalled by his lack of formal education and the robust language he used when getting them to do as he wanted. In the end Mr Murdoch eased him out.

Since then The Times, in terms of influence and readability, has gone steadily downhill. And Mr Wilson? He joined the Mirror Group. And is now that group's managing director.

It is because the Mirror Group owns 43 per cent of the Independent that Mr Wilson, by his own choice, I suspect, is now its temporary editor.

In just two weeks he has transformed the paper. Last week he published a page one story which caused the rest of Fleet Street to rub its eyes.

It was the revelation that, while most newspaper groups in Britain pay 30 per cent or more in corporation tax, Mr Murdoch's News International, which since 1986 has made profits of £979.4 million, pays virtually nothing. Thanks to the adroit, but quite legal, way in which Mr Murdoch's accountants have transferred profits and losses in his multinational company from one country to another, sometimes involving letterbox companies in offshore tax havens. It is a disclosure which must embarrass not only Mr Murdoch but his new friend Mr Tony Blair, too. It also explains how Mr Murdoch's BSkyB can afford to secure a virtual monopoly on all football matches played in Britain.

And how Mr Murdoch is able to wage a price war against other and weaker newspapers.

When Mr Murdoch eased Mr Wilson out of the editorship of The Times I wondered whether the day might come when he would regret that decision.

Might that be now?

*MR Mohammed Al-Fayed, the owner of Harrods, is not someone to whom I have ever instinctively warmed.*

*But, by spending £4.5 million of his own money in resurrecting Punch, he has shown a damned sight more guts and belief in British tradition than those toffee-nosed members of the Establishment who for so long have sneered at him.*

*Will the new Punch succeed? I hope so. If it continues to be crammed full of such splendid reading material and as many brilliantly funny cartoons as are in the first issue, then I think it will.*

# Shame of the TV assassins

THERE has been some critical acclaim for the Channel 4 programme in the series Secret Lives on the late Lord Beaverbrook.

For my own part, I found it disappointing.

Whatever faults Beaverbrook may have had, and he had many, he was a considerable force in politics and indisputably the greatest journalist of his age. A man of extraordinary fire and passion and with an instinctive gift for assessing character.

Nor were his assessments often wrong. Who can argue now against his deep distrust of Mountbatten?

He was a man also of quite remarkable generosity, although the programme depicted him as a skinflint. Above all he was a man who faced death with the same enormous courage and even audacity as he had faced life.

The programme trivialised him and turned him into a comic cuts caricature of himself.

The next famous man to be featured in the Secret Lives series is going to be Douglas Bader. Sad, isn't it, that Channel 4 and Michael Grade are going to try to destroy his character, too?

# Why Labour shoud come out in support of Hayes

MR Jerry Hayes is not a Tory MP for whom I have ever had the slightest regard.

But I am utterly appalled at the way in which he has been crucified by the News of the World, by a spiteful, venal 24-year-old homosexual Mr Paul Stone and by that obnoxious Labour supporter and filth-peddler Mr Max Clifford, who sold Mr Stone's story to the News of the World for £100,000.

Mr Hayes strenuously denies ever having had a physical relationship with Mr Stone. But even if he had had such a relationship, would that justify the treatment he has received?

Have there never been homosexuals in the Labour Party? Can we be quite sure there are none in it today?

Did they not once have a chairman, Tom Driberg MP, who used openly to boast to his friends about the number of kilted soldiers he had buggered?

Almost everyone in Parliament knew about his acts of gross indecency. The newspapers did, too, but nothing was ever published.

Compared with Tom Driberg, Mr Jerry Hayes is a simpleton who has been naive and foolish beyond belief.

But it would be a blot on our society if, thanks to the News of the World, Mr Paul Stone and Mr Max Clifford, he were forced to resign his seat.

IT WAS an appalling slur on the honesty and integrity of the Princess of Wales to suggest, as the Express on Sunday did last week, that she was personally going to pocket £1 million out of the auction in New York of the glittering collection of designer dresses she has discarded.

It was even more appalling that the following day, and despite denials from the Princess's office, the Express perpetuated and tried to justify the story under the headline 'So explain this, Diana'. In the circumstances the Princess had no alternative but to issue a libel writ.

Yet isn't the most appalling thing of all the fact that the next day the Express did not even publish the tiniest of news items to say that she had?

So where is it all going to end? I am not a betting man, but if I were, I would not be laying odds against the continuing survival in office of the editor of both the Express and the Express on Sunday, Mr Richard Addis. Or, come to that, of his newspapers either.

# Police

*J.J. so much wanted to write kindly of the police. Without them he feared we would all be lost. But he wondered why so many of them seemed to go deliberately out of their way to behave in an uncaring and objectionable manner.*

*It was a theme he was to echo constantly. He was forever critical of the police preoccupation with errant motorists at the expense of real criminals, which he saw an unnecessary harassment. Among other criticisms he had of the police were the high-speed chases which resulted in so many tragic deaths.*

What's in this for Branson?

The slow arm of the law

Let's see his face A credit to their

Not quite the ticket uniform

# Let's see his face

WITH memory of poor murdered Mrs Marie Wilks still fresh in her mind, I can understand the fear of 38-year-old nurse Pam Gilfoyle when in the early hours of the morning her Volkswagen Polo broke down on a lonely part of the M50 in Gloucestershire.

I can also understand her relief when, just five minutes later, she spotted a police panda car and flagged it down.

Isn't it almost unbelievable that the policeman driving the panda didn't even bother to get out of it but suggested that she should walk and call for help from a phone box half a mile back?

Isn't it even more unbelievable that when she refused to do that, his alternative suggestion was that she should try to coax the car along the road until she did reach a phone box? And that he then drove off into the night without even saying that he personally would telephone to have help sent?

Merseyside police, who admit that the officer acted badly, are now investigating the incident. Investigating? Why not just make public the offending policeman's name so that we can all have a look at a man who would leave a woman motorist stranded on a lonely road in the middle of the night?

IN SUSSEX, *police harassment of motorists continues unabated. In a letter to The Times Mrs Janice Phillips, of Isfield, East Sussex, tells how, during the course of a one-hour journey on the afternoon of Christmas Day from Robertsbridge to Isfield, a young friend of her daughter's was stopped at random four times and breathalysed four times.*

*He had not even had as much as a single glass of dandelion wine. Nor was he in the sort of flashy sports car which might excite police attention. He was at the wheel of his father's sedate, middle-aged Rover.*

*Nor are occurrences of this kind all that unusual.*

*The propensity of the Sussex police to stop and check motorists without apparent reason has become a byword in the South of England. It verges on the intimidatory. And all this in a country where random breath-testing has not even received the sanction of Parliament.*

*Mr Roger Birch, the Chief Constable of Sussex, may regard himself as the best thing since sliced bread. There can be few other thinking people in this country who do. But wouldn't he have been a real wow in Hitler's Waffen SS?*

# The chases that end in death

FEW road victims can have been more innocent, or more unsuspecting, than 48-year-old Mrs Jean Hollick of Bankside, Clayton-le-Woods, near Chorley, in Lancashire.

There she was at the wheel of her family Volvo, driving sedately along an M55 sliproad, when a stolen Ford Sierra driven by a 16-year-old joy-rider, in full flight from the police, came the wrong way down the road and smashed into her.

Mrs Hollick died. Her rear-seat passenger, 46-year-old Barbara Ayers, was also killed. Mrs Hollick's husband, John, aged 55, is in hospital with multiple injuries. It would appear that the Sierra had been stolen from Gretna just over the Scottish border and had been chased by police through Cumbria and Lancashire of speeds at up to 120 mph.

It is an appalling story, and in due course the 16-year-old, who has not yet been named, will no doubt face a juvenile court. I have no desire either to pre-judge his trial or criticise the police.

I simply point out that it is not the first time that there has been an accident of this kind. Time after time, there are accounts of innocent people and some-times the youthful joy-riders themselves being killed as police chase stolen cars.

When the registration number and make of the car is known, and the crime itself is in effect nothing much more than a minor misdemeanour, do the constabu-lary always have to act like Steve McQueen in Bullitt?

# Not quite the ticket

I REPORT an odd incident involving a lone woman driver and an unmarked police car.

A week last Thursday, around 10 pm, on a road leading out of Leicester, attractive 21-year-old Miss Alison Osborne was pulled over into the dark entrance of a cemetery by an unmarked car flashing a blue light.

Luckily for her the two men who jumped out of it were indeed uniformed policemen. It is what happens next which puzzles me.

The police officer asked her to leave the relative safety of her own car and get into the back seat of theirs. Only there did she learn of the offence she had com-mitted.

Earlier in her journey she had been clocked travelling at 45 mph on a city centre dual carriageway with a 30 mph limit.

Couldn't she have been given a ticket without leaving her own car? What was the point of tak-ing her into the back of a police one?

I so much want to write kind things about the police. Without them we would be lost. But do you sometimes feel that some of them seem deliberately to go out of their way to get themselves disliked?

**SPEEDY: Paula Hamilton**

■ ■ ■ ■ ■

MISS Paula Hamilton, the glamorous, long-legged, devastatingly attractive star of the Volkswagen TV commercials, is clearly a lady who likes driving fast. Magistrates at Witney, Oxfordshire, heard how police caught her near Curbridge at 1.47 pm driving on a 70 mph dual carriageway at 99 mph.

Nor was that the end of the story. Just 13 minutes later police nicked her again, this time driving in a 60 mph zone just miles away at 90 mph.

Now Miss Hamilton, who pleaded guilty, faces the loss of her licence when the adjourned hearing is resumed on January 27.

I will make no complaint if she does lose it. It is incredible that she should have acted so foolishly.

But isn't there something almost as incredible? The fact that the police should be out in such strength against motorists that they were able to nick the same lady for a second time just a few miles down the road?

I applaud the thoroughness of their campaign to keep speeding cars, save when driven by policemen, off the roads.

Wouldn't it be great if they could also be out in equal strength and thoroughness in the pursuit of criminals who beat up old ladies?

# The slow arm of the law

HOME from the US, but still on holiday, I arranged a game of golf with a formidable lady player.

We both arrived at Walton Heath Golf Club in Surrey at 10.40 am and parked our cars in the clubhouse car park, which is enclosed and invisible from the road. Although there were many other parked cars, there was not another person to be seen. My friend took her handbag from the back seat of her car and locked it in the boot.

Normally we would not then have returned to the cars for at least another three hours. But the day was so sunny that my companion decided in the clubhouse to take her golf jacket back to the car. She found that in the few minutes she had been away, the boot had been forced open and her handbag, containing her chequebook and credit cards, stolen.

Swift action was taken. While Janice, the super-efficient golf club assistant secretary, tried to contact nearby Epsom police on one phone, my friend was on another to her bank, asking them to cancel both cards and cheques. The secretary was less lucky. It took nearly ten minutes for Epsom police station even to answer.

When they finally did, and even when told the break-in had taken place only ten minutes previously, they sounded utterly uninterested. Yes, they would send a patrol car. How long would that be? They didn't know. That was at 11 am. At 12.30 pm the NatWest Bank in Dorking telephoned to say that a woman had entered the bank at 11.30 am, successfully posed as my friend and, despite the fact that the chequebook had already been reported stolen, cashed a cheque made out to cash for £1,000.

Thirty minutes later a woman had tried unsuccessfully to get money using my friend's Access card in Guildford. Odd little story, isn't it? How, in a car park empty of people, could my friend be spotted putting her handbag in the boot? How could a cashier in a Dorking bank pay out £1,000 to a stranger on a cheque already reported stolen?

And what about the police? We waited and waited for their arrival.

Three times I tried to phone them. On one occasion at 1 pm I failed to get a reply at all. On the two other occasions I was told: 'You will just have to wait until we arrive. We have more important things to do.'

It was 3.19 pm when a young, intelligent PC in a panda car did arrive. His late arrival was not his fault, he had been informed of the break-in only 15 minutes previously. Doesn't it make you wonder what it was that kept the police so very busy for such a long time when a prompt appearance might actually still have caught the culprit before he or she had had a chance to leave the club?

Having coffee breaks perhaps? Or lunch? Or engaged in chasing really serious criminals — like motorists who forget to fasten their seatbelts or even briefly park their cars on double yellow lines?

# Humour

*J.J.'s legendary humour enriched the lives of millions of his readers.*

*They turned to his column in The Mail on Sunday, not only for his forthright and acerbic views on so many important issues of the day, but for the special brand of humour which was his trademark. He was sometimes cruel but always perceptive, sharp and witty.*

*Nobody was spared, whether they were royalty, rich, famous or the ordinary man in the street*

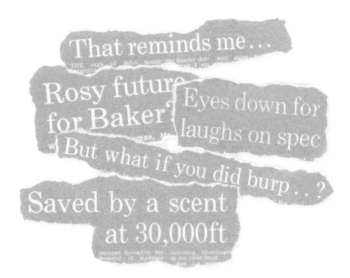

*THE editor of a once great but now, alas, ailing national newspaper says patronisingly of my move to The Mail On Sunday:*
*'Good wine clearly does not travel.'*
*Doesn't it? I had always thought that good wine travelled enormously well — which is why the great vintages and premier crus are enjoyed by millions of connoisseurs all over the world.*
*I also thought the stuff made of sour grapes was hardly worth putting into bottles at all.*

*DID you read that in the US an exception has had to be made to a new law which forbids smoking on domestic flights?*
*It will not apply to the men actually piloting the aircraft.*
*Why? Because a medical survey suggests that if they are smokers and are deprived of a soothing drag, their judgment in times of stress might not be as good as it should be.*
*But if that applies to the men up front, does it not apply even more — especially when the aircraft hits a sudden pocket of turbulence — to the poor wretches sitting in Economy behind them?*

# These so very devoted sisters

A FEW horrified eyebrows must have shot up in the Vatican at the story of these eight elderly Belgian nuns, all members of the splendidly named order The Poor Sisters of Clare, who sold their rambling, chilly Bruges convent for £1 million and lit off for the South of France on the proceeds.

Nor will, I imagine, the Catholic hierarchy be completely convinced by the subsequent sob story that they were forced to do as they did by a brutal handyman.

But need there be a criticism anywhere else?

Isn't it touching the way they stuck together and cared for each other?

And that while most of them travelled south in luxury limousines they also made sure that the eldest of the group, 93-year-old Sister Agnes, travelled in comfort in an ambulance.

I have never believed that God cares all that much for the ultra-good. I sometimes wonder how He can even love them at all when people who occasionally yield to temptation are infinitely more interesting and more human than those who never do.

So can He look down with anything other than love and understanding and maybe even amused approval on these eight old dears if, after a lifetime of serving Him, they have opted to end their days, a glass of champagne in their hards, warming their ancient toes in the Mediterranean sun?

# But what if you did burp...?

IN A report published by the Royal Society of Health, Dr Michael Turner tells us that the regular consumption of garlic is a wonderful protection against heart disease.

Not just little itsy bitsy pieces of the stuff to flavour, and to my mind utterly destroy, meat dishes. But great chunks of it. At least one whole clove per person a day. Dr Turner says three cloves would be even better.

Dr Turner also thinks it is better to eat natural garlic cloves than to take pills made from them. He also says that those who don't care very much for the stink of garlic on their breath could overcome that by taking garlic oil in capsules or dried garlic in tablet form.

'These preparations transfer the potentially smelly compounds to the stomach directly. If you do not burp, your friends may never know.'

If you do not burp? But what if you do burp — or worse still, with all that garlic bubbling around in your tummy, inadvertently commit an even greater social indiscretion?

Wouldn't it be quite dreadful if at a crowded concert or cinema you turned round and found that from the three rows of seats behind you people with handkerchiefs to their noses were stampeding towards the exit?

# Rosy future for Baker?

WHEN the Tory Chairman, Mr Kenneth Baker, was recording an interview for local radio during last week's conference he was asked by the interviewer what he would like to have been if he had not gone into politics.

He replied: 'A priest.'

One of Mr Baker's aides intervened to suggest that such a response might be regarded by listeners as a little quirky. So the question was asked again. This time Mr Baker gave as his reply: 'A gardener.'

If Mr Baker was being serious, and I have no reason to doubt it, don't these replies give a fascinating insight into the character of the man?

I have no doubt that if he ever gets the chance, Mr Baker will make a splendid Prime Minister.

And wouldn't he, with his cherubic, smiling face and gleaming benevolent eyes, also have made a

quite marvellous Archbishop of Canterbury? But at the end of the day, might not he, in common with most politicians, produce more benefit for mankind, and certainly more happiness for himself, just tending roses in a garden?

January 13, 1991

*I CAN think of only one good thing to say about randy old Graham Partridge who, at the age of 75, had his 27-year-old, long-legged, red-headed mistress so steamed up with jealousy over his relationships with other ladies that she smashed up his house.*
*Hasn't he put a new spring into the tottering step and a new swing into the sagging sporran of every other ancient laddie in the land?*

April 28, 1991

# When is a deer not a deer?

A FRIEND of mine had an unusual experience the other night while out walking with a mongrel dog in a field near his home.

Hot on the scent of something, the dog had excitedly and disobediently made off along the thick hedge which was the field's boundary. Seconds later it began barking furiously.

To his horror, my friend saw that it had cornered and was attacking a deer. He ran full pelt the length of the field and flung himself on the dog, which by this time had the deer on the ground.

As he pulled the dog away by its collar he turned his back on the deer. That was a mistake. The Bambi-like creature lowered its head and charged him, goring him quite severely in his thigh before it sped off.

Since his leg was hurting and blood was spreading over his jeans, my friend thought he had better get some medical attention and an anti-tetanus injection. So he drove to the casualty department of the East Surrey Hospital, where he explained to a nurse he had been gored by a deer.

She didn't seem all that surprised. She reacted instead as if people were trooping in suffering from the same complaint every day of the week. Nor did she seem to regard it as all that much of an emergency. He was told to sit down and take his place in the queue.

It was nearly three hours later before he actually received medication.

It was only later that he learned why he had been treated so casually. The nurse had misheard him and instead of putting on his chit: 'Gored by a deer', she had written: 'Floored by a door'. I don't in any way blame her for mishearing. I just wonder what she would have written, and how much longer he would have waited, if he had told her that he had been sat on by an elephant.

# Saved by a scent at 30,000ft

WHEN I checked in at Atlanta international airport for my Delta airlines flight home, I was dismayed to see that hundreds of American tourists — pot-bellied men in T-shirts, matronly women, and children, some of them babes in arms — were already waiting to board.

'Are all these people going on this flight?' I asked the man at the check-in counter. 'They sure are,' he replied. 'We haven't one unoccupied seat in economy class.'

I groaned and in a moment of madness had a most unworthy thought of which I should be deeply ashamed. 'How much,' I asked, 'would it cost me to upgrade my ticket to business class?'

He busied himself with his computer and came up with the reply: '1,800 dollars, sir.' 1,800 dollars. More than £1,000. Just to avoid eight hours of cramped discomfort. My moment of madness passed.

When I boarded the plane, which was about the length of a football pitch, I discovered that cigarette smokers were confined to the last three rows of seats at the very back of the plane. My own seat was one of two in the very last row. Any further back and I would have been perched on the tailplane.

But there were some pleasant surprises too. First, the leg room, which was remarkably generous. Then the food, which was brilliant — filet mignon, salad, cheese and dessert accompanied by as much free wine, including Champagne, as you could drink.

And just guess who out of that motley crew of fellow passengers was occupying the seat beside me? A quite stunningly beautiful Mexican girl who spoke the most deliciously accented English and who, it turned out, was on her way to Cambridge where she planned to take a postgraduate course.

As I fell asleep 30,000 feet above the Atlantic with the scent of her perfume still heavy in the air, I reflected on something my old mum used to say to me when I was a little boy: 'J.J., with your luck if you ever fell out of an airplane you would land in a haystack.'

There are times when I think she might just possibly have been right.

**ADVANTAGE: Gabriela Sabatini**

■ ■ ■ ■ ■

**TENNIS** star Henri Leconte is said to be in disgrace in France.

Hands are being held up in horror because, instead of training with the rest of the French team for their Davis Cup match with Switzerland, Monsieur Leconte jetted off to Florida to spend four days in the arms of his newest girlfriend.

And who was she? That gorgeous Argentine multi-millionairess Miss Gabriela Sabatini.

It is said that when he came back to France he looked very unfit indeed. So unfit that he was not picked for the match against Switzerland and as a result France lost.

Wasn't that disgraceful? Perhaps it was.

But wouldn't it have brought even more disgrace on France if a full-blooded Frenchman had given up the chance of four days with Gabriela just for a game of tennis?

# Eyes down for laughs on spec

THERE are few of us who have not experienced the anguish of arriving, complete with laden basket, at a supermarket check-out and suddenly discovering that we have left our money at home.

Can you imagine then how the Queen must have felt when on the very point of making a seven-page speech at the Commonwealth Institute she discovered she had forgotten her spectacles?

Luckily, Prince Philip was at hand to read out her address for her.

But the incident did set me wondering. What if, instead of at a relatively minor function, it were to happen just as she was to read her speech at the State Opening of Parliament?

Can you just visualise the panic that would ensue as Her Majesty searched desperately in her handbag? With TV cameras whirring away all the time, would Knights of the Garter and Cabinet Ministers be bobbing up and down offering the Queen their own specs to try?

I mean no disrespect, and I hope it never happens. But if it did, wouldn't it be just about the funniest thing on national TV since Laurel and Hardy?

June 26, 1992

# A girl with two rackets

IN the Australian Open Tennis tournament, Miss Monica Seles once again proves that if she is not the best woman tennis player in the world, she is certainly the noisiest.

Isn't it quite extraordinary the way she grunts?

I do not want to seem personal, but if she produces that sort of racket playing tennis, have you ever wondered what she must sound like when engaged in infinitely more pleasurable activities?

September 6, 1992

# Will Sandy find war or peace?

THERE would hardly be a middle-aged wife in the land who did not give a sigh of satisfaction at the news that 65-year-old Sandy Gall was leaving his glamorous 43-year-old mistress and going back to the wife of 34 years on whom he walked out last year.

'Wasn't he a silly old fool?' I can hear them saying, and 'Isn't it marvellous it is all now going to have a happy ending?'

But was he such a silly old fool? And will it have such a happy ending? I do not profess to know the answer to either of these questions.

Mrs Gall seems to be a formidable lady with more than a touch of temper. Remember how she bundled up Sandy's Savile Row suits, his beloved golf clubs and his claret into a dustbin liner and dumped them all outside the house of Georgina Gillan, his mistress?

Now that he is back home again with his carpet slippers neatly parked on his side of the matrimonial double bed, is she likely to be completely forgiving — with never a hark back to his nights of sin?

I wonder. My suspicion is that life for poor old Sandy from now on is going to fall a little short of being a bowl of cherries.

But still he has one consolation. If the worst comes to the worst, couldn't he always mount his mule and set off once again with a TV crew to cover the very next war in Afghanistan?

November 1, 1992

# A lunch I could not miss

I WILL long remember the look on the motorcyclist's face.

He had propped his motorbike up against a bollard and was standing there on the road near the edge of the pavement on one of London's main highways.

He seemed to be waiting for a break in the rush-hour commuter traffic in order to dash in to the road to retrieve something.

But to retrieve what?

The answer to that question came to me as my front wheels went over what had looked like a piece of cardboard.

There was nothing I could do about it. No way in that stream of traffic I could stop. But when I heard the crunch I knew exactly what it was — the motorcyclist's lunchbox which must have fallen off the back of his bike.

The look on that man's face was quite wonderful to behold. Anger, anguish, then resignation and utter sadness as he stepped back on to the pavement.

I do hope that by now he will have forgiven me. And I suspect that he will. Just one thing slightly bewildered me.

Could that really have been a victory salute he was giving as I accelerated away?

January 1, 1995

# That reminds me ...

THE SAGA of John Prescott's missing car reminded me of the story of the Church of Scotland minister in a country parish not all that far from Auchtermuchty who lost his bicycle and was convinced it had been stolen.

He deliberated on how to catch the culprit and hit upon a cunning plan. He said to his beadle: 'On Sunday during my sermon I am going to repeat the Ten Commandments from the pulpit and when I come to "Thou shalt not steal" I will pause and I want you to study the congregation to see if anyone looks embarrassed.'

After the sermon, a puzzled beadle remonstrated with the minister: 'You told me you were going to pause after saying "Thou shalt not steal", but you didn't.

'So I didn't have a chance to see if anyone in the congregation looked guilty.'

'That's all right,' replied the minister. 'When I came to "Thou shalt not commit adultery" I suddenly remembered where I'd left my bike.'

■ ■ ■ ■

MRS ALAN CLARK, wife of the former Government Minister who has so scandalised Whitehall with his account of his sex life, tells us that her husband eats only Force for breakfast and has done so all his life.

Force? Isn't that a name from the past?

Many years ago, it was one of the most popular of all cereals. I remember still the jingle with which it was sold: 'Over the fence jumps Sunny Jim. Force is the stuff that raises him'.

Because it is no longer advertised on TV, I did not even know it was still being produced. But clearly it is. And the disclosure that Mr Alan

SCANDAL: Alan Clark

Clark seems to have thrived so well on it will no doubt give its sales an enormous boost among middle-aged men seeking, perhaps, to emulate him.

I am all for it. But as for Mr Alan Clark, if Force really is the stuff that raises him, might he not be wise for the sake of his marriage to change to All Bran?

# Why Foot could never have been a KGB spy

I HAVE heard some daft things in my time. But never anything quite as daft as the suggestion that Mr Michael Foot may have been a KGB agent.

Mr Foot may have been for most of his life a gullible, naive Left-winger. He may have led futile, poinless marches on Aldermaston. He may have been the Opposition leader who affronted the nation by attending the Remebrance Sunday Cenotaph ceremony in a duffel coat.

But sell his country for money? Rubbish. He is not only a man of enormous personal honour. He is also someone who have never been interested in money. As I know well from personal experience.

He idolised the late Lord Beaverbrook, who was his proprietor when Mr Foot was editor of the London Evening Standard. Many years later, when I myself was an editor and Beaverbrook was clearly within months if not weeks of death, I was summoned to see the old man at his villa in the South of Frnace. Mr Foot, recovering from a car crash, was a house guest at the villa at the time. During my visit I seized the chance to plead with Mr Foot, who knew the old man better than anyone else, to write me an obituary in advance of his death which I could hold until the moment he actually died. I offered a considerable sum of money. In today's terms about £50,000. I also promised that the obituary would be kept under lock and key and that no one would know he had written it in advance.

We were walking at the time along the cliff top at Cap D'Ail.

I will never forget his reply. He ground the ferrule of his walking stick into the soft turf said: 'I can't do it. I care for that old man too much. I could not do anything that I felt was hastening his death.'

Is anyone going to tell me that a man who talks and thinks like that is going to sell his own country for a few miserable fivers?

Or is the next smear going to be that the late Lord Beaverbrook himself was a Russian spy?

November 10, 1996

# The way not to take one's seat

DID you chance to read the story of how 28-year-old Gary Foxley found himself stuck fast to a McDonald's lavatory seat in Knightsbridge, London, for five hours after some joker had smeared superglue on it?

It took six firemen, two women paramedics and two policemen an hour just to free him, still attached to the lavatory seat, from the vandal-proof cubicle. Then he had to be carried through the restaurant on a stretcher with the seat still jammed to his backside.

From there he was taken by ambulance to hospital, where it took doctors a further four hours to free him.

During those four hours, he presumably lay face down with his bottom and the loo-seat up in the air.

It is not, of course, the first time something like this has happened. In the annals of ancient history there is the authenticated story of the Auchtermuchty lassie who suffered exactly the same fate when she sat on a newly-varnished lavatory seat and had to be taken to hospital.

She was lying in bed with her bottom in the air and the lavatory seat still attached to it at a moment when a young American medical student was being showed round the ward by a consultant.

'Have you ever seen anything like this before?' queried the consultant.

The American student took another look and said: 'Yes, I have. But I guess it's the first time I've seen it framed.'

# The last farewell . . .

*WHEN you read this I hope to be sitting in the sun on the terrace of a French water-side cafe waiting for my croissants, strawberry jam and coffee to arrive and idly speculating as to whether I might have the sole or lobster for lunch.*

*At the request of Sir John Junor's family*
*a donation from the sales of this book*
*will be made by The Mail on Sunday to the*
*Royal National Lifeboat Institution.*